T0208885

BEGINNING *of an* EMPIRE

AN EGYPTIAN HISTORICAL FICTION NOVEL BY
JOSEPH HERGOTT

Joseph Hergott

authorHOUSE®

AuthorHouse™
1663 Liberty Drive
Bloomington, IN 47403
www.authorhouse.com
Phone: 1 (800) 839-8640

This is a work of fiction, everything besides the Kings'
names are fictitious. Most character's, places and incidents
portrayed are the product of the author's imagination.

Published by AuthorHouse   04/09/2015

ISBN: 978-1-5049-0403-2 (sc)
ISBN: 978-1-5049-0402-5 (e)

Print information available on the last page.

AUTHOR'S NOTE

I decided to write the story about the very first Pharaoh of Egypt or Kemet (black land) as it was called in the ancient times. As I studied, I found many conflicting stories about how and exactly by whom the north and south joined. I do know that Narmer was the one that is said to have joined them, but Menes is also a name that pops up. The problem is, there are some Egyptologists that hold to the thought that they were one and the same person, however, there are differing reports surrounding the death of each one of these kings. Egyptology is sometimes very confusing because of the many conflicting theories that exist. There are very few concrete facts about Narmer and Menes. Even though it is said by some that King Scorpion was Narmer's father, it is questionable. Who exactly was his father or mother for that matter? How did they die? Were Narmer and Menes the same person? No one knows for sure. . .

With this lack of factual evidence, I decided to have fun with my artistic licence and write these two historical characters as twins. This way both Narmer and Menes will be there at the beginning, molding the great country of Egypt. Enjoy!

THANKS:

Special thanks are given to Melissa Steffler and Geraldine Zahra for their dedication in helping to make this book come alive.

To my encouraging friends:
Derek & Ken
May we continue to lift each other up
through the mysteries of our lives.

Contents

Characters

Students
Kah [Kah] – oldest student
Anitka [ă-nĭt-kah] – student
Hayki [hā-kē] – Anitka's younger brother
Rayu [rā-yū] – youngest student
Ist [ĭst] – only female student
Weneg [wĕn-ĕg] – teacher

Royalty
King Scorpion - King
Osiris-King-Scorpion – the name given to the King after he dies so he is associated with Osiris
Nestuwan [nĕst-ū-wän] – Queen: Narmer and Menes' mother
Narmer [när-mer] – oldest twin son [prince]
    Eshe [ē-shē] – Narmer's first wife
        Hakizimana [hăk-ēz-ĭ-măn-ah] – Eshe's father
        Jendayi [jĕn-dā-ĭ] – Eshe's mother
    Neithotpe [nē-thōtĕp] – Narmer's second wife
    Hor-Aha [hōr-ah-hah] son of Narmer
Menes [mē-nēs] – youngest twin son [prince]
Hsekiu [hĕs-kū-ē] – King of the north
    Thesh [thĕsh] – son of Hsekiu
Alafin [ăl-ă-fĭn] – King of Semma [city in the south]

Priests
Hor-Nu [hōr-nū] – priest of Min
Meresamun [mā-rēs-ămūn] – High Priestess of Isis
Nakht [nă-kĕt] – priest of Amun
Masud [mă-sŭd] – Maya's son

Maya [mā-ah] – new High Priest of Amun-min
Neferenpet [ně-fer-ěn-pět] – High Priest of Ptah
Sem priest [sěm] – funerary priest in charge of embalming
We'eb priest [wē-ěb] – young priest initiate

Other characters
Aabab [ā-băb] – child from the Nubia
Betresh [bět-rěsh] – Eshe's body servant
Chisisi [chĭ-sē-sē] – dispatch runner
Dejati [dē-jă-tē] – administrator-of-the-works
Gahiji [găh-ējē] – sailor
Halima [hă-lē-mah] – temple prostitute
Her-uben [her-ū-běn] – security
Khu [khū] Narmer and Menes security and retired soldier
Liben [lĭ-ben] – Nubian interpreter
Mahut [mah-hŭt] family dog
Mbizi [m-bĭz-ē] – military captain
Minnakt [mĭn-năkt] – Narmer's captain
Nakhti [năkh-tē] – retired warrior
Nefrusheri [ně-frū-sher-ē] – blind albino oracle dream interpreter
Nephthys [něpf-thĭs] – midwife
Re'hotep [rā-hō-těp] – sailor
Sacmin [săc-mĭn] – midwife
Setaten [sět-ăt-ěn] – head of northern army
Wenemon [wěn-ě-mŏn] – young boy that befriends Narmer

Criminals

Teremun [ter-ĕ -mŭn] – prison leader

Weren [wār-ĕn] – criminal army leader

Definitions & gods
-gods and goddess'

Amun – chief god and creator of all things

Anubis – god of embalming

Hathor – goddess of women, fertility, children, beauty plus too many more to name

Hapi – god of the Nile

Isis – dutiful wife of Osiris and goddess of magic and healing

Ma'at – goddess of divine order [truth and justice]

Meretseger – dangerous and merciful goddess of protection

Min – god of male fertility

Natron – salt harvested from dry saltwater beds: used for washing and purification

Osiris – god of the underworld and leader of all the gods

Ptah – creator god

Sobek – crocodile god of the Nile and protector of the King from evil magic

Seth, Set – god of chaos.

Tarewet – protector goddess of women and childbirth

Wadjit – goddess of Lower Egypt [northern Egypt]

-Definitions

Field of Reeds – a place of utter content where they will be reborn [paradise]

Ghazye [ghā-zē] – temple prostitute

Hamsa [hăm-sah] – a hand gesture that extends an open face palm that wards off the evil eye

Hem nejer [hĕm-nĕ-jer] – servant of a god

Ka [kah] – soul

Naos [nā-ŏs] – a shrine that holds a small idol

Pesh-en-kef [pĕsh-ĕn-kĕf] – Egyptian adze magical tool used at Opening of the Mouth ceremonies to let deceased person walk, talk, see and smell in the afterlife

Senet – a Chess like board game

Shenti [shĕn-tē] – long ankle length shirt

Sister – this could mean a female family member or wife or close friend

Pure singer – an abstinent (from sex) temple servant that sings to a god

"Breath of Amun" – Narmer's boat

"Min's Wisdom" – King Scorpion's boat

* * * segue

* * * * segue from the main story with students to the past with Narmer

PROLOGUE

The floor felt cool under Nestuwan's bare feet as she walked the dim hallways of her home. The baby inside her swollen belly kicked in angry distain. She stopped and put her hand on her extended abdomen and clutched the Bes amulet that hung around her neck. *Maybe I should lie down on my couch,* she thought. *It is about time for my baby's arrival – so my midwives tell me. Nephthys and Sacmin are so wise . . .* She decided to return to her room. She felt a pop in her groin and then a light trickle down her leg. She smiled, let go of her amulet and placed that hand on the swell of her belly. As she walked a little a gush of what felt like warm water oozed out of her and splattered on the dirt floor. What happened next was a disconcerting rush of painful throbs deep inside her. The first wave of labour pains started like a tsunami, forcing her to her knees – another gush and now she was kneeling in mud.

"Help me!" she cried out, but her voice was swallowed up by the sun-dried brick walls.

Her abdominal walls contracted on their own as if she was a victim of her own body. Labour pains roared through her torso – leveling her. Terror seized her as panic threatened to take control of her mind. Her body now had a will of its own. *Is this supposed to be happening? What if no one finds me?* Yet it was strangely peaceful. Her body knew what to do. She would just have to endure it.

"Aargh," she moaned as she laid on her side in the filth of the wet floor. She grabbed her amulet again desperately searching for comfort. In her mind she saw Bes – the ugly dwarf god; protector of childbirth, of women, of children and of the home. "Give me strength Bes; protect this child inside me; give me strength to bare a son for my King; and make my baby strong." A third, fourth and fifth contraction washed over her body . . . slowly at first, then at a predictable pace before the midwife found her.

Nephthys had been waiting for her in the spacious whitewashed room preparing for the young Queen's impending child birth. The sixteen year old Queen had married King Scorpion on her fourteenth birthday – the day that all her dreams had come true. She had married the King – an older and powerful man, one that everyone looked up to. Now she was carrying the next royal child – "The future" so the oracle had told her. Nephthys patiently waited for the Queen who had told her she just needed to stretch her cramped legs. She had been gone too long and Nephthys cursed herself for not insisting on accompanying her. As she waited, Nephthys had heard a faint annoying sound she assumed had come from household cats that mewed repeatedly. It was only when she focused on the sound that she determined that it was not that of animal – it was different.

Nestuwan lay on the muddied floor as the experienced Nephthys and the calm yet excited Sacmin spoke reassuring words to her. "All is well my Queen. Your child will soon be here. We do need to go to your bedroom though and put you on the birthing block. We will need your help."

Nephthys got on her right side; assisted the royal mother-to-be to drape her arm around her neck; and helped her to stand. Once she stood, another contraction gripped her. She lost all strength in her legs and had to be carried to her room. In the bedroom Nephthys stood behind the Queen and held her up. Sacmin brought the birthing blocks and placed a clean white linen sheet between them. The midwives helped the Queen stand and then squat on the blocks – her legs parted. Sacmin then switched positions with Nephthys. Sacmin held the Queen up while the more experienced Nephthys squatted in front, ready to receive the babe. Another contraction surged through her body; it was all Sacmin could do to hold her in position. It would be another hour of moaning at each ensuing contraction, and the midwife's soothing encouragement before Nephthys could see the baby's head crown. By now the room was filled with priests chanting their doleful songs interspersed with Nestuwan's regularly timed wails. Officials crowded in wanting to witness the next royal's birth. The onlookers that had filled the room annoyed the Queen from time to time, but all-in-all she was able to ignore them.

"Majesty you need to push now" . . . a loud outcry . . . "Yes that is it! Push again," coaxed Nephthys . . . another determined outburst.

Nephthys smiled satisfyingly as she reached forward and cradled the baby's head and guided him out and into the world. A quick resounding slap to his bottom brought much crying as the infant prince protested. The umbilical cord was tied with a red string and then cut with a flint knife. The young Queen opened her eyes, but just as she saw the child, another contraction enveloped her abdomen.

"You have a boy, my Queen – a little prince!" Nestuwan was oblivious to the midwife's comment – she was in the midst of another contraction.

Nephthys saw the pain in the Queen's face and directed her concentration to the royal's pelvic area. There, you could see a second head crowning.

"You have twins your Majesty!" Nephthys said with delight.

Kemet

3125 BC

L IKE A MISSILE ON a mission, a colorful spinning stick flew through the air deep into the papyrus marshes that lined the Nile River. Though the duck was unsuspecting, it nevertheless died in an explosion of feathers and a quick guttural quack. The bird dropped into the water later to be picked up by Kah – a thirteen year old boy who, at the time, felt on top of the world. Kah was well-built for a boy of his age. He was of average height, short black hair and deeply tanned. His family was modestly wealthy; a fact that caused an attitude of pride within him. Bakenkhons, his father, had taught him to read and write.

At first glance what impressed you about Kah was his calm demeanor. He never raised his voice to curse at somebody. He just went with the flow. He struggled with and wasn't too proud of his easy nature. *Why do I have such a problem speaking my mind?* was the question that plagued his thoughts when he was in tough circumstances. During his life, Kah knew what his future would entail. He would follow in the footsteps of his father, who was the High Priest of Amun, and begin as a We'eb priest, a full-fledged priest and then a High priest. He would be a servant to the god – a Hem nejer. It was a noble job, a well-paid job, but not what he wanted. *Why must I be shackled to being a priest like my father?* He thought. *Yes it is a worthy profession, but is it what I want? I don't even know what I want,* he complained to himself. *My mother wants me to get married and yes I should, but the only one I am interested in, is far from my social caste.* Kah was thinking about Ist, a girl that lived a short distance away from him. She was a sweet girl that had grown up with him. As children they used to run around naked and go swimming together. At first he had not been attracted to her and never thought of her as someone he would be remotely interested in, but that was changing. As the years progressed, the time of being regularly together waned and maturity increased, he did desire her company more and more. He never revealed those feelings to her though.

Kah's home was nicer than all the others on the footpath which was connected to several others to the south, but he did not think about that fact very often. Kah's father had been away doing his duty as a priest for the last two months. One more month and his three month cycle would be over. Kah and his mother, Asute, eagerly awaited his return.

Kah poled his small reed raft closer to the papyrus to retrieve his felled duck when he saw five other agitated, but quiet water fowl nesting close by. His throwing stick lay stoically in the water just a little farther in the abundant grass like sedge than his raft could navigate. Kah used his pole to nudge the fallen bird towards the raft until he was able to pick it up. *Now for my throwing stick, I cannot lose that,* he contemplated. Kah cautiously reached the pole through the sedge and managed to tease the stick closer until he could grab it. The ducks were getting increasingly restless now, but they luckily stayed in place. A spinning vortex of color sailed a second time through the air felling another bird. A flurry of water fowl launched themselves into the papyrus in a cacophony of noise and feathers.

"At lease I got one more," Kah said to no one in particular.

Kah retrieved the second bird and poled home. *I wish my father were here to enjoy that hunt with me. That is one reason I do not want be a priest!* There was much to do to fill his days that it at least deadened the pain of the loneliness he felt in his father's absence. There was always weeding and trimming that needed to be done. Feeding of the livestock was a continual chore that had become second nature to him.

Kah started pulling weeds away from the base of the sandstone statue of Amun that had been recently erected. The complacent stone face of the god looked over the property showing little regard for those approaching him, but he demanded their respect. The image was gilded with gold, but the arms and legs were black. The impressive double feathers that stood in the crown atop his head were beautifully carved so that the intricate veins showed. The statue stood beside three pools that supplied water to Ficus trees that at that time were in full bloom.

"Kah," a voice from the house called.

"Yes . . . I am here Mother," the teen answered.

"Please remember to feed the fish while you are out there," Asute said in a sing-song tone.

Kah rolled his eyes. "Please feed the fish," Kah quietly muttered to himself. *I always feed these damn fish . . . well most of the time,* he thought. He remembered how he accidently forgot two weeks ago and three fish had starved and had been found belly up.

Kah reached into a sack that he was carrying and grabbed a handful of bread scraps and tossed them into the ponds. Small black and silver fish swam up to the crumbs and sucked them up.

"Well maybe another handful," he said as he tossed in more.

A cow mooed in the pen close to him which reminded him of more chores he needed to do. *I would like to go fishing,* he thought in frustration. *When will I be able to go?* It would be later that day that Kah was able to finish his tasks and collapse into bed. The next several days were filled with even more tasks – ones that his father had written down for him or his mother had asked him to do.

Finally at the week's end he had completed the jobs and he was finally free. Kah was then back on the raft, throwing sticks in hand and fishing poles laying neatly in the middle that he felt the most content. Kah poled the raft to the edge of the river and cast a fishing line into the reeds. Fastened on a copper hook, the bait he used was a small piece of roast duck he had saved from the previous meal that he had had. There were no takers for the treat right away, but when he cast the line closer into the reeds, the food was snapped up quickly. Kah was able to eventually land three nicely sized fish that would be roasted later that night.

Kah thought about his father's property just to the north. This property bordered the river as well, but this was a very special place to Kah's household. The family tomb was on this plot of land. This tomb was very important to Kah since his family was one of the only ones that had such a place. The tomb not only had a small secure structure that was beautifully painted, but also had a little grove of fruit bearing Ficus trees in front of its entrance. A nice touch to this tomb was on the river's bank, a span of naturally growing papyrus plants that hid the tomb's location from any river traveller. An added bonus to this property was the plot of land directly beside it, which had been given to Kah himself. It was his own land. For the last several years Kah had been clearing it and building a home, with his father's help of course.

Kah felt very important thinking about the land he had been given and in some cases bragged about it to others, which he knew he should not do. His convictions, however, gave way to his pride. Kah poled farther south where he came to Ist's home. Meretseger, Ist's mother, was at the river's bank washing the family's clothes against a stone with a small amount of natron; a soap made from salt deposits along river. Meretseger was a beautiful woman for her age and Kah thought that Ist was just a younger version of her. Ist's mother had let her straight black hair grow to her waist and held it back with a brown leather tie. She wore no makeup and thin lines had started to frame her eyes. Kah laughed at the memory of when his own mother told him how at the age of four he had said he was in love with her. Meretseger had taken it well and had said that it was cute.

"Hello Meretseger," Kah pleasantly called out.

"Greetings Kah," she replied.

"Where is Ist these days?"

"I believe she is swimming right now," she said motioning over her shoulder with her thumb.

"Oh."

Kah continued slowly poling towards the south and periodically casting his fishing line in the water. In the distance he saw Ist slowly swimming ahead of him in the middle of the river; this concerned him so he increased his pace. In a short time he was beside her.

"What on earth do you think you are doing Ist?"

"What!" she said.

He had obviously startled her. He could see that she was swimming naked. She obviously had not expected to be seen by anyone and tried unsuccessfully to cover herself with her arms.

"Kah!" she said surprised. "I'm just going for a swim by myself!"

"It is dangerous to be out here alone."

"Just a little," she agreed, "but I'll be fine," she said with a defiant toss of her head.

"Do you really think so?" he said as he pointed to two crocodiles that were on the bank sunning themselves.

Ist knew that he was right – she should not be in the river by herself.

"Come aboard and I'll take you home," Kah said as he offered her his hand.

This would not have been a problem for her when she was three or four, but she was twelve – pretty much a grown woman – and her body had gone through many changes.

"No I think I'll be fine," Ist said. She could not imagine being naked in front of Kah now.

"Now is not the time to be shy Ist," Kah said as he once again pointed to the place where the crocodiles once were. They had slipped silently away. He did secretly desire to see her naked as any boy his age would and he acted as if he were honourable, doing her a favor and that it was no big deal.

Ist looked at the bank annoyed, but quickly realized the stupidity of her actions when she noticed the crocodiles were gone! *This only means one thing – they are in the water!* Ist swallowed her pride and embarrassment and grabbed his hand. She quickly got to the back of the raft behind Kah and sat down hugging her knees to her chest. Kah did, nevertheless, sneak hidden peeks at her from time to time during their travel back to her home.

As Meretseger threw yet another sheet to wash on the stone slab, she heard muffled voices from further down the river. She looked up to see Kah poling towards her. Her daughter was sitting behind him naked – hugging her knees.

"Back so soon?" Meretseger asked humorously.

"There were crocodiles!" Ist said annoyed.

One farm to the south was the small family of Anum, his wife Bennu and their five children. They were as close to being homeless, without actually being labeled, as you could get. They lived on a very small plot of land and were always struggling to pay their taxes. Their oldest son, Rayu, played tag with his four brothers who wove in and out of the brittle scrub brush that covered the property. Rayu was ten years old and was approaching manhood, but had little to no skills to carry him into his adult life. He was raised with no belief in the spiritual world and nor did he have any desire for it. He was a particularly short boy with curly black hair, but the thing that surprised the people around him was the patch of white hair that grew above his left ear. He was a happy boy, always smiling, laughing and telling jokes. The nature of his family's financial situation was exceptionally dire. They could not even pay for what they owed. They had considered selling their children into slavery to pay the back taxes. A decision they were dreading to make.

Just south of Rayu's home there was another family farm. A family that was not as poor, nor were they as joyful. The oldest son, Anitka, sat under a small wild Ficus tree that only had given fruit once in his memory. He had always thought it was diseased. As a tall red haired boy, he was prone to acting out his frustrations with violence towards anyone that was close to him at the time. He also would viciously berate those who offended him. His face was lined with scars from the times that he had been on the losing end of one of his regular disagreements. His life was not one of peace and happiness. The only feature of his besides his red hair that made you want to pay attention to him out of curiosity were his perpetually watering eyes. Unfortunately, the reason for the unhappiness rested solely on his attitude towards his father's new wife, Uadjit. Even his two dogs did little to calm his spirits. He scowled when he saw his stepmother, methodically work the soil between the vegetable plants at the corner of his father's property. *The only thing my father ever gave me of any worth was teaching me to read and write,* he thought begrudgingly. He was definitely proud of that fact and he would look down on those who did not have these skills. *I wish he had been more careful with the water well, contaminated by the rats that had drowned in it. Maybe my mother wouldn't have died and he wouldn't have ever married that woman... why do I hate her so much?*

Hayki, Anitka's brother, walked out of the home and crouched down beside Uadjit and helped her to pull weeds.

"Mother, I milked the cow and the goats for you," he heard his brother say.

Just that was enough to annoy Anitka.

"Why does he ingratiate himself to her? Let her do it!" he muttered.

Hayki was two years younger than Anitka and much shorter. His head only came up to Anitka's chest, but what he lacked it height he made up for in stubbornness. Hayki was a quiet boy and was not one to make waves. He just accepted things as they were, much the same as Kah. He put up with his brother's aggression and truly did love his stepmother. In a lot of ways, Hayki had more fear than respect for Anitka and tried as much as he could to not show fear. He did not want to be like his brother who regularly was beaten by their father for his rebellion. More than once he had watched Anitka have his sides beaten with a rod until his ribs were black and blue. Hayki could see the tears well up in Anitka's eyes, but the older boy never let them out.

Anitka continued to watch both of them work together. *Why does he not have a problem with her, she has come into our home and wrecked everything,* he thought in spite of the fact that this was not true.

He had no clue as to what he would want to do in his life. One thing he did know — he wanted to be someone of importance, someone of significance, someone who others valued. For now, however, he needed to focus on surviving one day at a time.

O<small>N A BRIGHT SUNNY</small> morning Masud remembered receiving a royal summons from King Hor-Aha. A servant of the King approached him as he was preparing to fulfill one of his many daily bathing rituals. He recalled, that without warning, an elegantly dressed man appeared at the side of the cold water bath and handed him a tightly rolled scroll.

"The King is in need of your services to fulfill his desires," he had said.

Masud assessed the man that had disturbed him. He was of average height and not very muscular, but he had an air of authority in the way he walked. Thick black eye makeup, from lead sulfide kohl, surrounded his eyes, a heavy gold chain hung from his neck and large earrings swung from his earlobes. His hair was cut to his shoulders and he was clean shaven. Masud took the scroll apprehensively and opened it.

"Greetings Masud, High Priest of Amun,

I see your skills and wisdom are ever increasing. This great land of Kemet is thankful for your service, but I require one more thing from you. Search out Weneg and order him to teach a group of youths about the Beginning of an Empire! I am ordering this because for too long the truth about Kemet has been kept silent and people have become lazy in their memories. I intend to have the stories taught to the next generation so they in turn can keep the memory alive. Tell Weneg to search out viable students to give this instruction to. Do not fail me.

Signed by my hand, Hor-Aha, Fighting Hawk, Lord of the Two Ladies, Son of Amun, Faithful Protector."

Masud remembered he let the scroll roll itself up in his hand – it tickled his palm. *Weneg lives a long distance away – I must leave immediately to be able to get there before the week's end.*

* * *

Five youths sat on the packed dirt floor of a small hut; lit only with two sputtering oil lamps that needed constant attention. The shenti, the ankle-length shirts that they wore, were all in various states of disrepair. Some had unattended rips in their seams. While some were clean, others were just dirty. They met in the middle of the Qena sepat, a territory on the outer bulge of the Nile in lower Kemet. The room was cozy and inviting with no offending drafts like those that fought to sneak in. The hut's interior was calm unlike the wild exterior where prickly scrub brush grew. Edges of the room were filled with baskets overflowing with jagged pieces of broken red pottery that cast strange dark and mysterious shapes on the walls.

* * *

Weneg remembered how just a month ago, Masud, the young High Priest of Amun, had approached him and insisted that he take in some youths and teach them about the past.

"You have the wrong man to do this. I cannot retell that past. It is too hard for me. Besides I don't remember!" he had protested.

"You remember Weneg. You just do not want to face the memories." the Priest stated in a matter of fact tone. "You must do this!" he ordered. "Besides, it is your duty to pass this knowledge on to others."

Damn his wisdom! He knows that this is very hard for me . . . why can I not just be left alone to live my life in seclusion?

"You are to choose youths who represent our land. You are to instruct them. You are to guide them into the truths of the past. You are to impart the wisdom to those who will be faithful stewards of this knowledge. They must be wise. They must be trustworthy. They must be honourable. Search them out. It is a command of King

Hor-Aha. He has spoken and it shall be done." Masud said, not leaving room for debate.

"But how will I know who to choose? How will I find the ones who have all of these qualities? How will I know?" Weneg said, feeling overwhelmed and trapped in a task beyond himself.

"You will know!" Masud spoke unwaveringly. Weneg knew the discussion was over.

He did not want to delve into that part of his past. *This will be the death of me. I do not want to do this he cried out inside, but the High Priest commands it. The King demands it. Even though everything in me wishes to hide from this, I must do it.*

* * *

Weneg set off from his hut and travelled the beaten path north along the great river Nile. As he walked past the thin trees that grew between spiny briers, he paused to listen carefully to the river for any snorting or sounds from hippopotamuses. After he did not hear any he moved on.

The path split as a separate narrower trail cut to the left. The trail had wild grasses crowding its sandy sides. After several minutes of brisk walking, he heard dogs barking. It didn't bother him or even cause fear to rise up within him. He always had good experiences with dogs. He actually was fond of them. Two skinny beige dogs with pointed ears cautiously approached him wagging their tails. Weneg lowered his hand submissively and pet them. *I do not want to do this,* he said to himself as he thought about his task. Ahead of him he saw a small mud bricked building with a small corral to hold a few milk producing cows. There were only two goats and one cow. A man that had been tending the garden approached him.

"Greetings!" he said, as he quickly observed the old man.

"Greetings, Good Man! My name is Weneg. I am searching for Anitka and Hayki," he said as he glanced at the list he had spent hours, even days, pondering and deliberating over ... finally writing them carefully on a piece of papyrus. "I am to instruct them about the beginnings of this great land. I have been ordered by our great King to instill this knowledge to selected children. I will be teaching the lessons at my home. Do you have these children in your household? May I have your permission to share this knowledge with them?"

The man was obviously startled with this offering, sceptically looking at him. "First off my name is Asim and yes I have those two boys in my home. I have taught both of them to read and write – it was not easy though. I will send both the boys at the start of the week. Our two children are . . ." he said pausing as he yelled for the boys. As they waited Asim approached Weneg and lowered his voice, "Our oldest will be a handful though. He is bitter because his mother died when he was young and I have since remarried. His younger brother is not bitter at all. He is a well-rounded boy and obedient."

As Weneg waited for the boys to arrive he looked around the home. It was surrounded by fig trees. There was a small well that had been dug in a depression beside a hill that looked to be supplied by the river. Beside the house were large black stones surrounding an ash pit signifying the place they cooked their meals. The garden that Asim had been working in when Weneg first came was on a small plot of land next to a rundown building.

I am glad he was able to teach his children to read and write, Weneg thought. *So many people, children especially cannot do that these days. I wonder where Asim got his training – maybe he was a priest at one time?*

"Here they come," Asim said as two boys followed by a woman walked towards them.

The one boy was taller than his father and had short red hair. The other was shorter with black curly hair cut to his earlobes. Both of the boys had just a loin cloth on and wore no ornaments.

"Greetings boys," Weneg said joyfully. "Your father has enrolled you in classes at my home not too far from here," he said motioning with his thumb back down their lane. "You will find it exciting and interesting, but first I need you to find a small flat stone like this," he said as he pointed to a pendant in the shape of a slanted eye that he wore around his neck. "You will be making a token to wear as the months progress."

The tall red haired boy raised his eyebrows in a show of annoyance. *This must be the boy that Asim was speaking of. I wonder how his younger brother will be.*

The man stepped forward. "These are my sons. Anitka is the oldest," he said placing a hand on the taller boy's shoulder. "And this is Hayki – my youngest."

"Very good! I hope to see you both at the beginning of next week in my home," Weneg said, then he turned and left.

As he retraced his steps back down the lane, he was greeted by the same two dogs he had met before. When Weneg was on the main path, he headed further north until there was a separate road that once again headed towards the river. Down that short path he found an even smaller dilapidated farm. There were two goats tied beside a scraggily tree next to a very small, one room house. Five naked children ran around the yard screaming with joy. *Even though these children are dirty and malnourished, they seem to be happy.* As soon as the children saw Weneg, they ran over to him and begged for food. Even a black mangy dog that Weneg assumed was a pet walked towards him and wagged his tail.

"Okay, okay let's see what I have," he said as he opened his satchel.

Weneg found four pieces of dry bread and some cheese.

"Here you go," he said as he handed the food out to the greedy outstretched hands.

The small naked children grabbed the food and disappeared in an excited flurry. After the children left, a man not much older than thirty walked out from behind the house and greeted him. He had long thinning brown hair that was neatly kept back from his face by a tied cloth strap. Weneg greeted the man and they traded names Weneg informed Anum – the name he had given – of his goals for instruction.

"Rayu!" Anum called. He then looked back at Weneg and continued, "I have one child that is old enough that could benefit from your instruction. My wife Bennu and I cannot afford any type of payment though," he said cutting his words harshly.

Weneg shrugged his shoulders and replied, "I do not require payment from you. The King is providing for my needs, he just wants me to instruct a selected few and spread the knowledge of our history."

A young boy dressed in a tattered long shirt and followed by a middle aged woman, who had silver streaked hair, walked over to Anum. Weneg knew that the more expensive clothing – a linen shenti – was beyond what this family could ever afford.

"This is my son – Rayu," Anum said motioning with his hand.

Rayu began laughing – nervously at first – which he tried to contain, but he only got control of himself after Anum placed his hand on the boy's shoulder.

"Rayu cannot read or write – neither can we for that matter – so taking instruction will be difficult."

"I am not concerned whether he can do these things or not. He will receive help." Weneg said.

"Will I learn those skills?" Rayu asked excitedly. "I have always wanted to read!"

"Well it takes years to master the skills, but I recognize you have what it takes to succeed and we can get you started right away."

A wide smile broke across Rayu's face. This knowledge had been his desire for all of his life. Many times he had begged his father for instruction, but it was a pointless request since his father himself could not read or write. Rayu could not believe his good fortune – his dream of education would finally come true.

"All of my students are to bring a small black stone like this one," he said as he pointed to the pendant around his neck. "You will be given instructions on when and how to make this pendant and its purpose during my classes. I will hope to see you at my place at the beginning of the week then."

"Oh yes! I will see you then!" Rayu said overjoyed as he flung himself on the ground and kissed Weneg's feet.

This was a reaction that Weneg was not prepared for so he awkwardly stepped back from the boy. *What am I getting myself into here?* he questioned.

Weneg said his good-byes and then headed back home and enjoyed a slow leisurely walk to his hut. Though a pesky fly bothered him on the way, he loved the quiet walk with his own thoughts.

Weneg's home was just a small hut made out of clay bricks on the lower half and a wooden stick structure on the top part with a flat mud roof. He entered the building and walked to a side table and lit a wide red clay oil lamp. After it sputtered for a moment the flame caught and burned evenly. It cast gray oblong shadows on the walls. *Well that was successful,* he thought to himself, but still didn't know what to think about Anitka. *I think I will try to gather the remaining two tomorrow.* Weneg uncovered a basket that was pushed against the side wall. Dust swirled in the stagnant air making him cough and ultimately draw aside the window coverings. Fresh air muscled its way inside and refreshed the hut. In the dim light his cot seemed to call to him. It stood with its black legs, like curled scorpion tails, against the far wall. It was like an exquisite jewel in the midst of refuse – his most valuable possession – a legacy from a past life – a gift from a King.

After a restful sleep Weneg arose, packed a lunch for himself plus extras in case he met a few more hungry children and stepped outside. Early morning insects were buzzing around. Grey doves cooed as they sat in the trees along the path. He was glad he wore his reed sandals this morning since the ground still held the chill of the night. He walked past the laneway that had scooted off to the left where he had gathered Anitka and Hayki. The smell of the river was stronger at this place – something he had not paid attention to before. The river bulged at this point and crowded the path. There were a vast number of ducks and other water fowl sitting in the water at this place. *Those are easy pickings,* Weneg thought wishing he had a throwing stick.

He walked on and soon he came to Rayu's laneway. *Such a poor family,* Weneg mulled over in his mind. *I hope I can be a benefit to the young boy. He looks to be a boy that has the desire to soak up knowledge, but his ability . . . we will see . . ."*

As he walked on, he arrived at Prehirwennef and Meretseger's home – a couple he was familiar with. He knew that they had a daughter that still lived with them. The others had already married and moved into their husbands' homes. He knew that this family was better off than Rayu's. Prehirwennef had taken his daughters to be instructed by the priests at the temple. Ist – their daughter – could read and write almost as well as the priests.

"Greetings Weneg," A man called out as he raised his hand in salutation. "It is nice to see you again, Old Friend."

Weneg chuckled to himself and returned the greeting. He then informed the man about the new mission that he had been given. Before he could ask if he was interested, the man had agreed. *Another one!*

Weneg thought. *I have space for one more in my hut. Maybe Bakenkhons will want his son, Kah, to join my teachings. I know his family is wealthy considering he is a priest of Amun and his son will follow in his footsteps.*

The priest's home was larger than most other's in the area. The trees were immaculately kept clear of dead branches and no weeds grew around them. A feeling of unimportance swept through Weneg's mind as he thought about his own personal wealth. His low self-worth was magnified when he saw the small irrigated pools that had been stocked with fish and surrounded with bright flowers. A stone statue of Amun between two Ficus trees seemed to stand guard as he walked on to the property. He had been here before, but in a way he felt trivial.

A young man walked up to greet him. He was taller than most, had short black hair, brown eyes and wore a linen shenti that was of high quality. He wore papyrus sandals and a shell bracelet on his left hand.

"Hello Kah."

Kah raised his hand in greeting to Weneg.

"I have been commanded by King Hor-Aha to start teaching selected youths at my home about the beginnings of our glorious county of Kemet. I already have four students. I have space for one more."

"Are you asking me to join?"

"Yes I am, Kah,"

Kah thought for a while. *My father is gone to do his duty as priest of Amun, but that is coming to an end so I definitely have time for instruction and extra learning. My father has a high regard of this man of great wisdom.* "Yes, I will come to your lessons. Will they be at your home?"

"Yes, the lessons will be at my home, but I ask you to bring a small flat black stone so you can make a pendant. It must not be a purchased one, he stressed. You will have to make this pendant," Weneg said knowing what Kah was like. He knew that he would typically want to just buy a new pendant rather than put the effort into making it. He knew that Kah was a young man that prided himself on having the best of the best and was not afraid to tell you how much things were worth, or how much he had to trade for his possessions.

"If you are willing, I will see you at my home at the beginning of the week."

After Weneg had left Kah's house he passed Ist's home and was on the verge of arriving at Rayu's when he saw a young boy sitting on the path as if he was waiting for him. As he approached closer he noticed it was indeed Rayu.

Weneg raised his hand in greeting. The boy greeted him back.

"What are you doing out here Rayu?"

The boy stood and stared at him seemingly too embarrassed to speak. Finally he spoke.

"Would you have some leftover food that I could have?" he said, his voice shaky.

K AH, THE OLDEST STUDENT looked across the room at the old sage who had taught them about the origins of the gods. He told them about the Ogdoad; the eight creator gods that molded their world from nothing. The young teenagers; Ist, Hayki, Rayu, Anitka and Kah intently watched the old man as he spoke and held onto every word. These youths had been receiving history lessons for weeks now. The old teacher was a very slight man, almost bald, a chest that caved in like a ground depression and a quiet voice. However when he spoke, he did so with the wisdom and conviction he had gathered over his seventy years of life – an age rarely ever attained. Kah loved the stories the old man told. He stated the tales in such an eloquent way that it sounded like a poem. The one thing that Kah often wondered was, *what was the meaning of the scorpion tattoo that decorated Weneg's forearm?* He had never asked about it, but his eyes would sneak glances at it when the teacher used his hands to enhance the story. The five youths, all from various families had the same unadorned look – short hair, coarse kilt and bare calloused feet. Each one wore a black painted carved stone pendent tied with a red flax string. The stone was in the shape of a slanted eye, a token that they had carefully created and fashioned by themselves.

Weneg looked over the students sitting before him – all were bright and ready to soak up knowledge, but he saw their inner selves and understood them more so than they understood themselves. Hayki, calm and reserved, was definitely a loner. Rayu, the laugher, the youngest and poorest of all of them, prone to have giggling fits he could not control, but he did have promise and wisdom beyond his years. Anitka, the red haired, tall one, towered over every adult – a boy Weneg knew had a rough side that everyone had to be wary of. Kah, the inquisitive one and from a wealthy family, was always questioning, always trying to understand. Finally there was Ist named after Osirus' wife Isis – the lone female of the group. Even though she had short cropped black hair and a ratty complexion, Ist had a beauty that was fighting to burst out and nothing could be done to hide it. Weneg saw the inner strategy game the boys played unbeknownst to themselves to draw her affection. Ist knew – the boys didn't – but she knew.

The teacher raised his hand corralling everyone's attention to what he was going to say. "I have a story

to tell you . . . a story that changed our entire world."
And mine in more ways than one he thought to himself.

Immediately the room was silent. All laughing
joking and small chit chat was abruptly halted and
Weneg had their complete attention. The sage drew in
a breath and adjusted his seating, closed his eyes and
began to speak.

Do you remember when you first came to my
home and you all brought the small black stone? Do
you remember that I showed each of you how to carve
this pendant? I told you that the pendant signifies the
Eye of Horus. I told you that the pendant was for your
protection – protection not only for your body, but for
the knowledge you will carry. This knowledge is that of
royal power. This royal power is the history of royalty in
our great land. This must be preserved. It is up to each
one of you to protect this information. The pendant will
help you to keep safe. You are in the elite few that will
have this knowledge. I chose each one of you personally
and I was not coerced. Each one of you represents the
variety of citizens in this country.

* * * *

"You will not get away boy!" the bearded mouth
breathed. Narmer cowered under the grotesque face
that hovered above him "No . . . go away!" he tried to
scream as he writhed on the dirty floor. Black stinking
and rotting roots lashed his face as he squirmed free.
"Got you!" the man growled as he pinned Narmer's
shoulders with his thick dirt encrusted hand. "No . . ."
he whimpered. Narmer awoke in a sweat, away from the
bearded man and safely in his cot. Even though he was

the oldest and expected to be strong, he was ashamed that he was tormented by nightmares.

"Are you ok Narm?" the boy in the next bed asked.

Narmer rolled on to his side forced his eyes open and looked at his twin brother. "I'm fine Menes, I just had another bad dream again," he replied in a whisper.

"Just try to go back to sleep."

"I know," Narmer replied, but he couldn't and he lay there until morning.

The two boys got up at first light, dressed and folded their bedding. They would have had a servant do such things at daybreak, but their father – the King – insisted that they learn to look after themselves. Narmer was a tall boy, taller than most in his town. He knew that as the older son he would be the King someday, but not just yet – he had some maturing that needed to be done first. The task of being King seemed to be daunting in his mind. This was a pressure that he did not want to think about at his young age, but he accepted it. Menes – his brother – did not take this mantle of power that was to rest on Narmer's shoulders well. He desired it for himself. Many times he complained to their father about being left out only to be told that 'This is the way that it must be.' Their room was quite sparse; two narrow beds with wicker frames, two wooden chests for their clothes and bedding, two small tables each with an oil lamp and a low stool. Ako, the household cat had claimed their room as his own. He was as much a part of the furniture as the bed's headrest.

Narmer and Menes walked outside his family's home in the quiet town of Abydos that lay beside the great river that had been named the Nile. His home was considered a palace by the citizens in his Nome or territory. The short but wide, whitewashed, mud-bricked building was none-the-less the home of the King. The structure contained the living quarters with multiple rooms; a kitchen, bedrooms, a grand hall, offices and a large dining room. Green fragrant trees, purple, yellow and red flowers grew in abundance around the buildings. Outside there was a large courtyard including an army barracks with a grand training ground off to the left side. The Nile flowed in front of the house and barracks and almost touched the training grounds, the temple of Min sat behind the palace and seemed to be watching over it like a hen with a clutch of chicks.

At twelve, Narmer knew that the Nile was a mysterious river. It was dangerous. Great hippopotami and vicious crocodiles roamed its banks, unchallenged. The deadliest of which were the bulky, grey hippopotami. Even though several people died each year from these creatures, Narmer was never affected. He was fearful of the water and didn't get too close to the swirling brown liquid. Aside from the fact that the twins were very close, Menes did not like the fact he held a secondary status to his older brother and constantly pointed out the things he was better at. Menes did not share his brother's fears about the river and regularly teased him about it. The most surprising and awe inspiring thing this great river did was; every year it would flood its banks and deposit new wet soil everywhere encouraging plant growth. *This gift of the Nile that Hapi brings is sure a mess,* Narmer thought as he walked along the bank keeping a wary eye on the water.

The boy's father, King Scorpion – the name he was known by – consistently took his boat up and down the river trying to gather fighters to go north to Ta-Mehu and as he would say, "to unify this land of rabble." Narmer wasn't so sure that this could be done, but if it could it would be many years from now. He knew the northern people were hard to track down, but when they did find them they were extremely tough to fight. The Northern King wore a gaudy red crown which was unlike his father's more impressive, sleek, white, conical one. They also were behind the times, as Narmer's father stated that when it came to their outdated weapons being: plain short flint daggers, unhardened wooden maces and common axes that were all usually dull King Scorpion, along with his war advisors, had developed a new tool for fighting: a stretched cow hide over a rectangular wooden shield that protected them from the flurry of quick knife slashes and battering mace blows. A new type of mace was also invented by mistake Narmer was told. This new mace had a stone lashed to its end making it almost indestructible.

Khu plodded after the princes as they walked throughout the town greeting citizens. Khu was now – after his retirement – security detail for Narmer and Menes – an honourable position. He had fought in more wars than he could count and had the scars to prove it. He followed them to the outskirts of the temple and watched as the faithful servants cleaned and kept the grounds immaculate. The servants bent their backs with wooden hoes in hand on the plot of land they were given for their food needs. Khu tightened his grip on his spear as random people almost swarmed the young boys as they asked for handouts or some type of favour. *I never need to worry too much,* he thought, *the princes are so loved by these people that they would never harm either one of them.* He never the less kept a wary eye on them.

"Let us go to the practice grounds and throw the spear at targets for some exercise," Narmer said.

Khu nodded his head and followed the princes to the grounds. Behind them, a tall skinny dog with pointed ears kept pace and nuzzled the prince's dangling hands.

"Oh there you are Mahut. I was wondering where you got to," Menes said playfully. The dog's tongue lulled out of his mouth as he trotted along. Narmer placed his hand on the dog's back and ran it down to his curled tail. They passed the shops that had been setup one beside the other. They saw the pottery makers molding red clay on small spinning turntables and the flint knappers fashioning arrow heads and knives, while huddled over blocks of this much needed rock among a growing pile of stone chips. Four weavers were hard at work creating beautiful linen blankets and clothing. Narmer and Menes stood for a time and watched the men create the necessary goods and then moved on.

"I love that smell," Menes confessed as they approached the bakery kilns.

Menes and Narmer stood and watched as the cooks scooped up handfuls of sand and added it to the grains of wheat to speed up the grinding process. They watched as the flour was made into dough then formed and baked in giant ovens.

"That is going to be so good when they are done," Menes said licking his lips. They approached three women working a long loom that lay pegged an arm's length off the ground. One woman was making the linen thread by beating dried flax stalks with mallets and separating the chaff, then rolling the thread into balls. The other two women worked the loom and made finely crafted sheets. The white sheets they were making would of course be used for trading and making cloths. Off to one side were three bolts of linen sheets that were so delicate and fine, they were transparent.

"The Queen will love this," Narmer said as he held the cloth between his fingers and slowly rubbed them together.

At the practice grounds, five straw sheaves were set up at varying distances at the end of the field, with racks of spears on the far right side. Narmer picked up three sharpened light spears and walked to the twenty paces line aimed and threw. The minute he threw Mahut took off and tackled the tightly bound sheaf.

"Get back here Mahut!"

The dog dropped the mangled sheaf, lowered his head and guiltily walked back to the boy. Menes threw next – his throw was worse.

"Ha! I'm older AND better!" Narmer teased.

"You are only older by a donkey's fart . . ." Menes teased back.

"Hey!" Khu scolded.

"We are just having fun," Narmer said with a pouty smile as Menes nodded in agreement.

They reset the sheaf and Narmer threw again. It was not a bull's-eye, but it was close. Narmer hoisted a second and let it fly. It too was off, so was the third. Menes hurled his next javelin as well, still with poor results.

"If I can help, Prince. . ." Khu said. "If you plant your feet like this and hold the spear this way. . ." Khu instructed as he hoisted his own spear and stood in a particular stance. "You will find that your accuracy is much greater." Khu let his spear fly dead centre into the target.

"You have done this longer than me . . . I just need more practice," Narmer said as he shook his head.

"That is true, you do require more practice, but learning to use and throw a spear is an art, Prince."

Narmer and Menes listened for an hour and a half drinking in all the information – Mahut laid at their feet, his head outstretched. Khu taught them the finer points of throwing the spear; how to let the spear roll off your fingers as you release it, how to properly aim allowing for drop and wind and how to pick the best kill shot.

"Throw again."

Narmer and Menes stood back on the line and threw with much better results this time. They continued to practice until their hands hurt and muscles ached. Then they were informed that they were not allowed to throw from any other line until they hit the centre with every throw.

"You have more skills than just security, Khu, is that not so?" Menes asked.

"Yes I do, Young Prince. I have fought all my life. I taught weaponry and fighting under your father. I was even given a field to grow my food, but I am old and tired. I want to spend the remainder of my days with my young son who desperately misses his mother. She died before he had the chance of really knowing her. I want to relax under the trees and enjoy what years that remain of my life. Now I am retired from fighting and teaching. I spend my time planting and harvesting and doing security for the royal family."

"You taught us. . ." Menes observed.

"Yes it was an honour, Young Prince."

"But why do you not teach anymore! The people could use your skills. The King could use your skills!"

"I have taught for years and I am tired!" he said strongly.

Narmer and Menes could see an emotional wall rise behind his words. He did not want to revisit something, but what? Narmer was determined to find out.

"You say you are tired, but your skills are needed. They must be taught. At least teach me and maybe my brother here," he said as he gave his younger brother a playful punch in the shoulder. "What do you have to lose?"

"I have much to lose, my Prince. You have even more to lose," Khu replied.

"Why are you so fearful, Khu and what do I have to lose?"

Khu shuffled his feet staring into the glaring sun filled sky. Then he squeezed his eyes closed as he picked the exact words to say.

"You have your life to lose! The last students I had did not listen to what I instructed. They were too busy playing and have now died. At first I got angry and pleaded with them to listen, but they just kept dying. I thought *is it me, have I lost my touch*, but no I just teach the skills and then it is up to them. Then my star pupil, a good friend, received a grave injury using my signature move that I only teach my best and bravest. I taught him the move after much begging on his part . . . I should have known . . . I should have known he was too much of a hot-head to follow my instruction."

"What happened to him? Why was this any different than any other fight?"

"It is different because he used my move, a move that intentionally drops your defences when your aggressor is attacking so that he thinks he has the upper hand, but in fact it is a trap to lower his defences." Khu paused for a while . . . "I cannot do it anymore," he said as his voice became quieted. "I just cannot . . ." he stopped again as if the retelling of the story was too painful for him.

Mahut whined and wagged his tail.

"I want to learn from you, Khu. I want to be taught by the best – I need to be taught by the best."

"Me too!" Menes added not to be out done by his brother.

"You do realize I can command you to teach me," Narmer said as he placed his hand on the dog's head.

"Yes I realize that Prince, but understand what it is you are asking of me. I would put you through a battery of tests to harden your skills – I will not go easy on either one of you because of who you are. You must not give in to childish fears. You must obey every word I say no matter what!"

Narmer thought about Khu's words and agreed right away along with his brother, but Khu told them to spend more time thinking about it before agreeing to the training. *I need this if I am going to be the King someday!* Narmer thought. *I must be careful not to fall into the same trap as the others. I must use great wisdom and listen to Khu's instruction. I must not be reckless and irresponsible in this teaching.* Prince Narmer purposed in himself, *I will listen well! I will learn to be cautious and exercise good judgement! I will gain the foresight and discernment of my teacher! I will be a king of honour, integrity and wisdom!*

* * *

Narmer felt the wind blow in his face as he accompanied his father on one of his river trips. He leaned forward along the side of the reed boat – surprisingly unafraid. The brown water slid quickly underneath his outstretched hand as he smiled and laughed to himself as he leaned over the side of his father's ship. Min's Wisdom was the ship's name. It was a long and wide reed bound ship. It also boasted blue and white flags and a tall curving prow. A fish jumped at his fingertips trying to nibble them. He looked back at his father, but all he saw was the mid-ship cabin. "Father . . . somebody?" no answer – the sailors had disappeared. Then the small reed hut expanded and contracted like it had a life of its own and was breathing like an odd looking monster. The boards on the side of the small ship's cabin began to split wider and wider with every breath it took. Fear enveloped Narmer with every crack of the papyrus stalks. "Father?!" The hut exploded on its final breath leaving a large bull hippopotamus in its place. He frantically looked for someone to help him – there was no one there. The hippo began to lumber forward smashing the boat with every step like it was made of thin dry reeds. The beast never sank into the water, it just kept coming and Narmer kept retreating to the front of the boat until he was clutching the very top peak of the prow. With one final push forward the hippo reared up on its back legs, crashed down on the boy and the prow. Water flooded all around him as he awoke with a startling gasp. He sat upright in bed with sweat pouring off his brow. The nightmare was over, he realized, as he hyperventilated. He did not want to sleep again. He looked at the bed beside him. Menes was not awake; Narmer was glad, so he pushed the disturbing thoughts out of his mind and thought about Khu's instruction. He then slept out of sheer exhaustion, later waking lying in the same position on his sweat soaked, linen covered bed. He then heard the loud padding of feet outside his window.

It was Shumo – summer time – low water and time for the harvest. It was hot at noon. It would be so hot it was hard to breathe. Narmer rolled onto his stomach and in one fluid motion pushed off with his hands, pulled his legs under himself and stood up. He walked over to the window and yanked off Menes covers, pushed aside the reed blind and peered outside.

"Hey!" the drowsy boy lazily moaned.

During that morning he thought about Khu; his lesson, his offer to teach and his warning. *Am I willing to give myself over to Khu's instruction with no argument . . . I don't know, it is a big responsibility.*

What Narmer saw shocked him. The sound of the feet he had heard earlier came from the hundreds of men with leather covered wooden shields, others with sharpened poles and many more with stone tipped maces. All of the men he saw carried flint knives in a range of sizes. When he saw all of this he quickly put on a kilt and walked into the main part of the house. There he saw his mother Nestuwan having her makeup applied by a female body servant.

"Where is the King?" he asked.

Nestuwan looked bothered and a little annoyed. "He is out with the men," she said.

Narmer ran outside in search of his father. As he walked out of the palace he could see the Nile. It flowed through the property straight as an arrow, but it was banked up on each side with dark brown sludge. Many papyrus rafts filled and clogged the river. *Why are these men here?* he thought as he looked for his father. Off in the distance there was a crowd of men surrounding Hor-Nu the local priest, a stout bald man who wore a leopard skin draped over his right shoulder. He held a smoking red bowl that was sending bitter smelling fumes into the air as he chanted prayers in a doleful drone. Trumpets sounded and all the men lined up in large square formations – three groups of two hundred men – all farmers. Local citizens from the neighbouring towns had been arriving at a steady pace throughout the night and now the small town of Aswan had exploded from hundreds, to thousands of people. The horns blared again. A procession of acolytes appeared. There were six young men, their heads shaved and clothed in long white thin cloaks, carrying a tall golden box between two long bejewelled poles into the midst of the men. The crowd split and Hor-Nu raised his hands and bowed his head in supplication.

"Behold! The great god Min has graced us with his presence. Bless this journey north to Ta-Mehu to bind this land together," Hor-Nu called out.

A great cheer arose from the men who proceeded to stomp the ground and beat their spears together. Hor-Nu approached the golden Naos box – the box that contained the god's image – with outstretched arms as the acolytes lowered it to the ground. The priest said a prayer and then opened its doors. Inside a golden statue of the god Min, the god of fertility, stood between offerings of flowers and stalks of green lettuce. The god held a flail in his raised right hand and with his left, was holding his exposed erect phallus. He was ornately clothed in fine linen and had a stern look. He was a moon god, the god of the Eastern Desert, of agriculture and male fertility; so in his honor Hor-Nu started to sing a hymn.

You are the Great Male, the owner of all females.
The Bull who is united with those of the
sweet love, of beautiful face and of painted
eyes, Victorious sovereign among the Gods
who inspires fear in the Ennead.
The goddesses are glad, seeing your perfection.

[World of the Pharaohs – Könemann]

Narmer lowered his head and tried to sing along, but found he stumbled over the words and repeated lines. *I'll never get that song right,* he cursed. Beside him, Menes sang along unchallenged – he knew the words. Narmer watched his father surrounded by his guards and advisors mount the small dais, the royal platform that had been set up at the far end of the field. King Scorpion addressed the army of men. The young boy strained to hear what his father said, but could not. During his father's speech the warriors clapped and broke out into cheers as the King spoke. Hor-Nu held the bowls filled with incense high as Narmer's father continued to speak. Nestuwan, the Queen, under shade coverings held by nubile women servants, walked between the rows of bowing men and up to the dais. Narmer knew his mother would have prepared herself for being out on the grounds today. She would have had black kohl paint under her eyes and had her eyebrows plucked, false brows added and her favourite ruby red paint would have been applied to her fingernails and toenails. His mother always wore a long tightly braided wig that had golden charms attached to the ends and wore oil of roses and iris as a perfume that created a fragrant trail as she walked. A hush fell over the crowd of men as the King stepped forward and stretched out his hand greeting the Queen. He then turned to the crowd and addressed them.

"As you well know, Hsekiu - the King of the Northern marshlands, holds sway over many villages right up to the Great Green, that never-ending expanse of water we all have heard about. You all have known that we barely hold our borders against him because of the constant skirmishes that deplete our numbers so greatly. I have now been told that the King of the north is old and will not live too much longer. We do not have much time. His son Thesh is untried and very young. Now is the time to act. In one year we will sail under the protection of Min and take the Northern land and unite the north and south lands."

A cheer arose in the crowd, but a cloud of worry permeated Narmer's mind. He didn't like when his father left the palace – *if you could call it a palace,* he had always thought. *Besides, Hsekiu probably has a real palace with real guards, which is why he is so powerful,* the boy thought. *Besides, a year is a long time away.* In reality though, the year would feel as if it flew by like an eagle speeding towards its prey.

* * *

One year had passed and again the King addressed the farmers trying to prepare them for the journey ahead. He hoped they would have taken initiative on their own in the past year for the possible fight ahead. The King looked over the group of men; they were a naturally well fit group of men, but did they have the skills for battle? He stood on a platform facing the men and spoke to them.

"We will sail north in two days," the King said. "Pack your weapons and shields; say your prayers to the god so that he will keep us strong and be at the river at daybreak."

Hor-Nu, the Hem netjer had the god, Min's Naos shrine brought before the people and opened in preparation for the King's departure. The priest shouted out a blessing and then on his signal, the inlayed double doors to the golden shrine were closed. The young We'eb priests who surrounded Min's sanctuary, lifted it and carried it back to the temple.

Narmer did not like this god that was in fashion at the present time. He felt that Horus or Amun were more powerful and deserved his worship. In private, he had his own small shrine he bowed to every night, and that gave him comfort.

* * *

Smells of the upcoming meal enticed the crowds that gathered in the small reception hall outside King Scorpion's palace. Roast duck, seared spiced beef, salted steamed vegetables and crisp cool fruit had been all prepared for this very important meal. The dais had been disassembled and moved to the inner courtyard where the meal would be served and now the King and Queen were seated between two fan bearers receiving their due adoration. Hor-Nu – ever watching, was mumbling prayers with the We'eb priests on the left side of the royal couple. Narmer and Menes sat on soft cushions at the base of the dais, impatiently waiting for the food to arrive.

"Any time now!" the annoyed Menes said as he impatiently tapped his foot.

The King then stood and everyone quieted.

"Tomorrow we set sail to take the hostile territory to the north and squash the continual assaults on our homeland. We will bring Hsekiu to his knees, take his kingdom and blend these two lands together. There are not enough boats to carry all of our soldiers, so a group of warriors will march on the banks for one day and then trade with the sailors the next day. I will also be training shock troops along this journey and they will be the first to assault the enemies we will meet. While we are away, Queen Nestuwan will keep our land safe."

Narmer looked at his twin sitting beside him and leaned over whispering to him, "I'm concerned about our father." Menes looked back at him and nodded in agreement. "These are not fighting men. The only thing they fight are the weeds in their crops."

"That is true . . . We must talk to our father."

A S THE DAYS PROGRESSED closer to the time of his father's departure north, Narmer could not shake the feeling of doom he felt surrounding his father's plan of war. *I could prepare for this war much better than my father,* he thought boldly, in reality though he wasn't so sure. Menes felt the pangs of worry as well, but he kept them bottled inside, only sharing them with Narmer. Many times, Narmer had asked the King to create security guards that would be beside him at all times when he was away, but his pleas fell on deaf ears.

"You worry too much Narm," [the pet name he was called by only a select few]. Besides, I have you and your brother to confuse anyone who would do me harm," his father said trying to make a joke.

Narmer scrunched up his face and shook his head. "That was not funny Father, I am looking out for your safety and I will not be with you during the fight."

"Do not trouble yourself. I am bringing along many warriors. I'll be safe."

"You mean farmers."

"No, the men have been practicing," The King replied.

"Father, surely a great King such as yourself can see that these 'soldiers' as you call them, are not at the proper standard that they need to be for battle."

The King's mind was made up. "The men will learn quickly enough when the fighting starts . . . if the fighting starts."

Standing a little distance away, seeing his brother talking to the King, but only hearing parts of the conversation, Menes felt in some ways neglected by his father. *Look at him listening to Narm. Why does he not hear what I have to say?* Menes becoming sullen, realized that Narmer was beginning to receive private instruction from their father on the ways of being the King.

The next day was slightly cool and windless in the morning, as the soldiers prepared to march and sail north. Narmer looked out over the grounds where bright blue and white flags fluttered in the cool breeze. He saw his father arrive behind a group of men that flew the King's banners, followed by Hor-Nu. The Hem netjer, soon was surrounded by the We'eb priests and shaded by an expanse of cloth hanging from decorated poles.

"Hail to thee Min. You are The Great Male. You alone can give us victory over the north!" Hor-Nu droned on as Narmer listened uninterested. He thought about the praises given to the god. He didn't trust this particular god nor did he even believe in him. Narmer had never revealed his unbelief to anyone except Menes – especially not to his father. He didn't want to show his doubt to the King and jinx his abilities in the war. Amun was by Narmer's belief a more powerful god, but there was nothing that could be done now.

The King walked up the reed-planking to Min's Wisdom, the largest boat, and stepped aboard. He had dawned all his royal weapons; an ornate stone-tipped mace and a copper ax both hanging on a belt for this occasion. The town people cheered as his army formed into two separate regiments – infantry and sailors. The sailors boarded the boats and readied the small ships to catch the current north. The infantry formed into a column on the right side of the river and started marching north. While the musicians played on their lyres and beat their drums, Narmer saw his mother and brother at the water's edge standing beside Hor-Nu saying their good-byes to the King. Narmer then rushed to them and said his good-byes as well. Soon, the current caught the boats and swept them down river past wallowing hippopotami that were nearly submerged by the banks. They watched the boats glide down the river until they lost sight of them, only then did they turn away and walk towards the palace. As Narmer was walking he saw Eshe standing on the path to the palace.

"Narm!" Eshe called out as she ran towards him towing a little child who had captivated her affections at the present time. "Narm, did you see all the boats on the river? They were so spectacular I wish I could have gone on one of them. Don't you wish you could go?"

"No I don't wish to go. You know I don't like the river," he reminded her.

"Don't be such a baby Narm," she teased.

"Don't call me a baby. That is a baby," he said pointing to the young child that hugged her leg. "Do you know how many people died last year from hippos and crocodiles? Fifteen people, that's how many Eshe, fifteen!"

Eshe thought for a minute, "First of all this is Wenemon," she replied, but she didn't have a rebuttal to his facts. She knew there had been many deaths, but she had no clue of the numbers. She eyed the river pensively and felt a chill when she saw a crocodile stealthily slip under the ripples of water. The young girl began to understand his fear and rubbed the triangle of moles on her neck in consideration, but her only feeling was that of caution.

Narmer thought about Eshe – her name meant kitten. She loved children and was the daughter of an influential family in the town. The King and Queen approved of her family; that is all that mattered to anybody. He thought about his father, the King, sailing into the unknown. *One day I will be as bold as him and conquer this fear. I can't be a King if I am scared of a river!*

"I must go Eshe. I will walk with you later," he then turned leaving her to tend to the child, which she didn't mind at all. He walked to the palace and into the eating area where his family was waiting for the servants to prepare the noon meal. The room was a comfortable size with a small dais at the far end. Central to the room was the seat of power. The throne sat in the middle, flanked by vases holding rare trees and flowers.

A splash of the colors – gold, green and purple, radiated out on each side of the majestic seat. The throne itself was short in stature, but because of the dais, it sat high in the room. He often spent time inspecting its sleek curves and ornate symbols. Two huge ebony scorpions crouched on the floor on either side of the golden throne, with their shiny black tails serving as armrests, looking like they were ready to strike any assailant that would foolishly approach the King – an imposing sight that instilled fear to all.

"When is Father coming back?" Narmer asked later that week.

"Have some patience. It will be some time before we hear what your glorious father has accomplished. We just have to wait to hear from him."

"How will we know he is safe if we don't hear from him?"

"Narm, the god will provide safe passage for the runners to give us information about the King. We just have to wait and trust," Nestuwan said. "By the way Son, how are your new servants and teachers?" she asked changing the subject.

"They are infuriating me Mother!" he said as he pictured the fat teacher that hovered over him as he practiced his writing. "He consistently confuses me with Menes. The new servants are not as bad, although Baruti - the other teacher, is by far the worst."

Nestuwan raised her eyebrows as she looked at her son. "That should not be a surprise to you Narm, because you and your brother are twins."

"I know, but it does get tiring," he said annoyed.

"About your father," the Queen said steering him back to their original conversation. "You need not worry about the King, he is in good hands... he is in the god's hands," she repeated trying to stress the point.

That was cold comfort to a young boy who was missing his father, but he did have to wait and there was nothing he could do about it. Days turned into weeks and still there was no word from the north. *No news is good news* he remembered his mother had told him, but Narmer didn't believe that. During the day, Narmer searched out the priests of Amun to plead for prayers and seek blessings for his father and the soldiers, but Nakht - the priest, informed him that he could not.

"The King had asked for the blessing of Min for this war. Asking Amun for protecting a campaign that Min is in charge of, will be an insult to both gods and may cause harm to the King.

Be happy that he has some protection, not as much as I believe Amun could offer, but he has protection."

This was very limited consolation to him. He knew the High Priest of Amun meant well, but this was his family and he could not just do nothing. Narmer was determined to find extra protection for his father and no priest would dissuade him. In the palace he searched through the scrolls in the King's library trying to find as much about Amun as he could – how powerful was he and where were his shrines and temples? There was so much to find out and he felt that time was running out.

Narmer walked into the palace and weaved through the buzz of servants, who were busy in some capacity, doing the will of the Queen either by command or by fulfilling their regular list of chores. Along the hallways, small purple flowering plants thrived by the constant care and attention of Nestuwan's dedicated staff. The floor was hard-packed dirt under the young prince's feet, although the floor seemed to sag in the middle of the hall, but it was well kept and clean. As he got deeper into the house, quietness settled around him as determination to find answers enveloped him. Off in the distance at the end of the hall he saw the King's office. *That is what I want,* he thought. *If there is any solution to this foreboding in my Ka for my father, it must be in there. There has to be some type of guidance in the library.* Narmer approached the door and looked from side to side. He saw no one and then let himself in. *I wish Menes were here,"* he thought.

In a dark corner of the King's office, Narmer searched through papyrus sheets of spiritual writings that had been copied from the old clay tablets. As he searched the baskets, he found tucked away on the bottom shelf; old documents that had yet to be transcribed to papyrus. Narmer then saw red clay tablets that were stacked on end, leaning against each other in the dark recesses of the lowest shelf. He pulled out the basket and gazed at the rectangular plaques. They were coated in dust and covered in spider webs. He picked up the first tablet and read the heading, it said: The Unknown Duat; the second, Concepts of Life; the third, Ib, Sheut, Ka and Ba; the fourth, Transcending Life; and finally the fifth, Communication in Aaru. He could not believe it; here, hidden away was the template of life. Narmer knew he was not allowed to be snooping in the King's private office and it wasn't beyond Her-uben to discipline him. Her-uben, the King's chief of security, had on occasion given him a beating for insubordination. He never broke the skin, he just rapped his sides a number of times with a thick willow switch. The pain was palpable – a deep stinging pain. Narmer did not want to have that happen again. "Why were these tablets tucked away and unseen? They should be carved into the walls and preached far and wide, not sitting here with dust as their only companion," he muttered to himself.

He scanned the first text - The Unknown Duat - it told him of the time, before time, and how there was chaos in the midst of nothing. Amun created himself. He then created the other gods, his children were they themselves the gods of air, land, water, light, the underworld and the sky. Narmer stopped reading. *Why are we worshiping Min? All honor should be for Amun, he was the first – he had real power. I knew I was right!* Narmer put down the tablet and reached for the second; it grated against the others as he pulled it out, sending small wisps of powdered dust into silent room.

He then heard the creak of leather from out in the hall. *Oh no! It must be Her-uben* he panicked . . . *I'll be beaten for sure!* Pain from previous beatings seemed to start all over again in his ribs. He looked around the office to find some cover, he then saw a coarse brown blanket tucked away in the corner beside a red basket. Narmer grabbed it, flung it over the clay tablets, and pushed the covered evidence under the shelf. The door scraped open just as he folded himself between the wall and a stack of boxes. Her-uben walked in and stood silently waiting and listening - just a step inside the door. After a few minutes he walked in and stood behind the desk. Narmer saw his scarred broad back from his hiding place. *When is he going to move? I can't hold this position too much longer.* The bulk of a man, doubled over and glanced under the small table hoping to catch the boy unaware. *I am going to be in so much trouble if I'm caught,* Narmer worried. Her-uben moved closer again to Narmer's hiding spot – so close he could hear the guard's raspy breathing. *Please leave,* Narmer silently begged Amun, breaking out into a cold sweat. As if he was instructed by a higher power, Heruben walked out of the office leaving the prince curled uncomfortably in a ball in the corner. *What a relief – if that was you Amun, you have shown your power in even the smallest of things.* Narmer uncurled himself and picked up the first tablet and left the room.

* * * *

Weneg looked at the group of students in front of him; they were engrossed in his story. *That went well enough, yes I think I can do this,* he told himself. He stood up with the help of a cane and walked over to a nearby basket, lifted the reed lid and pulled out an old tablet. He then placed it on a brown cloth lying on the ground in front of the students.

"Come and look. You might learn something just by seeing this. There might be something you see that I cannot teach."

Kah walked to the centre of the room followed by Ist and Rayu. He kneeled down and absentmindedly brushed the dust off the ancient writing that filled every corner of the clay plaque. The words were not as familiar to him in their spelling as he was used to, but he could read the title without problem. It said The Unknown Duat. Kah quickly looked up at Weneg. *This is the same tablet he was telling us about.* Kah looked down at the writing with renewed reverence.

"This is really hard to read!" Rayu complained as he looked at the small letters on the tablet.

"Can you even read?" Anitka questioned the boy in an insulting tone.

Rayu hung his head feeling defeated and quietly said no.

"I will read it for you Rayu!" Kah said as he picked up the tablet.

Anitka rolled his eyes when Kah offered to help the underprivileged boy.

From the waters of chaos Atum created himself out of shear will, joined with his shadow and brought forth his children to create the world; air, land, day and night, good and evil.

"This is the basis of our life, our belief. Study it well," Weneg said. "You can just listen and soak up the information," Weneg said to the smiling Rayu.

Kah quickly retraced his steps to his spot on the floor, gathered up his writing supplies, returned to the clay tablet and copied the inscriptions. As he was doing this he noticed that Hayki and Anitka had not followed his lead. They didn't move forward to copy the pallet. Ist was the first to finish after him. Weneg stood up, walked to the middle of the room and picked up the old writing, rewrapped it and returned to his seat.

"If you would like, I will continue the story," Weneg said as he leaned forward on his stool.

"Please continue," they all agreed.

5

TWO MONTHS AFTER THE King had left to go north, the first message was received via Chisisi the runner. He held a tightly bound roll affixed with a bees wax seal. The deeply tanned man approached the dais and waited to be called in turn. The Queen sat on the Scorpion Throne surrounded by young servant girls holding peacock fans and the chief viziers sat beside her on short chairs. Dispatches from the small Nomes the King controlled, were swiftly ruled over – many were disputes over land boarders or small petty crimes by youths. Finally Chisisi was called. He bowed low to the floor with his arms outstretched and waited for the Queen to bid him rise.

"You may rise Chisisi, I trust you have secured news from the north for us?"

The man stood up and retrieved a small scroll from his satchel and handed it to the Queen who in turn handed it to the official on her right. Duaenre accepted the scroll and broke the seal and read:

To the Great Queen Nestuwan and respected officials:

We have taken the current north towards the Great Green to meet Hsekiu in battle and claim this land. I did not think that I would have met such little resistance from the villages along the way. We enter each town with the decks of our boats lined with soldiers at full arms. When they see us, they drop their tools and kneel in homage. We then pull the boat to a dock if they have one and disembark. I do have this planned so that by the time I arrive at each village the ground troops also arrive in full force. I have never had a group that didn't yield and swear their allegiance to me on the spot. Praise to Min, he has truly blessed me – you must sacrifice five bulls to the god on my behalf when you receive this. We now sail towards Thinis and trust that we will continue to be in the god's good graces.

Written and sealed by my hand and delivered to Chisisi my trusted servant.

King Scorpion,
May my name live forever.

Duanre let the scroll roll up in his hand and looked over at the Queen. Nestuwan considered the King's words and made the proclamation, "Tonight let us sacrifice to Min as the King has asked. We will keep our hopes and plans on our King's good fortune. Chisisi, where was the flotilla when you last received this message?"

"We were just outside of Thinis, my Queen. I did not see it, but I hear it is a large city of several thousand people. The small towns we had encountered so far had only a population of fifty or one hundred civilians."

After hearing that report, Nestuwan did not feel as optimistic as she had previously. Narmer and Menes were listening to the whole report and also felt the pangs of worry creep in. *I must do something to aid in my father's plight. I can't just put my trust in the mercies of a small unimportant god to protect my father. I must study those tablets and learn all I can,* Narmer thought. He then looked for an opportunity to leave the audience hall and study. His time to leave showed up soon after Chisisi left the steps of the dais.

"Where are you going Narm?" Eshe called when she saw him walking across the parade ground.

He turned to see his friend running up to him. He tried to quickly formulate a story to answer the impeding onslaught of questions he would undoubtedly be receiving, but came up empty.

"Greetings Eshe, can I help you? I can't stay and talk right now, I have to go," he said to the girl who had shoulder length black hair and was the same age. Surprisingly she was free of a usual tag-along child.

"What's the hurry, surely you can give me a little time? Where is your brother?" she asked grilling him with her quick-fire questions.

Narmer paused and moved his head from side-to-side stretching his neck until he felt a crack.

"I just saw you out here and wondered if you wanted to check out an old building I saw on the far side of the parade grounds? Don't you have a little time?" she said enunciating *a little* for effect.

He knew that as a prince he should have a security guard with him at all times, but today he had managed to slip the watchful eye of Khu. "Well I'm kind of busy right now, I don't know where Menes is or what he is doing. Where's your entourage?" he said with a slight smile as he shifted his bare feet on the ground – typically he wore papyrus sandals, but he didn't today.

"What is going on Narm? You never pass up a chance to go discovering with me," she said as she could see an inner struggle behind his eyes and was determined to find out the story.

"Hmm . . . I guess . . . well . . ."

"Hey I'm not getting any younger Narm and I'm free, let's go!"

Narmer looked around, trying to see if Khu had caught up to him – he didn't see him. "Well okay Eshe, just for **a little bit**."

She smiled and started walking with Narmer, keeping pace beside him, who was unusually quiet. They both walked past the tall palm trees at the three wooden docks jutting into the Nile and then followed the river to the far corner of the parade ground.

"What is going on Narm, you're too quiet?" she asked, not letting up as he avoided eye contact. Narmer turned his head to the side, away from her, his eyes darting this way and that searching for an answer. He didn't want to reveal his disbelief in the main god, but if he was to tell anyone, Eshe was the safest person.

"Have you ever thought about who the most powerful god is and who is the one we should pray to and trust in? We pray to Min and everyone tells us that he is powerful, right?"

"That's what I learned Narm, the same as you."

He glanced around to see if anyone could be listening, which was highly unlikely, but he had to make sure.

"Can you keep a secret?"

"Of course I can, you know that," she said as she remembered trading and keeping secrets with him throughout their entire childhood. "You tell me your secret and I'll tell you one of mine just to be fair."

"Okay. . . I was in the King's office and found an ancient tablet that mentions the old gods – the beginning of everything. I borrowed it."

"You mean stole."

"No, borrowed! I'm going to return it you know . . . I just need to study it a little first."

"If you get caught . . . maybe by Her-uben," she said with a wry smile. "you will surely pay for that."

"That is why you must keep this a secret."

"I swear. Are you going to tell Menes?"

"Yes, I can trust him," he said introspectively. "Well, what is your secret?" he said taking a step back and placing his hands on his hips.

"I have been praying to all the gods to bless me with a child," she blurted out.

Narmer eyed Eshe really annoyed.

"You have been going on about that forever Eshe," he said shaking his head. "You know you must wait."

"Yes, but for how long? I see girls my age with children and I just heard Her-uben tell his daughter she was worthless if she could not produce a child. Narm, I do not want to be worthless."

"Oh you are not worthless, maybe annoying," he said as a poorly timed joke.

Eshe stepped back and raised her brows – she felt a little hurt. By now they had walked a long distance along the Nile's edge and far from the palace. Narmer was somewhat unfamiliar with this part of the river.

"Where are we going Eshe? I thought this would only take **a little bit**."

"Yes, maybe it was a little further than I thought."

A bright light shone in Narmer's eyes startling him. He stepped back and lifted his hand to shield his face. *Hrrooonnh, huuuuuuuuuugh, huff, huff, huff.* Narmer dropped his hand and looked towards the sound. He saw the sun reflecting glaring ripples of light off of the gray back of a large wet bull-hippopotamus. He could see the massive head staring at him, its small rounded ears standing at full attention. Its nostrils sprayed jets of mist with each snort. Narmer grabbed Eshe's hand and slowly backed away into the trees. When he had retreated far enough into the brush, he stopped and the bull turned its head and settled into the muddy water. Eshe placed her arm around Narmer's shoulder and squeezed tight. The prince could feel his heart pounding in his temples and he was slightly hyperventilating.

"What have you gotten us into Eshe? You know it's dangerous to be so far from the palace."

Eshe scowled at him and replied, "You must know that I didn't plan to stumble on a lazing bull, right?"

"I know . . . I just don't like those vile creatures. They invade my dreams and then steal my sleep."

Back at the palace, Menes searched for his brother – it was soon obvious to him that his brother was missing. Menes walked to the temple of Min and watched the priests complete their morning chores. The priests all stood around stone vats of cold water and bowls of natron they used for washing. The salt and ash mixture that was used for bathing and purification, was in very high demand. *The King could use the natron to trade for anything and everything*, Menes thought, as he remembered watching raw sea salt chunks being crushed to a fine powder and mixed with ash. This natron was then packaged for trade or use in the temples. Menes walked around the temple searching for his brother, but the only person of significance was Hor-Nu.

"Can I help you Young Prince?" the High Priest asked.

"Yes you can, I am looking for my brother. Have you seen him?"

Hor-Nu thought briefly, but shook his head no.

"I will contact Her-uben to help with the search, he will find your brother."

"Yes I'm sure he will," Menes said, knowing that Her-uben had a knack for finding Narmer and punishing him for his misdeeds.

Menes walked out into the parade grounds, but it was vacant. He then walked to the edge of the grounds and to the edge of the river. There was no sign of Narmer. Menes looked up and down the river bank, but still there was no sign. A thought crept into his mind. *If Narmer does not come back . . . I will be King. Everyone will bow to me! I hope he never comes back.* Menes shook his head and cursed himself for thinking such an awful thought.

Farther down the river and hidden in the scrub brush and trees, Narmer and Eshe continued to talk.

"Yes, you have told me how you can't escape the monstrous beasts before they trample and eat you. I'm sorry you must deal with that each night, it must be frightening."

"It is, and it's not every night, but almost." He closed his eyes and shook his head to clear his thoughts. "Why again are we out here?" he said as he looked around searching for an answer.

"Do you not see it Narmmy?" she said in a baby voice and pursed her lips.

"You are infuriating Eshe!"

Narmer slowly scanned the overgrown trees and the thick underbrush, not only once, but twice. All he saw was primarily dead trees with choking green vines wrapped around their trunks, scraggily waist-high brush atop of soft black soil. He could hear the trickle of water all around him, as well as the calls of two medium sized birds. As he focused he could see a short-legged painted snipe with its brightly coloured plumage and could hear the *coo coo coo* of doves and pigeons, at the top of the trees. The red headed woodchat shrike's *chip, chip, chip* call could barely be heard. Monitoring all, the hovering falcons waited for any bird on the ground to drop their cover and become an easy meal. Narmer then noticed a short brown structure hidden by the overgrowth.

"Is that what we came here for?" he asked, as he motioned, he made the Hamsa gesture with his hand to ward off the evil eye.

"Yes it is. Let's check it out!" she said as she walked towards it.

They approached the remains of the building, its roof had caved in long ago and the mud bricks that formed the walls were un-repairable. As Narmer and Eshe got closer to the building, they pushed aside the vines that had overgrown the door frame, and entered. They saw that part of the collapsed roof still hung on the left side of the room at a 45° angle; the remainder lay on the floor mostly rotted away. The remains of one table and three chairs that had at one time sat in the centre of the space, had now been completely destroyed by the fallen ceiling.

"Wow, this is something!" Narmer gasped as he looked around.

"I knew you would like it," Eshe replied.

"I never knew this place existed. What do you think it was?" he asked.

"I can't imagine what this was, but I think it's time to explore."

"Agreed! My brother is sure missing this," he said as he eagerly entered the room.

Narmer noticed the walls had been once whitewashed and painted with rudimentary scenes, many of which were overly spiritual in nature. Unfortunately, a large amount of the plaster had flaked off the walls taking the pictures with them. There were empty niches in the walls at chest level. At one part of the wall there was a list of tasks; bread, wine, prayers, songs and honour. *Well I guess this won't hurt,* he thought as he picked up a sharp stick and scratched a picture of a fish on top of a wedge into the wall. Eshe looked at him and rolled her eyes and pursed her lips.

"Must you scratch your name into everything?" she asked annoyed.

Narmer just shrugged and then walked to the left side of the room, where the roof was laying against the wall. He then tried to see what, if anything, was being blocked from sight. He managed to squeeze himself along the end of the wall and looked at the underside of the roof and the wall. *A door!* His heart beat faster. *If I can only get through there, I can see what is beyond that door.* Narmer un-wedged himself and stood up planning his next move and then noticed Eshe trying to reassemble the broken table and chairs. He grabbed the roof and pulled, but he could not move it. He then reached higher along the frame and using his leg as leverage, placed his foot against the wall and pulled. The roof gave way and pulled back from the wall. It teetered on edge for a split second and then crashed down flat into the centre of the room. Eshe let out a short scream as she watched her neat little table and chair set get crushed, now for a second time.

"Hey! I was working on that, Narm."

"Sorry," he said with a sheepish grin.

Narmer walked over to the now exposed wall and entered the hidden door. It was dark and had the musty smell of a long forgotten cellar. It was rectangular and only a man's body-length wide, but full length of the building deep. Dead rats littered the earthen floor and scraps of their nesting materials lay damp in the corners. Three dark brown boxes also were there, a frayed and half eaten off-white canvas tried to hide them, but failed. Narmer pulled off the rotting cover and opened the first box. Unfortunately for him, there was nothing but shards of pottery to discover in this box, so he dumped it on the floor. The second box contained two tightly bound scrolls blackened by age. His fingers waded through the miscellaneous items that remained and found something heavy, the size of his hand that was wrapped in red linen. He unrolled it. It was a solid gold statue of Amun. Narmer had to catch his breath before he continued. The image seemed to carry a mysterious heaviness; both in weight and apparent authority – he didn't understand it. He placed Amun gently on the top of the box of broken pottery and bowed his head. *Come to me Amun, in this year of need, guide me in my doubts.* Narmer draped the red cloth around the static statue, all the while whispering prayers. As he prayed, he resumed exploring in the box. He found four amulets bound in a coarse cloth; a small lapis image of an eye – the eye of Horus, a djed-pillar – the human backbone, a silver scarab beetle – the symbol of creation and finally a small feather. *What are these doing here? They should be in the temple . . . unless . . . they were intentionally left behind. Oh Amun, guide my way.* Narmer picked up the amulets, rolled them in a cloth and tied it to his belt. The deity he held, Narmer folded into his clothing keeping it close. Narmer looked around the room again; there in the corner, Narmer saw a Kyphi incense burner. He then turned his attention to the third brown box. He pulled it towards himself and tried to open it. It would not open.

AAAAAHHHHH!! Narmer heard a scream from outside the room.

"Help me Narm!"

Narmer's heart dropped at the sound of Eshe's terrified voice.

6

NARMER DROPPED EVERYTHING HE had in his hands and rushed as fast as he could out of the room. Eshe was beside the door he just came out of; her back was against the wall and she was pointing a shaky finger towards a crocodile that had crawled into the building. **There was no way to escape**. . .

The crocodile was between them and the only opening in the wall – there was no window. The yellow Nile crocodile emitted a low cough followed by a loud hiss. He snapped his head from side-to-side and hissed again.

"What are we going to do Narm?"

"We could have escaped by climbing up the fallen roof, but we can't now," he said as he stared at their only means of escape laying flat on the floor.

The crocodile rushed towards them in a show of aggression, but stopped four paces short and hissed again. Eshe looked at Narmer – she was petrified and could hardly move as she knew she would die.

"Slowly come over beside me Eshe," it took all of her will, but she did.

Overcome with a strange sense of belief, Narmer pulled out the small golden idol of Amun. He held it out towards the fierce reptile and quietly whispered to Eshe to slowly follow him. Slowly he walked towards the animal. The crocodile hissed once and then lowered its head as if in submission. The two youths slowly walked around the animal and out into the scrubland. As soon as they were out of the entrance, Eshe ran to the tallest tree she could see and collapsed from emotional exhaustion. Narmer picked his way through the trees and sat down beside his friend. She was softly crying. Narmer put an arm around her and held her tightly.

"How did you know Narm, how did you know . . . We could have been lunch for that thing."

"I don't know . . . I just knew that we would be ok . . . Does that make sense?"

"No, that doesn't make sense."

How did this happen? I have never experienced the tangible power of a god before. This proves who should be worshipped. I must keep this safe, he thought as he fingered the image he still held in his hand.

They arrived back at the palace later that day. As they walked across the training ground, Her-uben confronted them.

"Where have you been Prince? Are you the instigator of this disappearance, little girl?" he said with a smirk, eyeing Eshe.

"This was not Eshe's fault!" Narmer said as strongly as he possibly could.

Her-uben eyed the pair skeptically – not believing them.

"You know the rules and yet you chose to disobey," he said forcefully. "I have been given authority to discipline you and that is just what I am going to do."

Her-uben forcefully grabbed Narmer and took him to the army barracks and pushed him inside.

"Lay down," he said pointing to the floor. "You are familiar with how this is done," Her-uben said smiling as he enjoyed what was to come next.

Narmer knew that Her-uben was in the right and he was in the wrong.

"Narm!" Eshe called from outside.

Her-uben leaned close to Narmer's ear. "I've never disciplined a little girl before; I'm going to enjoy this!"

"I will take her punishment. Just leave her alone!"

"But I was looking forward to that," Her-uben said with at pout. "Well, alright then."

Her-uben took a hard papyrus reed off of a table and slapped it on his hand; he then stood menacingly behind the cowering boy and whipped the boy's sides ten times. The pain was intense and brought tears to his eyes.

"Narm!" Eshe called again from the outside.

"Are you sure you want her punishment?"

"Yes I do," he said gritting his teeth.

Outside Eshe heard Narmer scream as he was given blow after blow from Her-uben's whip.

"Oh I cannot stand hearing him take my punishment!" Eshe moaned as she stared at the barracks. Soon the girl was openly weeping and trying to wipe her tears with the hem of her garment. This loud display of emotion brought onlookers that tried unsuccessfully to calm her.

"This is all my fault! If I had not persuaded him so much to do what I wanted, this would have never happened," she sobbed. "I will never hurt him like this again," she swore.

Fifteen minutes later, Narmer gingerly made his way out of the barracks being careful to not let his arms touch his aching sides.

* * * *

Weneg ended the story there and thanked the students for listening.

"Please come back tomorrow so I can finish the tale. Right now, though, I must rest as it has been a long day."

The students picked up their supplies, thanked their teacher and left, each going to their own homes.

Weneg slowly stretched as he stood and collapsed on his cot for the night. When he awoke, he trimmed the lamps, dragged the basket of clay tablets to the centre of the room and opened a covered window. He looked down at his shenti he had put on – it was stained from years of wear. *I remember . . .* he thought as he shook his head. *You are getting so old Weneg, long gone are the days of splendor and high-esteem.* He unwrapped a piece of cheese and a small chunk of bread and nibbled – his mind in his past. *The last time I spoke to the students went well enough, but as this story progresses I am not that confident that I won't be crippled inside,* he thought. It was early in the morning; a cool breeze blew outside, but now entered the stuffy space and refreshed it. The youths were not due to arrive for an hour so he had time to calm himself and to organize the next lesson and story. He sat beside the basket and walked his fingers through the individual plates of clay that held ancient knowledge and chose one.

* * * *

Early that morning, Kah walked down the twisted path towards Weneg's hut. The sky had the look of pure glass – blue with no clouds and calmness that soothed the mind. The birds nattered their calls back and forth; hoping to attract a mate and continue their never-ending life cycle. The doleful call of the ibis' was periodically interrupted by the impatient honking of geese. Crocodiles still lay partially submerged in the river, still digesting their previous day's meal. Soon, when the sun was high enough, these beasts would emerge and bask on the banks during the heat of the day. In other areas a pod of hippopotamus had gathered and were relaxing in the water, waiting for dusk when they would leave the comfort of the water and graze on the grasses on land. Kah thought about his home life, how he was raised in an upper middle-class family and how that was so different from Rayu's – he felt extremely blessed. He had three changes of clothes that he had washed and repaired; one shenti, one kilt and one loin cloth. His only adornment besides the necklace he made, was a shell bracelet on his wrist that his mother had given him.

"Wait for me Kah!"

He didn't have to turn around to know that it was Ist that called out to him, but he turned and looked anyway. Ist was jogging towards him. She carried a small satchel in her right hand and wore a rough apron style dress. She was unadorned.

"How are you Ist?"

"I'm fine Kah, and you?"

"I'm fine as well. What did you think about the story we heard last time?" he said, not waiting for a reply. "I thought it was very interesting, but how would Weneg know so much about Osiris-Narmer-Glorified or his brother for that matter? It seems weird."

"I also thought it was good, yet interesting. Do you think young Narmer will get caught for taking that pallet out of King Scorpion's office? What about Menes, not much was said about him?"

"I don't know about Menes, but remember, Narmer **borrowed** the tablets?!" Kah immediately said.

"Ok, **borrowed** . . . do you think Her-uben will find out and then beat him even more than he already had?"

"No, I don't think so – he is a prince remember, I don't think a security guard would have the right to beat a prince too much. Remember, the prince will be a living god someday."

"I think he would; he was not a god yet, remember. King Scorpion is gone and it would be up to the head of palace security to keep order."

"Hmm," Kah said thoughtfully. *That is a good point . . . but why would he have to sneak into his father's office? Could he not have just walked in and searched for what he wanted?*

"Ist, on a different topic . . ." Kah hesitantly said. "You are twelve years old, right?"

"Yes, why?" Ist answered with a raised eyebrow.

"Well, I was wondering . . . why are you not married?"

Ist stopped dead in her tracks and turned to face him, her cheeks flushing. "Kah, you sound just like my grandmother!"

"Ist, I was just curious. Sorry, did that offend you?"

"No . . . there are just no worthwhile men with any interest out there," she said shaking her head, yet lying, since she secretly had feelings for the young man beside her.

"Hello Kah, hello Ist," Rayu said as he trotted up beside them.

"Rayu," Kah said greeting the youth with a nod.

"Did you ever wonder why we have been invited to listen to Weneg's stories?" Rayu blurted out. "I was just wondering," he said with a shrug of his shoulders.

Ist half-smiled, raised her hand and gave back a glazed look. "Maybe there is no reason at all. He is just telling us stories. Just enjoy it," Ist said.

"Oh . . . thank you for reading to me Kah. I guess you have figured out that I never had lessons like everyone else."

Kah shrugged his shoulders and said it was not a big deal. They were soon joined by Anitka and his brother Hayki.

Anitka walked closely behind Ist watching the sway of her hips and tried to take in her scent, but was unable to. Even though he had watched her and greatly desired her for many years, he had never revealed his true feelings for her to anyone and felt as though he was running out of time to claim her.

"Ist, will you join me at the new year's festival at the end of the month with me?"

She did not have to think very long about her answer. She knew she did not ever want to spend any time with this boy.

"No I'm sorry Anitka, I am very busy with my family at that time," she lied.

"How about tomorrow at day break before our teachings? You and I can sit at the river and eat some bread that my father's wife can make for us, upon my request."

Hayki looked surprisingly towards Anitka and thought *it disgusts me the way Anitka thinks he has the right to offer Mother's services whenever he pleases.*

Ist cringed while gritting her teeth, lying again she replied, "I'm so very sorry Anitka, but my mother and I are washing clothes tomorrow morning, so I will have no time."

Anitka was not happy with Ist's excuses but did not display his displeasure.

They walked along the beaten path that was still cool from the previous night. They travelled through the short leafless scrub-brush, up and down small stony hills, in silence until they finally came to the hut. All but Kah rushed inside. Ist was in front of him as she headed in, but Kah caught her arm. She turned to face him.

"You look really nice this morning," he said with a smile and a nod.

She returned his smile questioningly and entered the hut, then took a spot on the floor. *Maybe . . .* she thought hopefully. *I never expected to have boys interested in me, let alone on the same day!*

"I am glad you have all returned. I hope the last story was not too long for you." Weneg said. "I trust you brought some questions for me as well?"

They all looked at each other not wanting to be the first to speak.

"I have one," Kah spoke up.

"Ask it then," Weneg responded.

"Ist and I have a question, actually."

He was quickly cut off by a short high-pitched laugh by Rayu.

Kah turned to him – peeved – and shook his head. "**Anyway** . . . Ist and I were wondering why Narmer had to sneak into his father's office . . . was he not the prince? He should have been able to have access to anything and everything."

"Very good questions Kah. I think he was afraid of him and rightly so. Her-uben was an opposing man. More will be revealed to you as my story continues." Weneg looked at the other students. "Any others . . .?"

Silence.

Kah and Ist looked at Rayu, waiting for him to ask his question, but when he didn't Weneg stated, "I will continue then."

IT HAD BEEN SIX months now since the last news of King Scorpion's campaign north and all of Abydos was on edge. Narmer continued to study the clay tablet he had 'borrowed.' He learned that Amun – the god of air, sun and sky – was replaced by Min as chief god following a dispute between priests and pressure from influential citizens. He spent his free time at the temple of Amun with Nakht and with Menes on the practice grounds learning from Khu. One day Narmer was alone in the temple standing beside the priest.

"I found a small temple in honor of Amun, a fair distance away by the river," he blurted out, pointing his finger in the general direction.

"Yes, that was abandoned during the reign of Iry-Hor. What of it?"

Narmer then proceeded to tell him about his discovery. "The building was in a terrible state of disrepair, it was overgrown and the roof had collapsed, the niches in the wall that held the image of the god were vacant, everything was gone . . . well almost everything."

"Almost everything?" Nakht questioned.

Narmer reached into his shenti and pulled out a cloth bag, opened it and showed him the image. Nakht clenched his hands together and fell to his knees.

"Where did you find The-Hidden-One," he cried. "I thought he was lost forever. What you found is the original totem that all of the statues are copied from."

"I found the image in a room I accessed through a small door in the wall."

"Very interesting . . . go on."

"After I retrieved the statue I was trapped in the temple by a large crocodile, but with Amun's help I was able to leave."

"It was very good that you told me about this. As you know, Sobek is linked to all Kings of this great land. He is there for their protection and safety. You are not yet the King, but you will be and Sobek knows that; he manifested himself as that crocodile to test you and see if you were worthy – you passed the test. Sobek the crocodile god honored you that day – rejoice. Now I have a request to make, Prince."

"Yes?" Narmer replied pensively, not fully believing the Sobek story.

"The image of Amun should be in the temple. Would you put him in his rightful place?"

Narmer thought about it. *Why was he left there in the first place? Was the issue that the priests of Min wanted more control and decided to raid Amun's temple? Someone – probably a priest – hid the small holy statue before they had to leave.*

"Yes I will Nakht, but I do not see why Amun and Min do not work together for the betterment of this land. Are not Amun and Min linked with the ram and bull?"

"They are, but it will be many years before the populous will accept them together," Nakht said. "You would do well as a priest of Amun, young Narmer. You will become High Priest of all temples as King when the time comes of course. At that time you could make that change."

I could change so much when I am King, Narmer thought. He handed over the totem and then later that day, walked to the palace in search of the Queen. He found her sitting on the throne flanked by fan bearers that slowly swished the peacock feathers back and forth overhead. His eyes were immediately drawn to his brother Menes, who sat on a small chair beside her. A security detail took up the first level of steps, the second held the viziers, Hor-Nu – the High Priest of Min, Nakht – High Priest of Amun, Dejati the administrator-of-the-works and finally Chisisi who was on his knees at the third lowest level. As Narmer walked into the throne room and prostrated himself, the Queen quickly bid him rise and snapped her fingers at the closest servant who brought a chair for him. He sat and looked at Chisisi and then back at his mother and then asked, "Did we receive a letter from the King?"

She nodded and then looked at Chisisi, "You may read the letter."

Greetings Queen Nestuwan, Hemet Nesw Weret, Great Royal Wife, may your light and beauty shine forever.

We have sailed and conquered the cities that hug the Nile up to Edfu, Tod, Naqada, Koptos, Thinis, Qau and Beni Hasan. They all fell easily and bowed before the King, professing their loyalty to him, but when we arrived at Lahun, they were not easily dissuaded and they would not bow or give their allegiance. Fighting lasted for two weeks. Our superior weapons benefitted us greatly, but we still lost a large number of men, as did they. I regret to inform you that an arrow found its way through the line and struck the King. He did not die, but he has a grave injury. We had to abandon the King's ship and set sail for Beni Hasan in a smaller, faster craft. We will then be sailing home when the King's body has recovered more. In his ailing condition the King still felt competent to leave two hundred troops as a fighting contingent to train and hold the land we have so far conquered. The King now commands that you gather all able-bodied men and set them through their paces and turn them into warriors for this great land. Recall Khu and Nakhti to help with training.

Written by my hand on behalf of King Scorpion, may he live forever.

Senbi, personal scribe to the King and delivered by my hand to Chisisi.

Nestuwan leaned forward on the throne and placed her hands on her knees. "Did you see the King, and if so, what are the state of his injuries?"

Chisisi shook his head and then looked up to the ceiling, but then brought his gaze back down to the throne. "The King is being treated by his personal doctor and by the doctors from Beni Hasan and is kept at the temple of Wadjet. I did see him oh so briefly – a glimpse really, as I was leaving to come here. He saw me, raised his hand and nodded."

"You did not see his injuries?"

Chisisi shook his head no.

"Well . . . I think the first thing we need to do is prepare additions to the army as the King commanded. Secondly we shall prepare an addition to the barracks for the new recruits. Thirdly we will send a team of doctors north to assess and help with the King's recovery," the Queen said.

Nestuwan called Her-uben forward and told him to bring Khu and Nakhti to the throne room. The two men arrived within an hour and prostrated themselves before Nestuwan. The two warriors had not seen each other or worked together since fighting under King Sekhen. They eyed each other contemplatively. Khu saw that Nakhti who had been young and vibrant, was now bald and frail, but he still had piercing eyes that missed nothing. He wore only a loin cloth since he had been out gathering wild grains and picking fruits along the river and did not have time to wash or change. Khu was dressed well; he had a short kilt and white streaked black hair that was cut no lower than his earlobes. He had dark eye makeup that circled his eyes to contend with the sun's glare and a wide copper band imprinted with a scorpion that encircled his right bicep.

The Queen viewed the men who looked to be at opposite ends of the caste system, but she knew that Nakhti was as much on the same level as Khu. "Greetings men. As you probably can see, Chisisi has arrived with a report from Ta-Mehu and it seems as though the King is requesting to recall your services again."

The men looked at each other, their eyes darting this way and that.

"What does the King require of us?" Nakhti asked.

Queen Nestuwan told them of the letter's contents; how the King had been injured and how he had called a new army to be fitted and raised. She also told them about the small army that had been permanently stationed to hold Beni-Hasan.

"We will require the lists of citizens from the temple archives to get knowledge of how many people are expected to fill the garrison. We will also need new weapons, since the King used the supply that we had and took them north."

"Hor-Nu, of course I am turning to the temple of Min to help fund this adventure," Nestuwan said, looking at the priest.

Hor-Nu darted his eyes back and forth and then spoke. "The god will provide the supplies for this war, but he demands more land and more tribute in the future," he said, his voice shaking.

Nestuwan waved her right hand in the air as if she was swatting a pesky fly, dismissing him. *That priest cares more about the finances of the temple then the welfare of the country we are trying to build,* she thought maddened.

Construction started immediately on the garrison expansions and practice grounds. The town also now swelled from two hundred, to over four hundred soldiers. Food was always a necessity in these times, so the Queen commissioned new bakery houses to bake bread, brew beer and a crew to fish the river so that a constant supply of fresh food could be maintained. A new push was on to create funds that could be traded so more looms were built. A larger amount of natron was also produced to satisfy the temples growing needs and also to trade. Since the citizens that arrived were all farmers and had no military experience, they all had to be trained in the very beginnings of warfare. Nakhti had never seen such a group of men – totally clueless in the art of war. The first week he taught them how to march and Khu taught them how to thrust with a spear – something so simple, yet something that the farmers had difficulty with.

During that time, a plan had been made to travel north with the best doctors and bring King Scorpion back. Two ships had been commissioned to be built with thick reed cabins, mid-ship for the trip. The cabins were outfitted with all the comforts needed to transport the King. The ships were sleek and didn't take much draft so they could navigate in shallow, as well as deep waters. Two oarsmen stood at the front and back of the boat, guiding it on the trip north and would then set sail to catch the winds south on the way home.

Narmer and Menes walked to the far side of the practice grounds and stared at the blue and white flags fluttering on poles at the front of the dark brown ships. They looked at the river – that mysterious river – it was flowing high on its banks. Narmer had lost track of time, *how stupid of me,* he thought. It is Thoth – the first month of Ache – the time that Isis cries and when the waters will break the banks. As he watched, a log floated by heading north with a stranded goat perched on its middle. "Hmpf," Narmer said as he smiled. *There were no crocodiles or hippos in the fast moving river to bother the poor goat,* he thought. *I wonder how the King is faring? How is his injury?* Narmer thought back to the power that Amun displayed to him and Eshe. *How I wish that I still had the image of the god to hold on to as I pray.*

"Brother, you are trouble?" Menes said. "What is in that head of yours?"

I hate how he knows me so well, it's like I have no privacy, Narmer thought. He then told his twin about his discovery and his plans to change the head god from Min to Amun.

"I have been thinking about that sort of thing as well. Since you are older, it will be your prerogative to do so. I will stand behind you in that," Menes said. He did secretly wish he was the older twin. He would be the one in charge in the future. *Everyone will look up to me and I would be a god on earth – the living embodiment of Amun. All would be grovelling at my feet!* He knew it wasn't to be and hated that fact.

Where they stood was calm, but a cool breeze blew and no clouds were seen. They heard Khu calling orders to the new recruits and Nakhti commanding similar orders to a different group at the opposite end of the grounds. He looked back at the river, the goat still stood on his life-raft, but was much further down the river.

Nestuwan stood at the water steps with Narmer, Menes, the King's visor and security detail. All new learning recruits formed lines on each side of her like rows of waves after a boat passes. The boats in front of them had been packed with supplies both of gifts for the new head officials of the conquered lands and new medical supplies to restock the hospitals along the way. The best doctors also went along to help with the King's injuries. On the path to the great boats, Hor-Nu led the temple dancers as they placed a layer of grain for the doctors, sailors and warriors to walk on as a blessing. Nestuwan stepped forward through the haze of thick incense that hung in the air. She looked past the military men that would soon bring her husband back to her. She did a quick tally of preparations in her head: food, supplies, weapons and of course anything they would possibly need for the well-being of the King.

"Sail swiftly to King Scorpion and bring him back; that is the will of the god, that is the will of me. Do not be dissuaded by any hardships you encounter. The people you meet are your fellow citizens, they are your brothers, they are your sisters. They might not know it yet, but we are one. That was the desire of the King and that should be your desire. Captain," she said as she looked at Mbizi, "launch the ships!"

Mbizi called out orders to the sailors, they obeyed without question. The helmsmen that stood at the front and back of the boats were ready. The order to cast off was given. Once they were in the middle of the river, the helmsmen guided them down the Nile with the second ship following closely behind. Narmer, Menes and Eshe stood together and watched the ships. *When will I see my father?* Narmer wondered. *Will they reach him in time or is it already too late?* He shifted uneasily on his feet. The boats caught a steady current and were soon out of sight. Narmer stood at the river's edge in a daze with Eshe. She looked over at him and she placed her hand in his.

"Are you okay, Narm?" she asked.

"I'm fine . . . I just can't help thinking that we are too late," he said, still staring down the river.

A crocodile slipped into the river from the opposite bank and seemed to follow the now missing ships. A frightening vision filled his thoughts; he could see his father writhing in a sweat-soak bed, with an arrow protruding out of a festering wound. He called for help, but no one was there. Fear poked at his soul again, filling his mind and he unconsciously squeezed Eshe's hand. She looked down at their joined hands and squeezed back; that small motion of reassurance snapped him back to reality. Narmer turned away from the river and ran to the palace. Eshe followed him with her eyes, but stayed by the water.

"You care for him, don't you Eshe?" Menes said startling her.

"Oh . . . I forgot you were here," she said trailing off. "Very much Menes . . . very much."

Narmer exploded into his room and collapsed on his cot. He then looked up at the bedside table at his right side. Behind the table was a small niche in the wall that held a cedar Naos box. The door on it was well worn since it had been previously owned by his grandfather and a temple before that. That box held an image of Amun – the god he worshiped. Narmer fell to his knees, opened the door and dropped a cube of loosely pressed incense on a burner and lit it.

"Hear me; Hail to thee, Lord of the thrones of the Earth; deliver my father I pray. You are the father of all gods. I have seen your power. I petition for my father's life. You are the maker of all things; maker of men and beasts and herbs; maker of all things above and below. Hear me."

Narmer bowed again and left an offering of food, applied kohl and malachite makeup, dressed the statue in fresh linen and closed the door leaving the image in the dark confines of the box. He looked at the smoldering incense cone that let off a blue-grey haze. It had the sharp scent of myrrh, but the initial sweet smell of golden honey, cinnamon bark and sandalwood mixed. It also had the scent of benzoin with a slight tinge of lemongrass added. These aromas gave off a calming sensation, a feeling he so desired. Narmer loved the smell, so he did not extinguish the smoldering incense, but left it to burn until it was used up. Narmer turned away as the last of the smoke dissipated into the room and looked at his baskets of treasures at the foot of his cot. He kneeled down beside it. Underneath the thick folded linen blanket, his hands found the clay tablet he "borrowed" from his father's office. He picked it up and began to read.

In the beginning was the Nu and out of the waters Atum created himself using his own thoughts and the sheer force of his will. He created a hill because there was nowhere to stand. Atum was alone in the world. He was neither male nor female. He joined with his shadow and spit out his son Shu and vomited out Tefnut. They had two children; Geb – land and Nut – air. As Narmer continued to read, he soon realized that Amun was the chief amongst the gods, but Atum was the creator god.

Narmer laid the tablet down. *We have it all wrong,* he thought. *I have to inform the King about this, but . . .* he then thought about the tablet at his feet. *Everyone will know about me taking this and I will be in so much trouble, but it is the truth and I need to tell them. I should go to Nakht and talk to him about this. Oh, why is this so difficult!?*

He stood up and grabbed the tablet, walked into the King's office and replaced the borrowed item.

Narmer walked out into the parade ground – the army had dispersed back to the barracks and the priests, singers, dancers, We'eb priests and acolytes of Min, had retreated to their temple. After a short while, Narmer arrived at the temple of Amun. Nakht had just finished his chores, looking after the god when he met the prince on the temple steps.

"Greeting Prince, how can I serve you today?"

Narmer told the priest about his discovery in his father's office, his belief and how he thought Amun should be instated as chief god and not Min.

"I do agree Prince, but as mentioned previously, that is something that only the King can do. You can change our history when you are the King," the priest reminded.

Narmer thanked him, turned and walked away. *I **will** change our history,* he promised to himself.

TWO MONTHS HAD PASSED when a boat flying royal colors had been spotted sailing towards the palace – it was the King! Nestuwan and the whole town came to the docks in front of the palace in silent anticipation for their King's arrival. As the afternoon wore on, the citizens crowded into the water and ignored the ever present danger that the Nile held. Mahut – the ever loyal dog – ran back and forth on the river bank yipping and whining in anticipation as if he knew it was his master that would be arriving shortly. After a brief time, they could hear a cry of jubilation from the river – the King's boat had been spotted. Minutes passed and the cheers became louder and louder until the royal barge bumped up to the water's steps. The priests on board filed out swinging incense burners and chanting prayers. The crowds fell silent – Mahut did not. A group of sailors hoisted a covered cot on their shoulders and carried it on to the land. Immediately, it was surrounded by doctors and chanting priests and then carried to the palace. Narmer's stomach turned over and sweat beaded on his forehead. He got a flash vision of the bad dream he had had about the King dying. Menes closely watched all that went on – the crowd's demeanor, the priest's actions and the returning soldier's nonverbal body language. The crowd looked worried, the priests were surprisingly quiet and the soldiers looked defeated. The crowd dispersed quickly. The princes followed the cot, the priests, doctors and the Queen into the palace. But the priests blocked their way into the bedroom.

* * *

It had been two months since the King had been back, life had gone on and he had not made an appearance in public yet. Khu and Nakhti assessed the men that were under their tutelage – they had come a long way from being farmers and craftsmen to a somewhat capable army. Nakhti now looked as impressive as Khu. He wore a tight white turban that had an emerald fastened with a gold chain and had re pierced his earlobes. He had a short white kilt that was held up by a black leather belt imprinted with scorpions – the symbol of the King. His stomach was flat and tight, he also wore black kohl eyeliner to protect his eyes from the sun.

"I did not think it was possible for this group to be anything worthy, but I was wrong," Nakhti said.

"We have both worked hard with them, haven't we?" Khu said in remembrance.

"Yes we have!"

"Look at young Narmer and Menes, they come every day to the practice grounds and work the skills like all of the men. They do not have the ability yet, but there is promise in them," Khu said as he slowly nodded as if agreeing with himself.

"They are becoming proficient in many of the weapons. Narmer excels at the spear more so than his brother though."

"He will be the new King, so we must take on his training in these matters. I have not mentioned his private training to the Queen, but I think she already knows," said Khu.

The two men parted ways and returned to the practice drills. Nakhti was pleased to see the prince drawing back the bow with the men, though he could not use a heavy draw-bow like the adults; he was more accurate. The King was taken care of at all hours since he had a fulltime staff of doctors and priests monitoring his every breath and was administered regular drafts of poppy to ease his pain. The arrow had been removed for some time now and the wound was healed over leaving a jagged scar.

* * *

Three years had passed by and the King was still unable to lead an army and march north, but he had maintained the army at Beni Hasan and it was growing.

Narmer was now sixteen; he was tall and lean with muscles bulging from his arms and legs. The sinews that protruded on the sides of his neck that were a deep brown colour, spoke of the hours he spent working and practicing outside – he had transformed himself into a human machine. One day he got the call to appear before the King.

"I am here, Father," Narmer said to the covered form reclining on the royal cot.

Mahut, who had never left the side of the bed, furiously thumped his tail on the floor and whined, but didn't raise his head

A hand jutted out from the side of the bed and waved a signal to the priests that made them pick up their spell books and vacate the room. Narmer made his obeisance and then approached the King. He heard the raspy wheeze of his father's breathing and thoughts raced through his head. *The arrow must have done more damage than I had thought! The payers of those damn priests are worthless! I can't stand their exasperating droning day after day.*

A faint whisper came from the bed. "Approach," the King said, followed by a cough.

Narmer obeyed and stood at the head of the bed. "I am here, Father," he said quietly as the dog's tail thumped louder at his approach.

"I do not know how or when we can join this land. This needs to be done. I can see this country strong and thriving for thousands of years, but I will need your help." The King's face contorted in pain, he then panted heavily; his fingers gripped the sheets tightly as a spasm ran through his body. Mahut whined again as if he was feeling the King's pain.

Narmer came closer and dabbed a linen cloth in rose and jasmine scented water and laid it across his father's forehead. The King moaned in pain. He motioned over to a side-table and mumbled something that was incoherent. There was a premixed draft of poppy, prepared in a clay cup on the small table. The opaque liquid swirled in the bottom of the cup as he picked it up. He examined the bitter contents that gave such comfort. *Poppy . . . such a beautiful flower – it gives peace yes, but it can give death as well.* He placed the rim to the King's lips. A thankful look washed over the royals face just before drinking it down.

"I will do my best on the quest you have begun, Father."

"Promise me," he rasped. "You and your brother must do this thing for me and the gods," the King paused. "Bring your brother to me," he said, then laid his head back and fell into a restless sleep.

Narmer placed an image of Amun beside the cot, said a prayer and left. The King slept for the remainder of the day with Menes sitting beside the bed. When the King awoke and was able; he spoke with the young man in private.

"You must support Narmer in the work I have assigned to him. [He paused] Narmer will be King . . . you know this. I have said there can be only one King and Narmer will be him. You have to respect that." King Scorpion said, as he ran out of breath.

Menes kneeled in front of his father. *This is unfair,* he thought and scowled. "He gets everything, just because he was born a handful of drips from the water clock earlier? How can I be barred and cast aside just for that?"

The King coughed up some phlegm and then relaxed back onto the bed. "You are not being barred or cast aside – no glory will pass you by. Narmer will have the weight of the world on his shoulders - you will not. Any mistakes that are made, he will have to answer for – you will not." The King coughed up some blood and Menes wiped the sides of his mouth with a white linen cloth.

"But Father . . ." Menes complained shaking his head but he could see by the look on the King's face that he was getting agitated.

"Do what I order, you are not to be King!" the King said surprisingly clearly.

Mahut whined and nosed the King's hand. After he drew in a raspy breath, he calmly spoke again. "Support your brother," he repeated and then fell into a deep sleep. *What have I promised*? Menes questioned as he shook his head and left the room.

Over the next several weeks, Narmer continued to advance in the skills of the army – he had forgotten about his personal life until Eshe barred his path on his way to the temple to pray. Of course, Wenemon was also with her.

"Am I anything to you, or am I just a friend to be pushed aside?" she demanded.

"What?" he said with a start.

How uncomfortable is this? Wenemon thought.

"I am at the age of marriage, you are too! We would be perfect together and you know it. You know my life-long desire for children, but you have not offered me a marriage contract yet. I cannot marry another and fulfil my desires. I have children around me yes, but they are not my children," she said as she tenderly glanced at the boy. "You know I am forced to wait for you and yet you do nothing. Why?" she asked as she shook her head and pursed her lips – obviously hurt. "I walk through this town and see girls younger than me with two or more children – they have a life and a future, yet I do not! The only thing I have is a possible promise."

Ok, now this is definitely uncomfortable! the boy thought.

Narmer opened his mouth to answer her, but he had nothing in reply. He just glanced at Khu's son and realized he too wanted a child. Narmer stood there in front of her, emotionally wilted.

"I am sorry Eshe, the time has just flew past me and I have not thought about that . . . about this," he said as he touched his chest and pointed to her several times and then to Wenemon.

Narmer stood looking at her, his eyes travelling up and down her body; she was tall, thin and had grown her hair to her mid-back. She had a dark brown complexion that matched her eyes and thought, *I could love this woman. I have been lazy in my relationships* and he shook his head, inwardly disappointed with himself. *I will be King one day and Eshe will be Queen – the Queen I want; someone to challenge me, but will be my friend as well.* A pleasant smile spread across his face. Narmer worried about his new responsibilities that would be quickly arriving on his proverbial doorstep. *Gone are the days of running around with no worries.* Narmer turned to Eshe and smiled.

"I will form up a marriage contract by tomorrow and give it to you; that is if you will still accept it, Eshe? I have been so busy this last while, I know that is no excuse," he said as he closed his eyes and shook his head.

"I know Narm . . . you have been very busy, and with the King recovering from his wound it must be a great strain on you . . . I was out of place."

Recovering? Narmer thought, *I don't think he is.*

"An apology was not needed, Eshe. Yes, we will be a good pair together and I will look forward to you moving your belongings into the palace. I will also need to build another addition to the women's quarters, so please have patience."

Early in the morning, there was a knock on the door of Hakizimana's home. Pahns, the prince' servant, stood back and waited under the short palm trees. Other than the palace, this house of an influential man, was the grandest in the Nome. The mud bricks had been whitewashed making it stand out against the dirty-yellow sand – a brilliant white beacon in an ocean of drab colors. Beside the home, a circular granary towered high above him. He had seen a secluded pool and an ornate lush garden behind the home; even though it was half the size of the King's, it was spectacular. On each side of the front door were statues of Bastet – the cat goddess – that had been placed in niches in the wall. The door opened and a servant appeared.

"How may I be of service?" a well-dressed servant asked.

"You may deliver this to your master – it is from the palace," Pahns said as he handed him a scroll.

The servant took the scroll, thanked him and retreated into the house.

* * *

Two months later, Eshe watched as her servants stacked her clothing into large boxes and carried them outside. She stood beside Wenemon in her room until all that was left were the reed mats canvassing the dirt floor. *Who would have thought my life could be summed up in these few boxes?* she thought, as she looked at her collection of belongings stacked at the base of several palm trees. *I almost can't believe it, I will be married to the crowned prince . . . The Crowned Prince . . . she let the words roll around in her mind. I will be Queen someday,* she thought, but then was worried. Did she have what it took – she did not know. *I know I will be a good wife. I know him. I grew up and went to the same school as him. I also believe in him. But can I provide my duty of baring children for him?*

Later that week Eshe stood in her new rooms in the palace – they smelled strongly of the fresh whitewash that had been applied just hours before. The boxes of her personal belongings were stacked neatly to the left side of the room. A bed with linen sheets and an ivory headrest sat in the center of the room. She looked at her belongings and located the proper box she desired and opened it. Inside was an image of the goddess Tarewert – she put her hand to her chest in reverence and bowed her head. Eshe placed the statue beside the bed and lit an incense cone. Joy filled her heart – *soon I will have my heart's desire,* she thought as she smiled. *I will fill this old palace with the happy sounds of children.*

As the days progressed, Narmer attended the throne room bureaucracy; sitting beside the Queen and the vizier and being instructed in the workings of the government. This he understood well and was soon able to assist without questions. The King's health slowly deteriorated as the years passed. Narmer was now fully integrated in the military and Navy, as well as fulfilling responsibilities in the temple.

"We are in need of more supplies before we march north again," Khu mentioned this in the throne room, when it was his turn to speak about the state of the army.

Narmer looked at Nakhti, "Is this accurate, Nakhti?"

"Khu is speaking the truth. We require new maces, bows and of course arrows. The bows will be the greatest cost I believe," Nakhti replied.

"It is settled then, I will go south with one hundred men and acquire supplies. I will need Khu to travel with me and pick out the proper weapons we need."

"Will we even be able to trade for the required weapons?" Nakhti asked.

Narmer thought briefly and then replied. "The previous Kings did go down south to Nubia, so I think the routes should still be open. It will be good to open a new dialogue with the Nubian Kings."

Nestuwan and the court officials agreed to the endeavour and put Nakhti and Khu in charge with selection of the soldiers that would be going along. After the throne room was emptied, Nestuwan spoke to Narmer; "This is a great undertaking that you have planned," she said nervously.

Narmer planted his feet firmly and shrugged.

"I hope you ask for protection from the gods . . . you never know who you will meet there," the Queen encouraged him.

"Amun gives me protection," Narmer replied.

TWO BOATS CARRYING ONE hundred of the best soldiers, floated calmly at the docks. The populous of the town had filled the training ground waiting for Narmer to head south. King Scorpion had been brought out on his covered golden cot so he could be part of Narmer's send off.

"What supplies have been packed aboard?" Nestuwan asked Menes – who was standing beside her.

"Narmer is bringing ten bolts of fine white linen, twenty sacks of natron, one hundred jars of wine and seven containers of kyphi incense."

Nestuwan nodded her head. "He is bringing a large amount of things to trade," she stated.

"Yes he is," Menes replied.

Hor-Nu walked to the boats, followed by four We'eb priests who were carrying smoking censers that spewed a sharp heavy scent. Nakht followed closely behind sprinkling blood and milk on the walkway. Narmer then mounted the ramp to the lead boat. As he stepped onto the deck, a familiar lump rose in his throat as he felt the rocking of the boat under his feet. Narmer closed his eyes. *Get yourself together Narmer,* he scolded himself. *Now is not the time to be afraid. How can you possibly be King if you still have the fears of an infant?* Narmer took a deep breath in, righted himself inwardly and faced the swarm of citizens that had gathered. The musicians that played the flute, sistrums and drums stopped playing and waited for the prince to speak. Narmer looked over the crowd and rested his gaze on Nestuwan who was standing next to his father's cot. King Scorpion raised his hand with much difficulty. The people that gathered, saw the King's raised hand, giving his blessing. Narmer acknowledged his father by raising his hand, but he was sure his father didn't see him.

The boats set their sails and cast off towards the south – which was nerve racking, as was for most of them, as they had never personally travelled south. The soldiers were comforted, somewhat, as they travelled into this unknown territory when they saw the same familiar animals and plants along the way. They travelled for many days not being able to see any dangers in the water since it was high flood time and the river had spilled over its banks. The banks of the river teamed with life – both plant and animal. Narmer stood beside Khu on the deck of the ship and marvelled at the new animals that were now revealing themselves.

Strange brown spotted animals with long necks he had never seen before, walked slowly with a herd of grey elephants. A pride of lions sat lazily in the shade of gnarled trees waiting for something.

"How would you like to go hunting?" Narmer asked Khu as a joke, pointing to the cats.

"You first," Khu said with a laugh.

Their attention shifted to twelve dark brown buffalo that were cautiously grazing – although they did not show it, the buffalo were keenly aware of predators. They sailed swiftly south until they arrived at what would be later known to them as the first cataract. The water rushed quickly over submerged boulders in this section of the river. After failing to pass these rapids by sail, they proceeded to pole and row the boats to calmer areas along the banks. Later in the afternoon they passed the turbulent water and began sailing deeper into the south. They stayed on this southern course for one month and navigated another cataract – this one was even more turbulent than the previous one. The area almost seemed dead since there was never anyone seen boating on the river or walking amongst the trees; this troubled Narmer since finding other people to trade with was the main goal of the trip.

"We might not find people to trade with and who knows what type or quality of weapons they will have." Khu stared at Narmer, "this could be a lost cause, Prince. We are getting low on supplies for the men. Let us go on a hunting trip to replenish our stocks and give the men some sport to ease their boredom."

Narmer did not have to think long before agreeing to, and taking part in the adventure. He was secretly glad that Menes had stayed with Nakhti at home to train the troops, but in a way knew that his brother would have really enjoyed the hunt. They pulled their ships to the banks of the river and the men departed, eager to hunt. The area they chose to hunt was a wide open area. Three giraffes slowly nibbled the leaves from high up acacia trees in the open woodland, while a small buffalo herd grazed at the base of the trees. The animals on the highest alert were the zebra, who were always ready to sound the alarm and run on mass.

Narmer led the hunting party towards the herd of grazing buffaloes and readied to shoot. The animal he had picked out to receive the first arrow casually raised his head and looked expectantly at Narmer, as if he had been tipped off by his sixth sense. Narmer let his arrow fly. What happened next was unexpected. The arrow had found its mark, but the herd turned on the hunters and charged at them, smashing through and over top of anything that barred their way. The hunters now felt like the hunted, as what seemed like a wall of angry beasts ran at them. A few men were able to keep their wits and place arrows into the buffalo's vital organs and quell their attack. Four of the animals ran straight into the hunters and trampled them, severely injuring them. Narmer and Khu stood just outside of the raging herd and used their bows and spears to dispatch the remaining hairy bovines. After the last of the beasts had been killed, a report of the men's welfare was brought to the prince. Three men had died and four had very grievous injuries.

"What have I done?" Narmer thought aloud while focusing on Khu.

"You did what needed to be done to provide for your men, Prince. Nobody could have known that the animals would return attack that way and men would be lost."

Narmer nodded in agreement to Khu's words, but he still felt responsible. *How am I going to deal with the hard decisions when I am King, if I want to shy away when there is a hunting accident – keep yourself together!*

The animal's meat was prepared and their hides were stretched on drying frames. Some of the meat was sliced thinly and placed on separate frames to dry as well, as quick snacks for the men.

"Let us roast a portion of this bounty and provide the men with a meal," Narmer said to Khu.

The meal consisted of fire roasted buffalo, freshly caught fish and some figs that were picked from the wild growing trees they found. After the soldiers had eaten their fill and the men had rested during the heat of the day, they sailed north once again.

The first civilization they arrived at was a cluster of dome shaped huts that were close to the river. The first person they saw was a man fishing in the river, who seemed to be driving fish into a trap made out of tightly spaced sticks that formed a U-shaped wall. Narmer and Khu watched as the man who was black as midnight, shut a makeshift door on the enclosure when the trap was filled. Amazingly, the man did not see or hear Narmer's boats at first, but was very startled when he did.

"Greetings," Narmer called to him.

The man jumped back and knocked the door to the trap open, accidently releasing the fish and then yelled back to Narmer in a language that was unfamiliar. He then tried to communicate something else, but that again was not identifiable.

"Where is your King?" Narmer asked as clearly as he could.

The man stepped back with a confused look and replied in his native tongue. Narmer looked at Khu and shrugged. He then held his hands above his head making the shape of a crown and emphasized as clearly as he could.

"King." He pointed at the man and then to the small group of huts and repeated again, "King."

A smile spread across the man's face. "Alafin?" the man said as he copied Narmer's action. Narmer made a second gesture as if he was pretending to place a crown upon his head "Alafin?" the man smiled and motioned for Narmer to follow him. Khu looked at Narmer and smiled.

"I guess we are going to meet the King," he said as he stepped off the boat and walked towards the man.

They followed the black man through the tiny village that had very few people. Their homes appeared to be built from a bound stick frame that was covered in leather hide. Some of the hides were black, while there were others that still had hair on them and were placed in a decorative rectangular pattern. Three children rushed past the men in some sort of game of tag. One boy had painted green stripes across his black face and appeared to be the one who was 'it'. The children laughed as they finally caught the striped boy who was quick to announce his displeasure. Although Narmer could not understand the children's foreign language, he did understand that the painted boy's name was Abab. Young children, Narmer thought, of his own were the one thing that was missing in his life, but he had plenty of time to remedy that. The man motioned again to Narmer and the prince followed. The black man brought him to a hut that had zebra pelts on each side of the door and walked in. The man later emerged with a tall woman who brought out a small basket that was filled with breads and dried fish. Narmer gladly accepted the basket and thanked her, even though he knew she could not understand him. Narmer offered her a small amount of dried buffalo meat that he had just caught and prepared, in return.

Narmer again made the crown symbol and asked for the King. The tour guide motioned again for the prince to follow him and ran down a bush trail. They ran into the next town which was much larger. This town was situated beside a casual bend in the muddy river. There were many women washing clothes, children swimming and men fishing at this location. The buildings and houses were much more appeasing to the eyes, even though the streets were boring and bland; the houses were brightly colored green and yellow. The green they had used was the same color as new shoots of tender leaves and growing grass in a damp meadow. Narmer saw men scraping stretched animal hides in the streets. Just like in his own town, there was a gutter in which waste was thrown that seemed to dump into the river. The streets seemed to all lead to a mid-sized building in the center of the town. Two wooden statues stood in front of the doors to this temple. These statues seemed to be twin images of their gods Zaire. The images were what appeared to be that of a male and female goddess, but every time a citizen walked by the statues, they turned their backs to the images. Narmer and Khu realized the people did not seem to honor, like or respect them for that matter. The priests for these strange gods walked around this temple humming and were all wearing slanted-eyed face masks that were painted completely white. They wore hairy buffalo hides and necklaces that sported long antelope horns. Narmer stood mesmerized watching the priests, until the dark colored man touched him on his shoulder. Narmer turned to face him. He pointed to his chest.

"Azizi."

Narmer pointed to himself and said his own name. Azizi stared back at him and motioned him to follow. Azizi led them to an even larger house and pointed to it and then held his hands above his head and said "King" the best he could. By now many of the towns' citizens had gathered. The one thing that was obvious to them was – unlike the people of his town – these people were as black as midnight. The citizens were mostly just wearing a small piece of animal hide across their groin. The women were all bare-chested, but had thick ornately beaded red necklaces that were interspersed with bones. The women had large earrings that spread the holes in their earlobes to a large diameter. The men seemed to have painted their faces in bright yellow and orange paint. The men's hair was cut short and a red paste – they later found out was cow's blood – had been applied. In front of the building they had been led to, naked soldiers carrying long spears stood four men deep, barring the entrance to the main doors.

"I think this is the palace," Khu said to Narmer in a hushed tone. "Look at the maces – they are all wood – we definitely should not trade for those," Khu said as he pointed to a man carrying a wooden club.

The soldiers parted and the palace doors opened. A man dressed in a white leather military vest stepped forward. He had thick gold chains decorating his neck and a headdress of beads and tall colorful green and black feathers that perched on his blood pasted hair. Azizi stepped closer to Narmer and pointed to the man and said "Alafin." Narmer bowed as he greeted the man, but it was obvious that this King did not understand Narmer's words or actions. Alafin called for Leben who had been standing close to the palace doors. A man stepped forward and bowed; he was of a lighter skin color and had a familiar facial structure. Alafin whispered something to the man.

"King Alafin offers you his greetings," Leben said.

Narmer stared at Khu and then at Leben. "Greetings . . . my name is Narmer – son of King Scorpion from the north."

"The King would like to know why you have come to his great city of Semma, entering his boarders' uninvited?"

"We have come here to trade for supplies," Narmer said. "I have brought wine, linen sheets, incense and natron.

Leben turned back to the King and interpreted what was said. The King then opened his hands and asked a question – Narmer did not need any interpretation to grasp what he had asked.

"Tell King Alafin that we would like to trade for weapons, like bows and arrows."

After the interpretation was relayed, instantly Alafin's demeanor soured sharply. "The King will not trade for weapons," Leben said. "He would like to see your supplies though."

In the middle of the afternoon the next day, Narmer, Khu, Alafin and Leben approached the prince's ships that were moored in the river. On the banks, the soldiers had made a small camp and were playing a game that involved spears and a rotten tree trunk. Alafin had never seen such a well-crafted spear before – it was obvious he wanted one. The soldiers brought the linen and natron down from the ship and placed it at the King's feet. Alafin reached down and held the end of a linen sheet, marveling at its fine detail. A large woman that stood by Alafin's side gasped, when she saw the white sheer cloth and excitedly spoke to him.

"The Queen wants to know what you want in exchange for these supplies," Leben interpreted.

"Bring some chairs and wine," Narmer said to a nearby soldier. "I got them now," he whispered to Khu.

Chairs were brought and they sat – the King and Queen sat directly across from Narmer and Khu. Narmer had wine brought to them in gilded cups and fine sheer cloth was piled at the Queen's feet. The Queen gasped. A box of Kyphi was then placed beside her so that the scent of the incense would rise to her face. Eight jars of fine wine were then added to the pile, as well as sacks of natron. The Queen's eyes sparkled with anticipation.

Right then, three hyenas boldly walked towards the town looking for a meal. They stealthfully crept just on the town's outskirts, looking for any wayward animals or children that could be an easy kill. The hyenas stayed on the outskirts and periodically burst into spurts of unsettling cackles.

Back at the gathering the prince continued his dealings. "All of this," Narmer said with a sweep of his arm, "for this," he said as he showed them a bow and arrow.

Alafin stood up and shook his head and said something to Leben. The Queen grabbed a bolt of linen and franticly spoke to the King.

"The King is scared that one day you will use these weapons on him, so he will not trade," Leben said.

The Queen then stood up as well and appeared to plead with her husband. Finally Alafin threw up his hands in frustration and yelled at his soldiers who then ran off.

"He has agreed to your terms. The Queen was overjoyed and scooped up as many sheets as she could hold and nuzzled her face into them.

"Get my spear," Narmer said to one of his soldiers.

Later that day, rows of bows and boxes of heavy arrows were set at Narmer and Khu's feet. Narmer picked up one of the bows and pulled back its draw string.

"This draw is heavier then what we are used to," he said.

Khu picked up a bow and fitted an arrow on the string and drew it back. Khu's arm's quivered as he aimed at the closest tree. After he focused himself, his arms steadied and let the arrow fly. The stone-tipped missile slammed into the tree and split the small trunk in half.

"The men will get used to the heavier draw," Khu said.

Narmer was impressed with the power of the weapon and picked up his personal spear and offered it to Alafin. The King's eyes grew large as he took the finely engraved weapon. Alafin saw that the copper-tipped spear was inlayed with gold scorpions both at the butt and middle of the shaft. Alafin was obviously thankful and grateful as he held the spear. He then spoke to Azizi for a short while.

They could hear the hyenas as they started cackling again, this time more aggressively. They were closer this time. A sorrowful piercing scream came from the village. The scream was then joined by shouts of panic.

"Men! Come to my side."

Fifty soldiers formed ranks beside Narmer with their weapons drawn. Three men from the village ran towards Leben speaking franticly.

"The hyenas have attacked a child and a herd of goats," the men cried out.

Narmer took charge of the situation. "Let's move out and chase these vile animals down. If we hurry, they might not have ran too far!" he yelled.

The soldiers quickly fanned out through the town looking for any trail the hyenas might have left behind. Just on the far side of town, the men came across small residual remains of a bloodied goat skin and a child's arm, that the hyena's had dropped when they made their hasty retreat.

"Aabab, can you hear me! Call out if you can!" the men franticly called to the boy as Leben quickly interpreted for the benefit of Narmer.

The hyenas laughed as if they were taunting the people searching for them. Villagers that followed the soldiers, could now be heard wailing in utter grief as they had just found the boy's arm. A small goat with a wounded leg hobbled out of the brush and towards the men, as if it had been seeking for protection and finally found it. With renewed hope, the soldiers pressed forward determined to find what was taken.

"Aabab," the men called again, but there was no response. "Aabab . . . can you hear me?!" they called again and there was still no response – only the cackling of hyenas.

After the soldiers pushed through a dense, thorn filled section of briers that ripped at their bare arms; they came upon an area that very few trees grew. Short knee-high dead grasses that were filled with crisscrossing animal paths, covered a large field in front of them. Ahead of the men they saw that hyenas had gathered in a circle, eating, squabbling and making their blood curling giggle, something that they were so known for. Narmer and his soldiers hoisted their spears, aimed and threw. All of the spears found their marks. When the soldiers retrieved their spears and moved the dead hyenas, they found the bodies of two goats and a young boy – who by now were unrecognizable.

Cheers mixed with sadness erupted amongst the men as the hyena carcases were pulled apart from the tangle of death. In a fit of rage and loss, the men of the town repeatedly stabbed the dead animals and picked up what was left of Aabab and wrapped him in a gray cloth.

One day later, the boy had been buried in a shallow grave and the hyena carcases were burned. Narmer then prepared to leave and head north. King Alafin and Leben approached Narmer.

Leben turned to Narmer and said, "The King is honored to have received this spear. He has told me that he feels in your debt as well, with the help of the hyenas and asks if there is anything he can do to repay you?"

Narmer thought for a while and then replied, "I will maybe ask for your assistance later on when I become King like you are, but for now I am pleased that we have helped you and opened a comfortable relationship.

Two days later Narmer boarded his ships that were now filled with the weapons that Narmer had traded for and caught the current heading north.

10

NARMER WAS NOW EIGHTEEN, but had still been unable to have children with Eshe which was of great concern. Eshe worshiped every god or goddess of childbirth and pregnancy she could find. Narmer sacrificed bulls to Hathor, Tarewert, Isis, Min and Bes and asked for favor in their quest to become pregnant. As the months wore on, Narmer himself became worried about their inability to get pregnant, but he just prayed more, sacrificed more and tried to comfort Eshe who had been going through states of despair and feelings of worthlessness. During this time of sorrow she brought Wenemon and multiple children with her everywhere, but even that did not stem her wants. She felt a small comfort talking with Jendayi her mother – the only woman she could tell her sorrows to and had complete trust and confidence that it would not then become common knowledge to everyone.

"I am doing everything right and still no sign of a child!" Eshe said strongly, but in a quiet defeated tone. "What more can I do?"

Her mother thought for a while and then replied "When I was young, I too was having a problem conceiving, but I spoke with an older woman in the village. She told me if you place a small onion into yourself overnight; that surely will prepare your body for a child. I did that for two months and prayed to Hathor and you were born nine months later."

Eshe stomped her foot and stood up. "I have done all of those things!"

Jendayi pulled her chair closer to her daughter and leaned in. "You might not be the problem," she whispered.

"Mother! That is no way to talk about my husband . . . he will be a living god you know."

"Just think about it daughter. He is not a god yet, and if you still cannot have a child, then what? [She paused] There are many other men . . . and if you do get pregnant, tell him it is his."

After she said that, Eshe angrily ordered her out of her sight.

* * *

During this time of sorrow, Narmer filled his days with providing Eshe with the best medical care possible. He also became proficient guiding Eshe through her disappointments by regularly having one-on-one time with her to just talk – nothing else.

When Narmer was not with Eshe, he focused himself on military planning; focusing on the Navy. Menes also poured himself into the military, focusing himself on the army.

* * * *

Weneg dragged the basket of tablets closer to him and selected one and then placed it on the floor in the centre of the room. *I got through that one with minimal trouble,* Weneg thought comforting himself.

"You would do well to study this one – it will benefit you greatly," Weneg said as he took out a new tablet.

The students gathered around the flat clay tablet that was entitled 'Concepts of Life'. The writing was very small, so after they retraced their steps and retrieved writing supplies, they began copying the vast amount of knowledge in front of them.

"These are the same tablets that Narmer discovered are they not?" Kah stated.

Weneg did not answer; he just smiled with self-satisfying pride.

Kah copied the first lines of the tablet.

What thou sow on this earth shall be what thou reap in the next. If thou sow evil, how cursed will your Ka be? But if thou sow good seeds like seeds of love, your life will be everlasting. He looked at the others in contemplation, *how is my sowing?*

"Rayu," Weneg suddenly said. "I sense you are troubled. What is on your heart?"

Rayu was caught off guard, his uncomfortable laughs now silent. "I do not know why I am here. I am young and I do not know anything; what can I possibly do to contribute to anything?"

"You have great value Rayu. You just do not realize it. It has not been revealed to you yet, but the gods created you for a reason."

It was cool comfort to the boy who just wanted to belong.

"Will someone teach me to be smart? I want to read . . . I want to learn . . . will someone teach me?"

"I will teach you Rayu," Weneg said. "I will contact your father and ask his permission for you to spend extra time here with me."

Finally I will be able to do the things other boys are capable of! Rayu thought.

"I will continue tomorrow," Weneg said after he took a drink of water. "Have a pleasant rest of the day and come back to hear the rest of the story."

* * *

Rayu ran home after his lesson with Weneg, pleased and excited with how his life was now changing. He was getting lessons along with others way above his caste and he finally felt worthwhile. *My dreams are coming true for the first time in my life!* Rayu thought in immense pleasure. *There is nothing that will stop me now!* he sang to himself. As he ran down the path to his home, he knelt down to greet the family dog. The dog sensed Rayu's buoyant mood and slathered the boy with multiple licks. "I am finally going to learn, boy!" Rayu almost shouted in jubilation. He then leaned forward and kissed the animal on the head. The dog wagged his tail furiously and licked him again. Rayu then skipped down the long path to his home. *I bet the other boys do not have a home like me! I have no responsibilities that tie me down. I am free to do what I want,* he was proud of that. As he approached his house, his siblings crowded around him and asked for any food he might have been given. Weneg had given him a mid-sized bag of food privately, so he gave it to them. The hungry children crowded around the bag greedily and opened it hoping that there would be something that could satisfy their groaning bellies. Rayu smiled as he could see that there was enough food to satisfy them for now.

Rayu walked the short distance to his home and happily waved at his parents when he saw them. His eyes were alight as he told them how the lessons were progressing and how he now had the opportunity to learn one-on-one with the teacher.

"Please allow me to learn more," he begged. "This is what I have always wanted!"

Rayu's parents looked at each other, but denied his request since they were scared that Weneg would then be asking for some kind of payment that they could not pay.

Rayu's tearing eyes said everything, "My teacher will not ask for anything!" Rayu assured them, but they would not listen.

Weneg had of course told them previously that no payment was needed, but they did not remember or did not believe it.

"Father, please let me learn! I do not want to be like this for the rest of my life! I want to matter, I want to be beneficial."

"We are doing everything we can do, Rayu!" his father yelled giving the boy shivers. "Tell you what, Rayu, if you can learn for free ... go ahead! I wash my hands of you! You are not worth anything to this family."

Rayu's mother just sat and did not try to defend her son, she just listened to the verbal abuse that was increasingly regular from her husband.

Rayu walked out of the house feeling chastised and unwanted. Even though he felt as though he was worthless, his spirits were quickly lifted when his dog started nuzzling his arm.

"I have missed you boy," Rayu said as he stroked his black head. "I **will** be something boy! You just watch. I will have enough to provide food for you and my family after I learn to be smart. I do not care what others might say, I will show them I am worthwhile.

The next day Rayu was excited to continue learning and make something of his life. In no time he was at the teacher's hut ready to gobble up knowledge so he could put it to use and prove his worth to everyone. Weneg started his lesson immediately after he drank a mouthful of water and greeted his students.

* * * *

The glorious war ship, Amun Breathes, gracefully bumped the wooden docks in front of Narmer. The parade grounds were crowded with newly appointed soldiers ready for war. So much had changed in the past year; the temple of Amun had been greatly expanded due to the support of the prince. Even though the palace had been greatly expanded, as well as for possible royal children, there was no sign of Eshe conceiving. She was determined to provide a child for Narmer, so much so that she gave herself to him every night and prayed unceasingly to Taweret – the god of women's sexuality and pregnancy. But as the months progressed, Eshe slipped lower and lower into depression as no signs that her prayers had been answered ever showed. Narmer had her rooms added to, with a side room for her servants. Narmer was now involved heavily in the bureaucracy of the courts and was performing rites in the temple of Amun. It was two days later, on a cool winter morning in the month of Phamenoth, that King Scorpion died. This was not a shock since he had been unwell and suffering for so long. The King's death brought a new level of realism to the prince. The first thing he felt was fear. In an instant the weight of responsibility felt like it was going to drown him. A strange feeling almost overwhelmed him and he wanted to run; run away from the impending onslaught of officials wanting this or that or demanding answers to their questions and problems. Visions of him as a young naked boy playing at his mother's feet and looking up at the King in awe had disappeared. The King had been a powerful man in whom everyone had put their hopes and dreams in and was now gone. *My father is forever gone*, Menes thought sorrowfully. He now felt alienated in his own world and diminished as a man and the prince, now that Narmer was truly in charge.

* * *

A long procession wound its way out of the town of Abydos and far into the desert. Along the way, the wailing of unpaid female mourners pierced the air, in an utter display of sorrow. The women ripped their clothes, baring their breasts. They scooped up handfuls of dirt and sprinkled it on their heads – leaving tear-streaked brown lines on their faces. Queen Nestuwan, visually distraught, let her tears flow unchecked and unwiped. He had been the love of her life – she had given him sons; the test of a perfect wife. Although bull-headed at times, he was the perfect husband – he juggled running a country, instructing his sons and providing for his wife. The Queen gazed at the lifeless body that held so much warmth and power *it is all gone now . . . he is gone now. What now?* Menes thought. *Must I now watch as all power is placed in my brother's lap? I will be left behind,* he cursed. Just then the memory of his father's voice, as clear as if he were standing beside him, pierced his mind. *Narmer will be King. Support him,* the voice said. "This is not fair," he muttered to himself.

King Scorpion was placed in a short mud-bricked, unroofed enclosure, along with his favored items that he would take and use in the afterlife. The tomb had two rooms which were unadorned. The first room primarily held two hundred jars of fine wine from the north. There were painted bowls, both clay and stone, that he would use in the afterlife. The room also contained the King's disassembled bed and a table with his favorite meal – broiled duck and cooked carrots. The Queen looked into the second and final room. She glanced around the tight quarters and had to catch her breath. The King lay on the ground, covered with a decorated blue and red beaded mat. At his side she saw Mahut the loyal dog, the two young servants that cared for him and much to Narmer's delight – Her-uben. *These people had to be sacrificed by ingesting poison, so they could continue to serve the King in the afterlife. Of course Mahut, I will miss. I will miss his cold wet nose on my leg when he wants something. I will miss his love, even after he had been disciplined. He deserves to be by his master's side for eternity,* she thought.

Narmer and Menes entered the room followed by Hor-Nu, who was chanting prayers. The small room quickly filled with the sharp scent of myrrh. The room was crowded and Narmer was pushed up beside his twin allowing the other attendees the opportunity to see the slight differences in their appearance. Narmer had a leaner jawline compared to Menes, but only slightly. Hor-Nu stepped forward and stopped chanting. In his right hand he held a Pesh-en-kef – the ceremonial adze that was used for such an occasion. The mystical tool was a bent gilded stick that had a copper blade, bound to its top at a right angle. He then approached the deceased body and touched the King's mouth and feet.

"May you speak again, may you walk again," Hor-Nu said.

I will miss you so much Father . . . I will look for you in the afterlife," Narmer thought. Menes was also deep in thought. *You were so wise, and a great King. Even in death I will look up to you and honor what you said to me, even though I think you were wrong.* Nestuwan cried out again and collapsed to her knees.

115

"May you speak again. May you walk again," the priest repeated.

A loud chorus of wailing could be heard outside the room. Hor-Nu then touched the adze to the King's eyes and mouth.

"May you see again, may you taste again," This he said without interruption and then pulled the mat over the King's face. The ceremony was over and everyone filed out of the room to partake in a celebratory meal, allowing servants to fill the rooms with sand; burying the King.

Outside, Narmer again felt the weight of responsibility rest on his shoulders, *can I do this?* he questioned himself. He felt eyes on him, eyes with anticipation behind them. *I must fulfill my father's quest,* he swore to himself. Menes came and rested beside him with a clay plate full of food.

"Things will change for you now . . ." he said. As he grabbed a cooked chicken leg off of his plate and bit into it, he wiped his greasy fingers off on his previously spotless white kilt.

Narmer looked at his brother and gave him a wry smile. "What if I do not want this responsibility?" he said as his words trailed off.

Menes looked at him with raised eyebrows. "What are you saying, Brother? You know as the eldest it is up to you to complete our father's work. You must . . . it is your duty."

"I know it is my duty – I'm well aware of that!" he said annoyed.

"Father talked to me about the struggles you will face."

Narmer looked at his brother – surprised.

"He made me promise to support you in all you do." He turned towards him and placed a greasy hand on his leg. "I will do that – I will support you."

Narmer thought about what his brother was saying, squeezed his eyes shut and slowly nodded. He did not want to give up on the vision his father started. *Maybe . . .* he thought. "We could work together, you know?"

"Narm, you will be King . . . What could I possibly do?" Menes said questioning his train of thought.

"I was thinking if we split up – I will take the Navy and you take the Army; it will be like the King is leading both parts of the Military. This way the men will always be in the presence of the King to some degree. Oh I wish I could ask Father's advice."

"That is true, very shrewd Brother . . . you do have the workings of a King!"

Menes was delighted that the doors to becoming King, were now starting to open – his father's warnings now evaporated from his mind.

"Humpf," Narmer snorted.

"You will be coronated as King at the end of the week. Have you decided which priest you will promote to do that honor?" Menes questioned.

That was something he had not been considering, but this in his mind, was a non-issue. "I have talked to you before about my beliefs – I will ask Nakht and align myself with Amun."

"You know that will cause problems for those that are used to having the support of the King; going towards Min?"

Narmer bit his lip and nodded. "I know, but this is my desire. Will you still support me, Brother?"

"You know I will, Narm."

* * *

Eshe stood in her room and dismissed her servants. A short while later she looked at her naked reflection and her still juvenile hips with disdain, in the polished bronze mirror. She was still unable to bare Narmer a son – or any child for that matter. *What must I do to be a worthwhile woman?* she cried to herself. Her desperation to have a child consumed her. Her eyes stared at a vial of poison she kept on her dressing table that she had used for rats. *What must I do!* She placed her hands on her stomach – it had never grown signifying that a child was on the way and her time of the month came and went like the predictable seasons. *What is wrong with me – the gods do not care,* she thought gritting her teeth. In a fit of rage she slapped herself in the face and then dug her fingernails into her stomach drawing blood. She collapsed on the floor and sobbed. *I am a failure.* Betresh, her body servant, rushed in upon hearing the Queen cry out. Betresh found the Queen lying on the floor – her hair in a major state of disarray and her makeup streaked down her face. Pots of makeup and incense littered the floor from a turned over table, she immediately kneeled down beside her.

"Everything is okay, your Majesty . . . what is your desire?" she saw the blood drips staining the Queen's fingernails and abdomen and quickly dabbed them with a cloth she always carried on her person. "Don't fret, Majesty, I will clean this up," the servant spoke softly.

Just then a second servant opened the door. "Can I . . ." the servant started to ask.

"Get out!" Betresh yelled – the servant made a hasty retreat. She quickly turned her attention back to Eshe who was still sobbing.

"I am a failure . . . I am no better than the rats that creep into my room." she said as her words trailed off and tears streamed down her face. Eshe reached towards the vial of rat poison, but Betresh grabbed it first.

"Not true Majesty, you are not a failure. You are the Queen, the Queen of this great land. You are married to a living god and your best friend. Any woman would be jealous of you . . . they want to be you!"

"I am the one who is jealous," she said fighting back tears, "jealous of them. They are able to have . . ." she stared off into the room and her eyes locked on the corner of the wall. "Children."

"Majesty, there are many women who cannot have children. Some by choice, some by the gods' plans."

"Well damn the gods plan!" she swore, then quickly made the sign of protection against the gods' wrath. "I need children. It is up to me to provide the King with heirs. Our line must go on. I cannot disappoint my husband like this! I caused him pain in our youth. I will not hurt him again!"

"Your family could continue if Menes has a son," Betresh said wryly.

"Menes have a son? He would have to show interest first. But no, I want a child! The King **needs** a child," Eshe said firmly.

T HE BROTHERS STOOD AT the water-steps and looked at the ship moored at its end. Brown water swirled around the mooring posts right at his feet, rocking the boat up and down and back and forth like an impatient child tugging at his mother. Narmer stepped onto the dock – his pangs of fear of the river long gone – and boarded the ship. Narmer stood at the starboard side and raised his arms silencing the crowd.

"I come before you pledging my promise I made to my father, that I will complete his desire and bring the north and south together." *I am still wary about completing this great work. Will this plan even work . . . I do not know, or will I fail and be a laughing stock and be a disappointment to my father's Ka who watches me?*

He took a breath in and put on a bold face. "I will bring Ta-Mehu into the glorious comfort of Ta-Shemau . . . we will be one! They are our brothers and sisters – they just are not aware of it yet. Pray to Amun and all the gods for it to be so." A weight lifted off of his shoulders as he said these words.

The gathered crowd erupted into cheers and Nakht and Hor-nu each placed incense on their burners. A tremendous crash of cymbals came next, followed by lutes, drums and guitars. Temple dancers stomped a rhythm on the ground and twirled around. The crowd cheered again. *What am I going to find out there?* He thought with pangs of fear gripping him. *Will I find peaceful citizens going about their daily lives or will I find major resistance? How could I doom them and let my army destroy them? I'm so torn.* He turned back to the canopy that was set up, mid-ship and found cushions to sit on. The captain gave the order and the two sailors that manned the oars at the front and back took their positions. The lines were cast off and the river greedily grabbed them and took them north. Narmer found his cushions, sat, and watched the fields speed by. Within the first hour the throngs of onlookers had dwindled out, but the lushness of the river bank crowded in. On the deck of the boat, a young boy approached him holding out a cup of water. Narmer eyed him curiously.

"I did not think I had such young warriors in my army," he said humorously. "You are that boy that hangs around Queen Eshe, are you not?"

The boy bowed his head and dug his toe into the boat's thick reed floor.

"Majesty . . . I . . . I have . . . I have been . . . been asked to serve you as much . . . much as I am able," he said with a stutter. *Why must I stutter like an idiot in front of the most important man in the world?*

The boy looked up at the King with wide eyes and a nervous disposition.

"Who asked you to do this for me?"

"M . . . my father did," he said as a fearful glaze swept across his face.

Narmer looked at him, raised his eyebrows and tilted his head wanting more information.

"Oh, sorry. K . . . K . . . K . . . Khu."

So this is Khu's son. Kind of a nervous young boy it seems.

"You want to help do you? Well the first thing you can do is clean the soldier's weapons, but you must work on your speech as well . . . your father sent you to school to learn how to read I assume?"

The boy nodded vigorously.

"Good. Then you must read all of the soldier's names who were dispatched, out loud, as you clean. You will read them and everything else I give you until you no longer stutter. Can you do that?"

"Y . . . y . . . yes."

"What did you say?"

"Y . . . yes," he said with frustration in his eyes.

"What did you say?" Narmer asked tapping his finger on his leg.

"Yes."

"Good. How old are you and tell me what your name is."

"Wen . . . Wenemon."

Narmer looked at him with raised eyebrows.

The boy closed his eyes, gritted his teeth and inhaled. "Wenemon, my name is Wenemon," he said slowly. "I am seven."

"Very good Wenemon, very good."

The boy smiled, he had rarely heard those words; words of praise directed to him by someone other than his father, let alone King Narmer himself, the most important man of them all. He was a child that was routinely subjected to ridicule because of his speech. No one, it seemed, was willing to or had the time to work with him on it. Wenemon bowed and walked to the cluster of soldiers that had gathered at the bow of the ship. He just pointed at the weapons and said "clean?" This one word he had been practicing over and over under his breath, so that he didn't stutter by the time he addressed the men. Many of them looked at their ordinances and handed them over to the boy, but when he could not hold them anymore, they just left them on a growing pile at his feet. "Th . . . th . . . thank you," he said.

Day after day, he sat with a linen cloth and bucket cleaning and scraping dirt off of spearheads, axes and knives – all of this he did while reading out loud the things the King had given him. They sailed past small cheering crowds at villages. Narmer and part of his army lined the deck of the Amun Breathes at full attention. Menes marched with the main army along the banks when able; if suitable footing was unavailable they would march further inland.

At each village, the boat was docked and the army disembarked and officials were gathered for personal meetings with the King. At each stop, Narmer was able to gather a handful of men able to fight and all swore their allegiance to him. After several days, the army had grown to well over two thousand men. Training was non-stop as they marched; they practiced moves; thrusts, shield blocks and knife slashes. These men also had an extra job of gathering spent arrows fired from the boat, by men practicing with the new bows they traded for in the south and returning them at rest stops.

As they floated by, Narmer kept an eye on the river – *there was a lot of hippopotamuses on this part of the river, as well as crocodiles,* he thought as he saw five crocodiles slide into the water from the muddy bank. Narmer decided that since his men needed some meat, he would try the new bow's power. Narmer saw a large male crocodile sunning himself. He picked up a bow and fitted an arrow onto the string. He drew back the arrow, aimed at the beast's heart and let the missile fly. With a loud smack, the arrow buried itself into the reptile and killed it instantly. The crocodile just lowered its head slowly and never moved. Minnakht called to the sailors to retrieve and butcher the animal.

"That was a powerful shot, Majesty."

"It's a powerful bow, Minnakht," Narmer said as he looked down at the bow.

* * *

He later arrived in Qau on a sunny morning and they were greeted with much fanfare as the boat slid into the dock. Nekura, surrounded by his town officials: Nebetka and Sabfi approached the dock.

"Greetings King Narmer, welcome to our glorious town," Nekura said with a sweep of his arm towards the tightly packed buildings.

Narmer let his eyes roam through the visible town. He could see that this town was kept very clean. There were no piles of refuse that stained the beauty of so many of the other places he had stopped at. There was something off about the little town though, something that he could not place. It seemed that the whole town was holding its breath pensively and was waiting to relax and to be able to breathe again. Narmer walked off the ship, but soon heard the soldiers that were marching beside the boat these past days. Menes army filled the town and sat down for their own nourishment. Loaves of bread, dried fish and pitchers of beer were given out by the towns' folk, much to the pleasure of the men. Even the town people put on pleasant masks of smiles. Narmer could tell it was a show.

"Stand up, Nekura!" the King ordered.

"How may I serve you, Majesty?" Nekura asked ponderingly.

"I sense you are holding something back from me. Speak plainly to me and tell me what is in your heart."

Nekura was taken aback and physically retreated a step.

"Great one, I mean no offence to you, but we hear that King Scorpion has died and you are now the King. We do not know if we will be treated with the same mercy from you, as he treated us. We are scared."

"Yes the King has died and he has joined his father Amun in the realm of Osiris. I am your King now. Do not be lax in your respect Nekura, or my respect and mercy for you, or your town will falter. I expect you to stand with me just as you have done with my father." Narmer looked at him, his eyes raised. "Can I count on you?"

"Yes, your Majesty, yes you can."

"Hmpf," Narmer said flicking his head up. "I will be staying here for a short while and will need lodging for my men and myself, are you prepared for that?"

"Yes Your Highness, Yes," Nekura said with a flourishing bow. "How many soldiers do you have?" he said as he turned to face the army and rose up on his tip-toes to see them better.

"Two thousand, one hundred and twenty five, including myself," Narmer offered.

Nekura's eyes widened. "Two thou . . ." his voice cut short as he looked even harder at the large group of men.

"Will you have room for them?"

"Yes we will, Majesty," he said as he swallowed. *How will I feed these men?* he thought, *we do not have enough supplies for them.*

"I see you are troubled . . ."

"We do not have the supplies to feed so many Majesty, but if we could set up a hunting party, we could fulfill the needs. We could do it," he said confidently.

12

ON THE LUSH FIELDS beside the river, hunting parties tracked down antelope and drove them into waiting hunters who had set up a large trap. Forty of the nimble footed animals rushed away from oncoming hunters only to rush into the waiting arrows and spears of the men. The same was done with a small herd of gazelles, but the ostrich were dispatched with much more difficulty. While this was happening five boats that sailed the Nile preyed upon crocodiles, fish and fowl. The fish were caught by a series of nets that were cast over an artificial pinch point that was constructed in the river. Large quantities of Tilapia, Elephantfish, Nile Perch, Catfish, Sharks and many others were caught. The papyrus plants that lined the river waterfowl were hunted as well, using curved throwing sticks and locally trained dogs.

Narmer stood at the bow of the lead, flat-bottomed, hunting papyrus boat, spear in hand and searching the brown water for signs of life – something he did not have to do for very long. A group of crocodiles slid into the murky water and disappeared from sight. *It won't be long now,* he thought. His eyes were intently searching for the quiet, but deadly eyes of this prey. He saw something and using hand signals to helmsmen manning the oars, he guided the reed boat a little closer. His spear felt so comfortable in his hand, it was almost just an extension of his arm. This was a skill he had developed by the long practice sessions under Khu. Narmer held the weapon parallel with his shoulders; his throwing arm was extended behind him as he picked his target. He let the spear loose. The small crew stood and watched in anticipation, but just as it was about to find its mark, the crocodile ducked his head underwater. There was a sigh of disappointment as the spear knifed into the river and disappeared. *I should have used a bow for this,* he thought to himself. The other remaining crocodiles on the bank made a hasty retreat into the water in a fury of large splashes. Still, Narmer stood quietly at the bow of the boat.

"Majesty, it's gone. Shall we try to retrieve it?"

Narmer was not used to missing his mark. He stood for a while not answering, but then biting his lip, he nodded and relented. *In front of my men . . .* he scolded himself.

"Yes, we should retrieve it if we can."

As the oarsmen guided the raft over to the place they thought that the spear landed, the bank of the river became alive with grunts and bellows from the hippopotami that had taken up residence there.

Narmer remembered back to the time Eshe and he had been so close to the massive violent beasts – they had been lucky to get out alive. He then noticed the yellow colored end of his spear just barely under the surface of the water. He saw little red bubbles popping up on the surface, half a boat length away.

"You got him!" one of the crew called out.

Narmer smiled to himself feeling proud, but that was replaced with concern as he saw a large bull dislodge himself from the muddy bank and head straight for the boat. Narmer looked for a spear, but could not find one. Arrows smacked into the fast moving beast, but they had no effect on it – it only enraged the animal more. The hippopotamus now looked like the familiar crested porcupine. *Hrrooonnh, hrrooonnh!* The hippo screamed as it splashed through the water, *huff huff huuuuuuuuuugh, huff, huff, huff.* It bellowed as it seemed to run through the water towards them. Blood was now frothing around his mouth and the beast seemed to have only one thing on his mind – ATTACK.

"M . . . Majesty!"

Narmer swivelled around and saw Wenemon holding a spear, offering it to him. He quickly grabbed it. The yelling men onboard were continuing to shoot arrows and bang their shields and axes together. Narmer hoisted his spear and quickly threw it just as the beast crashed into the craft – it was not a direct hit. Now, the hippopotamus had a spear in his thick skin which went through a fatty part of his side, came out the opposite side and hung into the water. The infuriated beast backed away from the now injured craft and charged.

His gaping mouth, full of wicked twelve inch canines, snapped shut on the side of the boat. It left a massive hole as if he had taken a bite out of a loaf of bread and let the water pour in. He slammed into the boat again and then submerged. There was a moment of silence where all that could be heard was the gurgle of the water pouring onto the deck. The balking of the baby hippos on the far bank could be heard and then what seemed like slow-motion, the water around the boat exploded. The boat bowed in the middle and snapped in two; Narmer was sent flailing into the river as the hippo proceeded to smash it to pieces. The unlucky sailors who got in the way of the beast, were stomped to death with its eight-thousand pound frame. Dazed, Narmer held onto some floating debris as the destruction continued. As he floated in the water, his leg bumped into a shaft in the river; he looked down and since the sun was high in the sky, he could see the glint of gold – it was his spear.

"Help! P . . . please!" Narmer heard the frantic cry. "Wenemon?"

He then saw the boy struggling to stay afloat a short distance away.

The rampaging beast now stopped and was swimming in his direction. The animal probably hadn't seen him, but he needed some protection. Narmer reached down and pulled at the weapon. Even though the spear seemed to be stuck deeply in the mud, it suddenly came alive, pulling this way and that. There was a crocodile on the end – and it was still alive!

"Help me . . ." he heard the boy's voice getting fainter and weaker.

Narmer started to panic as he was faced with this impossible situation. The crocodile's head surfaced.

There was a crazed look coming from the reptile's eyes, whose nictitated eyelids opened and shut repeatedly. The crocodile submerged again as Wenemon was carried by the current closer to the reptile. He held the end of the spear and evaluated his situation; *big angry crocodile . . . just below my feet. Wenemon now on top of him. . . I am pretty close to the bank though and if I can reach the boy in time, maybe I could swim us to shore? Oh no, the bull is swimming right towards us. Amun help me!* As the hippo got closer, Narmer swam between the hippo and the bank, managed to grab the boy's flailing arm, but still succeeded in holding onto the moving weapon. Wenemon held onto the King's back as the hippopotamus' piercing eyes zeroed in on Narmer, getting closer, and identifying him as his enemy. The animal almost galloped in the river. *There is only one chance,* he thought. *How I wish Menes was here to help me with these beasts!* The hippopotamus got closer and closer – when he was about a body length away he suddenly stopped, the spear stopped moving as well. Narmer was able to fully remove the weapon from the submerged reptile. The hippo stuck his head into the water as Narmer quickly swam to the bank, towing the spear and the boy. As he achieved the bank, the hippo stomped the crocodile to death, who was now under his feet. The bank smelt strongly of decaying wood mixed with an earthy, fishy scent of the muddy river. He pushed Wenemon ahead of him as he tried to climb up the bank, the mess of rotting roots made this an easy task. When they achieved the embankment, they tried as much as they could to blend into the overhanging brush. The boy started to cry as he faded into the trees. *Listen to yourself you are such a baby, Wenemon! The*

King is looking after me. Show him that you are strong,
the boy thought. With the snapping of dead limbs,
Wenemon climbed over and the crying he could not
contain alerted the beast to his position re aggravating
it. The beast coughed and foamed blood, keenly aware
of his foe. Behind the large beast, two rafts poled
towards them and slowly got closer. The men onboard
hollered out and beat their weapons together, trying
to get the animals attention away from the King. The
beast ignored the men's ranting and focused on Narmer
and the boy. It saw them and charged, slamming into
the branches, driving some arrows in deeper; some just
snapping off. Narmer and the now sobbing boy backed
further into the trees, still maintaining a grip on the
spear. He found better footing and adjusted his grip.
The monster charged again. Just as it did, Narmer raised
the tip of his spear and let the hippopotamus's weight
and inertia, drive the spear down its own throat. It let
out a gurgling whine and spat out a stream of blood and
mucus, covering Narmer's leg and spraying the boy's
face.

The men finally reached the King and boy with
their remaining rafts; they had seen the entire fight and
cheered when the beast tipped over on its side as it died.

"Oh, Your Majesty, we are glad you are alive! After
the hippo destroyed the boat and killed all the sailors
we had lost hope! When we saw the wreckage and dead
bodies we thought you too were among the lost," Gahiji
proclaimed.

"All were lost?"

"Yes, all on your boat and another – ten men in
total."

"How did the hunt go, do you know?" the King asked.

"Yes I have some results for you. We got nine crocodiles and many fish – so much that we had to unload the catch on shore. I do not know what the hunting parties on shore have been able to get, but with that," he said pointing to the hippopotamus, "We will have a great deal of food for the soldiers."

Wenemon had stopped crying by now and had come out from behind the trees – he felt ashamed that he had not shown his strength or courage.

"We surly did not expect you to survive boy," Gahiji said motioning to him.

Narmer smiled and tussled Wenemon's hair. "He was brave, this young one," Narmer said with a chuckle.

No I wasn't! I just cried and needed saving, Wenemon thought, but he managed a sheepish smile.

"Alright, let's get you both aboard. That beast won't be going anywhere," he said pointing to the bloodied monster. "We will retrieve it later."

* * * *

You could hear Ist breathe in the hut. All eyes were glued on Weneg as he ended the story.

"Wow that was really something to hear, teacher. I would have died!" Rayu exclaimed.

"I wouldn't have," boasted Anitka.

"I think that would have been frightening for anyone, Anitka," Kah scolded.

"You don't know how I would think! Why don't you keep your ideas to yourself?" Anitka snapped.

"Students!"

Chastised, the teenagers gave their complete attention back to Weneg, who sat comfortably in his chair. "What did you learn from that story?"

Rayu looked around the room waiting for someone to speak. There was a lull in the room as one of the teens coughed. Ist leaned over to Kah and whispered something in his ear that made him smile.

"Anyone?"

"Stay close to the King?" Hayki offered.

"No." Weneg said, his face scowling. "You can do better than that."

"Well, definitely stay away from hippos," Ist said hopefully.

"Trust in your abilities?" Kah asked.

"Not quite, but that is a good one."

Ist looked at Kah and nudged his arm. Kah looked back at her, smiled and shrugged. There was a long, awkward pause where everyone just sat and looked at each other.

"If you remember from your reading about the gods, Narmer called out to Amun for help, that was good, but what was the change of tides in this encounter?"

"The spear!" Anitka called out.

"Yes, the spear changed the tides. If he had a used a bow or had had a spare spear in hand on the boat, he would have been able to kill the beast without letting it destroy the boat; which resulted in the loss of the lives of the men. Remember, praying to the gods is helpful, but you must take your own initiative in your life and trust in your abilities. Remember you can't just expect the gods to think for you. The King should have prepared for the possibility of things going wrong before he threw his spear. Even the most powerful and important men make errors in judgement, no one is above that. Think ahead, not only in hunting, but in your daily lives. What are you going to be when you get older? What do you want to be?" Weneg paused for effect letting his words sink in. "Do you want to be a scribe, a soldier, a business owner, a teacher?" he then looked directly at Ist. "A wife? Another thing to think about [he paused] is this; surround yourself with loyal people. Be a loyal friend to others. Be a loyal worker. Think about this . . . what if the men on the boat had left and not searched for the King, even though it looked like he had probably died? Then Narmer and the boy too, would have perished."

The students were silent, all seeming to stare at the floor in the middle of the room in deep contemplation. *I want to be a scribe – they are successful and that is what I want, to be a success,* Hayki thought.

Business owner sounds good to me, Rayu hoped. "I want to be a business owner!" Rayu said without encouragement to speak. "I will be a success," he added with determination.

That will be the day! Anitka muttered under his breath.

"And I believe you will!" Weneg said encouraged with the boy's boldness. *I like this young man*!

I want to be like you, Kah thought as he looked at Weneg. *I want to be wise like you, master. How did you get so wise?* Anitka was also deep in contemplation; *I want power . . . I want to be the King,* Anitka imagined; staying true to his aggressive nature. Ist was lost in her own imagination . . . *a wife, yes that is what I want to be. I will run the household and have many children. I too, will be a success!*

Weneg looked at his students, all seeming to be lost in their own thoughts, *whom of these will reach their potential? I wonder . . .*

"That is enough teachings for today. Go home and consider this lesson. Consider what you want to make of yourself."

The students all stood up, thanked the teacher, gave him a short bow and walked out into the dim light of the evening. It was uncomfortably humid and muggy. There was no relief in the hot dead air. As the students made their way down the path, Kah was the first to speak.

"What do you guys think about the lesson today?" he asked.

Each of them said what they had desired; some of them received understanding nods and some, like Anitka, got a demeaning laugh. The question was then put to Kah.

"You have been silent Kah . . . what do you want to be?"

Kah looked up to the sky and focused on a fluffy white cloud. Just then, the loud, high-pitched buzz of a cicada started singing; after one started it was joined by two others making a chorus. The sound was almost deafening, but Kah replied. "I want to be like our teacher. I like his confidence, I like his stories and I like the morals he teaches."

"I thought you wanted to be a priest," Anitka scoffed.

"My **father** wants me to be a priest," Kah corrected.

"I want to know where he learned those stories he tells us," Rayu said breaking the tension.

The path they were walking split to the right at a grove of palm trees. Anitka just headed down the trail not bothering to say anything; he stopped after a while and turned. "You coming?" he called to his brother.

"I'll be right there," Hayki called back and then followed his sibling.

Kah looked at the boy and raised an eyebrow in annoyance.

"Sometimes I forget that they are brothers . . ."

"Half-brothers," Ist corrected him.

"You're right, half-brothers. How did that go again? Anitka's mother died from some sickness of something right?"

"Yes, some kind of sickness in the water."

"Very strange," Kah said as he shrugged his shoulders.

They could smell the river again, hear the birds that frequented the muddy banks and knew the next road was coming up. Soon they saw the brown river to their left and could smell it; it was a hint of wet earth, decaying plants with an overtone of dead fish. Kah unknowingly walked a little closer to Ist, she looked over and smiled as they continued. Rayu suddenly laughed. Kah and Ist slowed down and turned towards him.

"What are you thinking about, Rayu?" Ist asked with a chuckle.

"I was just thinking about what the teacher asked us today. You know, about what we wanted to do in our life."

"What did you think of?" she asked

Rayu raised his eyes up to the clouds and waved his head back and forth. "A business owner," he said in an even tone – sure of his statement.

Kah stuck his lips out and sucked in, contemplating Rayu's statement, "I can see that . . ."

"Don't know what business though, maybe I will make pottery," he said as he shook his head.

"I could see you do that."

Right then the path turned left and again they could hear the squawking of the birds in the river. They heard the Nile flowing by, even closer now, and they could smell its muddy scent. The trees thinned out and now they saw it; wide and majestic – the river held every animal they would ever need to survive. A large flock of ducks and ibises had gathered – some in the center and some at its banks. There were hippos wading on the far side and monkeys hanging from the low-lying branches of the sparse trees. The path had now followed the edge of the bank, so close that the youths could splash their feet in the water as they walked. Rayu stopped at the water's edge and bent over to pick up a stone. He flipped the small rock up and down in his hand. He turned his head to look at his friends and gave them a mischievous smirk. He adjusted his stance placing one foot in the water, turned back and threw. The stone sailed into the middle of the wading ducks. In unison the birds exploded into a frenzy of feathers and screams, as they took to the air.

"Woo-hoo," he yelled out and jumped as he lifted his hands in triumph.

"Nice, but I wouldn't do that," Kah said.

Rayu burst into another one of his laughing fits to which he was forced to bend over and place his hands on his knees, pausing to catch his breath. There was a large splash of water at his feet and a crocodile grabbed his leg in its wicked jaws. Rayu screamed and tried to remove his leg but it was hopeless. The crocodile's jaws of death had locked and it was unchallengeable. He screamed again as he was pulled into the murky water. The vicious reptile rolled over and over and fiercely ripped Rayu's leg completely off. Kah, although stunned at what he was witnessing, yelled out and tried to make as much noise as he could to stop the attack. Rayu managed to call out one more time before a second alligator joined in and seized the boy – within a second Rayu was gone.

They were stunned.

Ist cowered behind Kah in a state of shock. A swirl of water was all that was visible a short distance from the bank. A larger crocodile had obviously grabbed Rayu and would not be returning. This was a shocking reminder of the dangers of the river, when anyone is careless and does not pay attention for possible threats. Farther out on the river, more bubbles appeared this time, mixed with red.

"No . . .!" Ist screamed.

"He's gone . . . I can't . . ." Kah said dumbfounded – unable to grasp what he had just seen.

Both of them knew that those type of things happen, but neither of them had actually encountered it firsthand. Besides being so shocked she was barely able to speak, Ist was terrified. She was scared at the ease that Rayu was taken. She was scared for her own safety, *one moment he was here and the next he was gone . . .* she rehashed in her mind repeatedly. She couldn't get the memory of his high-pitched laughter out of her mind.

His laughter was quickly replaced with a cry for help. His laughter brought tears to her eyes and the emotion reddened her face – she was now openly weeping. Kah circled her shoulders with his arms and drew her against him, letting her cry while enclosed in his embrace – he too felt the loss.

When Kah was at his home he decided to sleep on his roof for the night. He brought his bedding up the steps at the back of his house and relaxed under the shade of a branch that hung over the back of the house. Saddened, Kah lay down on the bedding under the sparse shade and stared at the stars. He considered whether or not Narmer and Menes had spent large lengths of time staring at these same stars back when they were young?

13

THE HUT WAS QUIET as the students sat facing Weneg. *I did not want this to happen! I just started to know the boy. He had great potential, such a young vibrant mind. I hope the words of condolence I offered his parents were satisfactory. I have lost so many of my friends, why do I have to lose my students too?*

The feeling of loss was palpable in the room as the students couldn't help but glance at Rayu's now vacant spot. Ist sniffed quietly.

"Let's talk about what happened last week," Weneg said as he looked around the room.

Kah cleared his throat; Ist looked at him and moved closer. "Last week when we left here," he said gazing around the hut, focusing on each person, "Rayu was having fun beside the river as is always his way . . ." he paused. "Ist and I," he said putting his hand on her leg, "watched him jump around in the water, but there was an unseen crocodile lurking below the surface and it grabbed him." Kah paused as he felt his tears begin to well up. "The beast ripped his leg off and a second crocodile took him under the water."

"It happened so fast that we could not have done anything!" Ist said choking back tears.

"We raced to his house," Kah said, "and told his father. He then assembled a search party to see if there was any chance to retrieve his son. We searched for the rest of the day, but could not find his body . . . we could not find anything."

"I am sorry that you have been through that pain, but you must realize by now that Rayu has gone on to live in the bosom of Osiris. He is enjoying his life in bliss right now – do not be distraught," Weneg said.

"If he made it past the Scales of Judgement," Anitka said woefully.

"Yes, he must pass the scale to be worthy – if he wasn't, he will be snuffed out like a dying flame," Weneg said honestly.

The room was dead silent, each one contemplating Weneg's words. As he spoke, a black scorpion scuttled across the floor between two of the baskets lining the walls and a jackal yipped in the distance.

"That is hopeless," Anitka said angrily. "Life is hopeless! What can we do to pass this awful life that these stupid gods damn us to? I hate this, as a matter of fact I hate them too!" he ranted.

Everyone in the hut quickly made the Hamsa symbol so they would not incur any god's wrath – Anitka did not.

"No, life is not hopeless, and be careful what you say Anitka," Weneg said furrowing his brow. "Life is difficult yes, but not hopeless."

Anitka raised his hands in resignation then said, "Well I don't see how we can get through this impossible Judgement Hall."

"By careful study and determination, by living a pure life and one that the gods will be proud of. I have been giving every one of you the beginnings of that very thing, by allowing every one of you the keys. The keys are the tablets. Study the tablets I have brought in. Through them, close study will help you gain insight and knowledge to pass the Judgement Hall and into the Field of Reeds – our paradise."

Anitka's mind stopped short, *I didn't even copy them down! That was so stupid,* he thought cursing himself. He looked up at the teacher with a woeful gaze. "Could I have the chance to copy them again, teacher?"

Weneg smiled and nodded, motioning to the basket of clay tablets. "I will continue on with the story . . ."

* * * *

Narmer spent three weeks at Qua, this gave the army time to relax and hunt again. The time in the town allowed more meat to be gathered and preserved and bread to be baked. After the respite, they gathered all their supplies on the Breath of Amun and pushed north. They glided past Badari, Asyut and multiple small villages, all of which gave full honor to Narmer as their King. They cheered as the boat glided by and greeted the marching troops Menes led. One town in particular made an odd impression on Menes. This town had no formal name; it was just referred to as "The Town". The people seemed strange as well. Their homes were propped up on poles that lined the river and they had rope bridges that connected everything. Even though there was no shortage of papyrus stalks to build rafts, there was not a raft or boat in sight. The citizens of The Town seemed to express a real fear of the water, so much so that they never seemed to have washed themselves either.

"This must be so nice for Narmer," Menes grumbled. "All glory is heaped on him and passing me by. When will I get my chance for honor?" he complained under his breath.

Narmer shut his eyes and rested in the mid-ship cabin. He heard the calm and sometimes excited talking of the sailors that seemed to surround him. *What happened to my father that handed him such unfavorable luck when he was in this area last time?* Narmer remembered asking Nakht about praying to Amun for his father's safety. He then remembered the priest telling him that Min might be offended since his father prayed to him for protection. *This is my fault! I ignored Nakht's wisdom and followed my selfish desires.* Narmer rolled over onto his side, resting his head on his arm – *I must fix this,* he thought.

Narmer gradually realized he was sitting at a dinner table; steamed vegetables mixed with savory spices of cumin and cloves filled plates in front of him. Jars of wine and cups of beer were at his right and left. At the end of the table he saw a copper mirror unlike any he had ever seen before; the frame glowed white and in its middle swirled a counter-clock-wise vortex. Then a plate of meat was placed in front of him by an unseen person. It looked dainty and succulent as he was considering devouring it, when it brayed like a donkey. He shook his head and clasped his hands.

"Eat of me – your destiny awaits," the meat said.

He felt like he was being sucked into the plate and the mirror all at once. He sat back in his chair and heard laughing all around him, but could not see anyone there. He held himself back from the table and the meat repeated its command; then he was in a field where two avocado trees stood – the tree's limbs were interlaced. One tree was full of fruit and strong; the other was beautiful, but was barren. He then awoke distressed at the strange dream. *I must consult a dream interpreter at my first opportunity*, he thought.

Another week slipped by and they could see Beni Hasan in the distance – the place where his father was held up as he healed. As the boat glided into the town, a welcoming party had gathered at the docks. Narmer could see the troops that had been left there by his father – they looked to be in good health and obviously very fit. A group of officials stood at the end of the dock and they bowed in unison. The first thing Narmer noticed about the town was the lack of cleanliness; streets were cluttered with broken or discarded objects. One spot close to a row of short buildings had many white and brown feathers around tubs that were possibly filled with water. Another area had a public drain that appeared to start further in the town and empty into the river. Muddied pigs roamed freely and rummaged through the discarded trash eating what they wanted. *What a mess,* Narmer thought.

"Greetings . . ." an official said, but then dropped to his knees when he saw the golden armbands Narmer wore, designating him as the King. Narmer looked at the official bowing in respect, but still wasn't used to the reverence.

"You may rise."

He rose and said, "We welcome you to our city, Majesty."

"I welcome your greeting," Narmer said after he stepped off the dock and onto the hard-packed ground.

"My name is Menkhaf, I am the Chief of this town. We of course were lucky to have your father stay with us when he was injured . . ." he said, but his words trailed off.

Narmer eyed the man disapprovingly. "You have just recently come under my authority," he stated. "I do not know what King Hsekiu of the north expected of you, but this," he said, sweeping his hand at the piles of trash mixed with human waste and clogged drainage ditches, "this is unacceptable! You should be ready to have any official arrive in your town; this town will be the gateway to the north. It must show off the power of the King. This does not show power, this shows mire and filth."

Menkhaf looked like he had been chastised severely by a parent and hung his head in shame. The other officials took a step back from him leaving the chief to stand on his own. "You are as much to blame as your chief," Narmer also stated pointing to the others. It was at this conversation that Narmer felt the authority of his father begin to course through his veins. He felt bold and strong. He did not know what had come over him, but he liked it. "Furthermore," he continued, "you will never again have this town looking like this." The officials stepped forward as if to rebut the proclamation, but they stopped short when Narmer raised his hand and pointed to them. "Or you will be replaced," he finished.

"We will do as you ask, Majesty," they replied fearing for their stations.

"Very good," Narmer replied unsure if he should believe their words. Narmer walked down to the dock, along with the military that was on the boat and stood before the town officials. Narmer observed the chief close-up; he was shorter then himself, had short cropped white hair and as with the rest of the officials he met, he wore a beard as well – his was white.

"You are no longer servants of the vile north," he said as he touched his own shaven face. Narmer remembered the nightmare of the bearded man when he was young and felt sick. "Do your best to fit to your new master's ways," he said as he reached out and grasped Menkhaf's greasy beard.

Menkhaf dropped to his knees, grabbed his beard with his left hand, pulled a short dagger from his belt with his right and cut the beard off. "I will follow the ways of my new masters," he proclaimed.

Narmer thought about this newfound willingness to please him – *can I trust them or is this all a show?* he wondered.

* * *

Menkhaf's office was slightly spacious and clean – a total opposite of the cramped filth outside.

"Tell me . . . What awaits me outside this town? What is the state of their army and their towns?" Narmer asked.

Metkhaf rubbed his now newly shaven face. "Lahun is the town to the north, it is smaller than my town, but it has a well-established military – it is greater than here."

"Where are their barracks located?"

Metkhaf revealed all that Narmer asked without any pause, even offering his scouts and the services of the priests. "I have one more question for you: do you have an oracle – someone who is skilled at interpreting dreams?"

Menkhaf did not take long to answer. "Yes, there is such a person who works at the temple of Amun, she might help you; her name is Nefrusheri. Ask for her at the temple gates and the priests will lead you to her."

* * *

Narmer and Menes stood before the army who had gathered on the parade grounds. Narmer looked at the army that had been left there – they looked eager to continue the fight. *What am I doing?* he questioned himself. *Am I ready for this? Will I die in this stink hole of a land and leave my Eshe alone?* He could see his wife in his mind's eye, walking the grounds at the palace. In his thoughts she was wearing her favorite pale green, long flowing dress. She wore three gold bracelets on each wrist and had an anklet – the gold one he had given her. She also wore a braided wig that touched her mid-back. *I miss her so much.* He then thought about the promise he had made to his father. *I must not retreat from that oath!* He was torn, never the less; *how could I be a good King and a good husband if I do not fulfill my promises? I can't.* Soldiers of the army that had been stationed by his father, had married the citizens of the town and many of them now had children – they were committed to this place. Narmer looked at the army that he had brought along, standing there as well – *these men trust me and I must trust in myself. Oh, how I wish Khu was here guiding my path. What if I die? What will happen to Eshe? I have no children. Menes will marry her - that is for certain! Will he want her though? He has been a bachelor for so long and he has shown no interest in her – at least not that I know of. I will talk to him about these matters.*

Narmer raised his hands commanding the soldier's attention, "You [he paused] warriors of Beni Hassan, warriors of Abydos, bind your weapons, shields and skills to me – to your King and make this land one. Be proud of the good graces of our god Amun, and I as your King, and fight for us! Ahead is Lahun and the vile army that almost killed my father; they did not want to accept peace and rest under King Scorpion's rule. They wanted to kill him – they have succeeded for now . . . think of that the next time you see the army of the north." The army hooted and stomped their feet. "We will sail under my command and march under my brother, Menes' authority at first light tomorrow." They hooted again and banged the butts of their spears on the ground.

That evening surrounded by his security guards, Narmer walked through the beaten copper doors of the temple of Amun. The smell of myrrh was strong in the air and a thick blue-grey haze filled the rectangular room like a fog. A bald priest immediately stepped in front of him and bowed in obeisance and waited for the command to rise. The remaining priests turned their attention to Narmer and also bowed.

"How may I serve you my King?" the We'eb priest asked just as the prayers started again.

Narmer was amazed at this young priest's inner authority and made a mental note to ask after him if he required future services. "I am in search of Nefrusheri, the oracle. I would like her counsel."

"The Wise Women," he stated nodding his head. "Follow me," he said as he turned to the left and walked to a different room.

A woman covered with a shawl sat on the floor; her hair was white, but her face was that of a young girl. The room was very sparsely furnished; it had one chair, one short table with a red oil lamp and one cot.

"You come to me with a troubled mind, King Narmer."

"How do you know me?"

"I know a lot of things, Majesty. I have thought about this meeting with you for a long time," she stated. "The gods have already whispered many things to me. What you want from me is very hard for you."

Narmer did not know how to respond to her immediate bad information.

"I, none the less, do require your counsel no matter what it is," he said as he questioned if this was going to be a disaster or not.

The woman faced him and spoke. "My counsel will not be pleasing to you right away, but your desires will cut you deeply in your life. I know you had a dream that troubles you and want my help to interpret it."

How does she know these things? he wondered, being oddly drawn to her. "Yes that is correct."

"Bring your chair closer to me," she said.

He brought the chair over to her and sat down; she then reached over and held onto his calf – something that made him uncomfortable, but also at ease. She hummed to herself quietly. *This is odd . . .* he thought, but didn't dare swat her hand away.

"What a powerful dream, my King . . . a bad omen, but maybe not."

Narmer reached over and with his left hand placed under her chin, he lifted her white face to his. Her eyes were a cloudy red and rimmed with white lashes. He noticed that the eyes he looked into did not return his gaze – she was blind. His thumb caressed her cheek as he held her chin.

"How do you know my dream . . . ?" he asked. He could see her hidden tortured spirit. "I do not understand."

"I was born like this . . . being able to see hidden things. It is a curse and a blessing," she said retracting her hand. "You do not want me to interpret your dream," she said as if almost in a daze, but with a hint of sorrow.

Why is this a problem for her? She hears dreams all the time, why is my dream any different? he thought. The woman pulled back, away from Narmer. *One moment she seems open to me, the next she is not,* he thought. "What did you see Nefrusheri – they call you 'The Wise Woman' so please, in your wisdom tell me my dream!"

The white haired women raised her head, her unseeing eyes blankly stared back at him. "I saw your dream. A buffet and talking food . . . a slab of donkey meat. You saw a mirror, you also saw yourself in that mirror."

"Yes that was my dream . . . what did it mean?"

"You will have a new life."

"Yes I will have a new life . . . does that mean I will be successful in my campaign?" he said as he was getting frustrated. *Getting information from this woman is like counting the fish in the river.*

"I see good luck in your future and your name will last for centuries, but you will share that future with another. Your brother is to help you and share in the victory for a time. Follow your father's wisdom and do not fret at these words - you need Menes just as much as he needs you."

Narmer felt taken aback, but he could feel that there was something else. *I must share this victory?*

Nefrusheri continued, "But, there will be a price to pay. You will have a new life [she paused] and a new wife."

"Eshe?" he asked raising his brows.

"She will die, my King."

Those words stabbed him deeply. *She will die,* he repeated to himself and then closed his eyes. "Are you certain of this?" he asked not believing her words.

"Yes I am sure . . . everyone dies," she concluded. You also saw two trees – one was full of fruit the other was barren. The Queen will never have children. One final thing my King; this path that you are on will be too much for Menes to bare. Heed my words and your father's: **you** are King - not him."

Narmer stood up, turned and left. *Of course everyone dies!* He cursed to himself, *how ridiculous. How can she possibly know Eshe will never have children?! What does she possibly know about Menes?* He walked out of the temple and into the cool evening outside. The stars shimmered brightly that night, but the smell of the silent street still remained. Although a vast amount of refuse had been gathered and burned, this town was far from the crisp cleanliness of his home in Abydos. Narmer then walked to the town's parade grounds where tents had been set up to bunk the soldiers. There were some awake, gambling with knuckle bones and betting with their rations – a piece of bread or dried fish for this or the promise of a cup of beer for that. He knew he was getting close to his cot by the smell of the river and as expected, saw The Breath of Amun rocking on the river.

* * * *

Weneg adjusted his legs and sat up stretching his back since he had been slouching – a bad habit of his. "We all die . . ." he said as his words trailed off. "We don't know when, but it is how you live your life here, before you are called to the scales of judgement, that truly matters. How will you answer the gods when they ask you the tough questions? Will you study now so you are prepared? I am giving you all the information you need to be successful," he said, motioning to the basket of tablets in the center of the room.

"This is stupid. How could Rayu have ever studied those tablets – he could not read," Anitka said. *I can though, so what is my problem?* he thought. He then sat right beside the basket, pulled out the first tablet and began to copy the script as he continued to grumble to himself.

Kah and Ist walked together alone back down the path towards their homes, reflecting on the latest events.

"What is wrong with Anitka? Just being in the same room as him is stressful," Kah said.

They both were glad to have copied the tablets previously and had the ability to read. Soon they came upon the place where Rayu was taken and they walked further on the right side of the path, distancing themselves from the river's edge. After they passed the place of the boy's death, Kah thought about the continuation of his own life – where it was going and what he wanted to do with it. *I must study more than what I am doing, if I want to be like my teacher. But what of my life beyond that? Do I want to join my life to this woman?* He considered as he looked at Ist.

"Remember when the teacher asked us what we wanted to be in life? I never heard your desires for the future?" Kah asked out of curiosity, but wondered whether he was worthy to have her.

She looked at him shyly and stopped walking. "I want to be a wife. I want to run my household, and I want to have children. That is my desire, it has always been my desire," she replied.

Kah stopped as well, *humph* he thought as they both stood side by side. He then reached into his shenti and pulled out a small clay tablet and gave it to her. She took it with a quizzical expression. The tablet was small but full of tiny writing, she smiled and looked back at Kah.

"What is this?"

"Just something I wrote for you . . . just read it," Kah said as he bit his lip.

Ist raised an eyebrow and looked at the tablet again.

The earth trembled as you passed by,
Turning everything sacred as you walked.

And you set your blue eyes upon me for the first time,
speaking at me with the depth of the night
...like a nightingale who doesn't need its wings to fly.
What a blessing it is to be worthy of your look.

I have seen rain on the desert,
and all impossible things coming true.

All of my prayers carry your name.
I wish to be pure so that I can desire you.

Take me as you will.
Your slave...
[http://themagentahornet.com/ancient-egyptian-love-poems.html]

Ist put her hand to her chest. "That was beautiful, Kah," she replied. "How long have you been feeling this way?"

"Honestly . . . since we were young, but ever since we started learning at Weneg's and he challenged us to act on our desires, I decided to pursue you."

"Hey, I thought your desire was to be like the teacher?" she said.

"Yes it is, but marrying you was always my first desire," he admitted.

Ist thought about it – not too long though. "I accept," she said and then kissed him on the cheek, clutching the love poem tightly to her chest.

They started walking again. A path split off to the left and Ist headed down it, followed by Kah. The two soon arrived at a small estate – Ist's home. She turned to face him, smiled and jogged into the house. Servants were tending the small flock of goats – feeding or milking them. Ist's father, Prehirwennef, who was tending a small vegetable garden, looked up at Kah's approach.

"Greetings," Kah said raising his hand in acknowledgement.

"Greetings," he replied. "How is your father?" Ist's father prodded, realizing Kah was there for more than just a visit.

"He is well. My father just attained the role of High Priest of Amun in this Nome, so he is very happy," Kah replied smiling.

"Yes I know, your mother will be pleased too. What is on your mind, young man?"

Kah looked at the garden and considered the harvest that would be coming for the man this season, *this is what Ist is used to being provided with, will I be able to maintain this level of lifestyle?*

"As you probably know, I have a home being built on a plot of land next to my father's."

The older man nodded and then felt a little shudder in his emotions, *my precious daughter will be leaving, how can I bear with the pain of having her taken from me? My sons have all left my house now with their wives, I will be alone; my wife as my only companion. Can he provide for my sweet little goddess? This is the way of things though, I must let go.* He knew what was coming and resigned himself to the inevitable.

"I would like to draw up a marriage contract between your daughter and I. I think that we are well suited together and she would be a good wife for me."

"Have you talked this over with her and does she agree?" he questioned feeling the loss of his daughter, but happy that his family will be now be joined with a more prominent one than his own.

"Yes I have. I will have my house prepared for her, the beginning of next month," Kah replied.

"Ist's mother and I will write up the marriage contract for you then, to sign later this week and she will move her belongings to her new home under your care.

14

K AH WALKED TO HIS new house that was being built by
the river that meandered by slowly at an even pace.
The front entrance wasn't yet finished – it just needed
extra mortar, some bricks and whitewash. At the far
end he saw workers bringing in the dried and hardened
bricks that had been made three weeks previously. He
had built a large rectangular structure that sat waist high
off the ground that had a ramp to the front door. The
roof was made out of wood, mud and straw – perfect
to sleep or relax on at night under the stars. A second,
three story structure would be built with an even larger
ramp adjoining this main house, but that would have
to wait a few years. Kah bounded up the ramp and
into the home and was met with a whitewashed wall

that sported a picture of him harvesting crops with flint bladed sickle. He was particularly proud of this picture – it made a statement of his prosperity. Now he turned to the left and walked deeper into the house and into the bedroom. There, the local painters were at work painting scenes of daily life. A large bed sat folded away in the corner beside an off-white mattress. The painters looked up from their work and greeted him.

"It is a pleasure to see you again, master." Kwab said as he put down his paint brush.

Kah raised his hand in greeting. He never thought being called master felt right, especially from someone much older than him, but these men were in his father's employ and now that they worked for him he was indeed their master.

"Will we be able to complete this painting soon or shall we hold off on this longer still?" Kwab asked as he motioned to an unfinished detail in the artwork.

The piece showed a husband and wife holding hands and standing overlooking their fields with servants reaping the grain and piling the sheaves. The missing detail of the beautiful piece was the portrait of his wife, their children and their names. The running commentary below that was to tell the story of their lives was also missing detail.

"Ist will soon be the mistress of this home and will be arriving when the construction is completed. Hurry to do your work well and you will be given a second ration of food!" he said with a smile, anticipating his future.

"Kwab smiled and said, "Thank you master, and congratulations. May you have a blessed life before the god."

"Thank you. I wish you to be blessed as well. I would like to know how the kitchen is progressing. Is it completed yet?" he said changing the subject.

"Follow me master," he said waving him towards the door.

Kah followed the man to the back of the home and into an open air kitchen complete with a clay dome shaped oven and an unused open fire pit. The back of the house had a wide door opening – not as wide as the front though. At the back of the house was the river – wide, deep, full of fish and crocodiles. There was a flock of white ibis that were cautiously sweeping their curved orange bills from side to side in the water in search of crabs and crayfish. These slow moving birds, regularly the prey of crocodiles, were still boldly hunting even though their teammates would disappear in a splash of water and feathers quite close to each other. Kah laughed every time a bird disappeared in a flurry. The banks of the river at some parts were densely overgrown with papyrus plants, which was a perfect home for all manner of fowl. The other areas of the river bank were flat and had no vegetation, a perfect place for a dock – one that had not been built yet. *Ist will love this place!* he thought to himself. *Why must I be a priest? I know that it is a place of honor and everyone would desire that as a career, but it is not my desire. My longing is far from that, mine is wisdom, but how do I get wisdom? How do I become like my teacher?* He did not know. Kah chuckled and mumbled "Well I can ask him." He turned back to the house, skirted it, walked through the unfinished wall and walked home.

The next day Kah followed the same path to the teacher's hut at the road that led to Ist's home – the girl was waiting. She carried her usual sack, the one that contained her meal for the day, her charcoal writing tool and a few pieces of broken pottery to write on. They greeted each other with an awkward kiss and made the trip to Weneg's hut, joining up with Hayki and Anitka on the way. Anitka was in a particularly foul mood and was carrying an obsidian dagger that he was flipping up in the air and fondling like a favored toy. Kah and Ist found this unsettling and odd.

"Be careful Anitka, you don't want to drop that and break it."

Anitka turned and held the knife towards them and swiped at the air. "I know what I'm doing. You are not my father!"

"Just put it down Anitka," Kah said as he stood between the knife and Ist.

"I am just having fun!" Anitka said as he flashed a rare smile.

"It was not funny," Ist said.

For the rest of the walk to Weneg's, nobody spoke.

Kah's mind was travelling in many directions as he sat in the dimly lit hut. He thought about the recent confrontation with Anitka, his house, his career, how to achieve that career, or is it a career – to be wise, but primarily he thought about the short-haired girl sitting beside him – Ist.

Weneg stood up and grabbed a small jar, walked over to an unlit oil lamp, trimmed the blackened wick and filled the lamp with the oil from his jar. The wick was soon lit; it snapped and sparked for a brief time and then settled into a constant soothing glow. Weneg was now comfortable with this new job of teaching and he looked forward to seeing his students grow.

* * * *

Menes army had been marching now for many days after they left Beni Hasan, but luckily their bellies were still full from the bounty they had been given. The soldiers had been very comfortable under Menes leadership and most of them now referred to him as 'King'. Menes enjoyed that title and even though it was incorrect, he did not rebuke them. A half day east of the river, Menes army came upon a small settlement that boasted five quaint homes and seemed to be peaceful in nature. Ahead of the columns of soldiers that filled the town, naked children stared with their mouths agape as the soldiers filed past them. Even the stray dogs seemed to pause when the men walked by – they didn't even bark. There were few planted pots that beautified the place – the only ones were in front of a modest house – a house that was no bigger than the others. There were a few torn reed baskets piled between two rows of cut papyrus stalks, near a vacant cold fire pit. As Menes approached the decorated house, a man with a stained shenti exited the home.

"Why have you come to our village?" the man demanded.

Menes was taken aback by the affront.

"Who are you?" Menes asked hoping he was the leader.

"Never mind who I am!" the man said obviously perturbed. "Who are you that you bring an army in to my village?! King Thesh will hear about this and will loose his wicked army on you if you do not leave immediately."

"I am here on King Narmer's behalf to join the north and south together. Will you join me in this great plan?"

"I do not know of this 'King Narmer' that you speak of and neither will I bow to this request! The true King is King Thesh – we are loyal to him. King Thesh's army will be a nightmare that will swoop down on you and grind you to dust," he said as a warning. "Those men have no souls and are un-beatable. They are like the goddess Amit – un caring and vicious."

Menes stepped back from the man in contemplation, *what would Narmer do?* he thought. *No, what am I going to do? If I want to be King, I need to make these decisions!* Just as he thought that the man swung the mace he had been holding.

"Attack these slime!" he yelled at his men.

The villagers picked up whatever they could and attacked Menes army. Menes easily dodged the mace and thrust a spear into the man. The out-numbered villagers screamed and fought against the army with vigor. One of Menes soldiers who had been careless was even killed, when a villager attacked him with a rake.

"Lay them to waist," Menes yelled to his men.

The soldiers attacked the townsmen and killed every one of them. It was only when the soldiers started killing the women and children, that Menes put a stop to the soldiers. *What have I done?* Menes questioned himself as he walked through the town square that was now littered with both men and women. Children gathered on the outsides of the square and cried for their parents, not knowing if they were among the dead or if their mothers were one in the few that were spared.

Guilt flooded over his mind like a wave that had no end.

"What will the gods do to us?" he said loud enough that the guards standing beside him heard.

"Why did you do this?" cried a woman who was on the ground cradling a deceased man.

Menes looked at them, but had nothing to say. His Ka condemned him, as if the gods were passing judgement right there. He knew he could have stopped his soldiers, but he didn't. Menes tried to ignore the crying of women and children that surrounded him by pushing his thoughts and feelings deep down inside him. Menes saw some of his soldiers light torches and approach the buildings.

"Stop!" Menes yelled. "We cannot do that to these people . . . They have gone through enough."

The men snuffed out their fires. After they spoke with Menes, they began digging graves for the fallen men and then buried them. The pain of guilt needled his mind like a bad sunburn on his forehead. He tried to push the thoughts away, but every time he closed his eyes, he saw and heard children wailing. He wanted all of the painful memory to go away.

* * *

One day later, the army found another small town – this one was much larger though. There were twenty homes and one small temple dedicated to the primal creator god – Ptah. The whitewashed temple had red and yellow flowers planted by its cedar doors and scenes of King Thesh destroying his enemies. The small temple was overwhelmed by many white clad We'eb priests in the midst of their daily chores of washing and cleaning. The citizens of this town watched cautiously as the army marched into the streets and stopped in front of the temple. Within minutes a High Priest of Ptah, who was wearing a leopard sash draped across his shoulder, walked out of the temple. His head was freshly shaven and he had thick kohl around his eyes. He was followed closely by five other priests who wore bright, white linen tunics and new reed sandals. The High Priest bowed in submission to Menes. Menes told him to rise.

"Greetings, Master . . ." he said. "My name is Neferenpet – I am the High Priest of Ptah," he said as he reverently motioned to the temple behind him with his hand.

Menes intently watched the man and tried to judge his character. *I am no good at judging people like my brother*, he cursed himself as he shook his head.

"Do you know why I am here, Priest?" he asked blatantly.

"I do," he said.

"Do you think the ruler of this town will yield to me?"

The High Priest smiled and shrugged, "The leader of the town left when he heard you were marching this way. He left the town under my authority," he said. "We have suffered under Thesh's control. I was hoping that the stories were true – that you had come to join the north and south together."

"Yes, I have come to join these two lands. Will you yield to my quest and turn away from Thesh and accept a new King?"

The priest bowed once again at Menes feet and kissed them. "I will do your bidding, my King."

I like this, Menes thought – again not correcting the man who had assumed that he was the King, not his brother. "I see that you will be loyal to me. Tell me what you know of this 'dreaded army' I have heard about. Where are they, what are they?"

"This army you speak of . . . They came through here two days ago. The men were taken from the worst jails in the area. The men were given 'freedom' for their service, but Thesh owns them and they are fiercely loyal to him. Be careful when you meet them. Do not trust them."

This new information troubled him, but finding the location of the army was the main priority. Menes army left Neferenpet's town and marched steadily, yet quietly north. They could see a definite path that this mysterious army had taken, by the discarded empty beer jars and colorful black and red damaged reed baskets. Every so often Menes saw a pair of papyrus sandals that had been discarded because the thong was broken or the sole was wore out. Menes also saw small bundles of damaged arrows at regular intervals – these he assumed – were places where the army had attempted to do repairs. At one spot, they found the brutalized body of a man. His right arm had been cut off at the elbow; his lips, nose and ears were removed as well. The shocking state of the body was compounded by the fact that his wounds had already healed over. The man seemed to have been killed by some type of poison, since he had white foam still bubbling from his mouth and an expression of agony in his twisted face. Menes was shocked and stepped away from the body. *What type of men are these?* he questioned. *I know that I have been told that these were criminals, but are they killing each other as well? They must be very brutal men!*

As Menes army marched forward trying to catch up with the illusive criminal warriors, one of the soldiers looked up to see a hail of arrows descending towards them, which pelted their ranks and killed fifteen of their men.

"Get to protection," Menes screamed. Nock your arrows and return fire."

Fifty men quickly fired their own arrows back in the general direction of the onslaught, while one hundred soldiers rushed ahead brandishing spears and maces. The criminals pulled back into the tall scrub brush giving Menes army the ability to advance even further.

The area they had advanced to, had changed from short green scrub trees, to tall date palm spires with heavy green leaf fans at their tops. Large red-brown clusters of dates in varying states of ripeness that looked like masses of small protruding fingers; hung like large baubles from the trees.

"I see them," Hanif – one of the soldiers – cried out.

Menes could also see the back part of the army as well. The army had fanned out and were pressed up against the river. Menes pushed them even harder until they had nowhere to go.

"We got them now!" Menes screamed out.

The criminal army turned and attacked, like the fury of a wronged lover. They could now see the faces of this new army – they had the look of the worst demons of the underworld. The sight of them brought fear to Menes core.

"Who are these devils," Menes asked out loud to no one in particular.

The northern soldiers had the look of misshapen painted gargoyles that had been turned into brutal mercenaries. He saw a naked soldier with a full black beard that had an arrow protruding from his arm, run out of the foliage and charge into Menes army, screaming and swinging a mace. The man killed three of Menes soldiers before he himself was dispatched by a spear. The small surprising skirmish was all the criminals needed to advance their troops and gain the upper hand. The criminal army swarmed around Menes before his men were able to fight back. Menes pulled his men back into the thick date palms and tried to flank the feared army on the left side, when he saw their archers split off and head towards the river. Menes pushed his men hard to gain as much ground as possible, but it was going to be a hard battle to win seeing his dwindling army numbers.

NARMER STARTED HIS CAMPAIGN north, he gathered his military and set off on The Breath of Amun. In eight days they reached the outskirt border of Lahun. Narmer sent out a call for the town to set up talks between the leaders and send an emissary, but no response was returned.

"Look Majesty, a ship!" Minnakht the commander-of-fifty called out.

Up ahead a boat sat in the middle of the river, the sails were down and no sailors appeared to be on board. To the right side of the ship, tall stalks of papyrus gently swayed in the breeze. The front of the ship seemed to have sticks tacked on for one reason or another, but it was unclear. As Narmer's ship got closer, Lahun eerily sat silent in the distance behind the mystery boat. The closer they got, the clearer the 'sticks' came into view – they were not sticks, they were skeletons nailed to the bow of the boat. A sense of fear mixed with disgust crept into Narmer as well as the sailors. *I don't think they want to talk* he thought. *This is an absolute insult and I will not stand for it!* The ship slowly coasted closer to the seemingly anchored vessel. They saw that this was Min's Wisdom – King Scorpion's ship – the ornaments were broken and flags were now tattered. They brought The Breath of Amun up to the front of the anchored derelict ship and began to remove the tacked-on bones. Knowing who was whom was impossible, but never-the-less, they removed the skeletons making sure they were kept together as individuals. Later in the day they were just about finished retrieving the cadavers when a hail of arrows peppered the river and sides of the boats. A sailor screamed as an arrow sank itself deep into his hip.

Startled, Narmer yelled out orders to the crew. "Detach from the ship and swing around to the far side of this boat. We need cover!"

Another volley of arrows were loosed killing fifteen sailors who were not protected with shields. Narmer held his shield like an umbrella as hail after hail of arrows fell around him. He heard the smack of arrow heads landing a finger width from his arm through the wooden shield. As he looked around him, a sailor stared back at him and through the noisy rain he could see him try to mouth the words 'HELP'. Narmer moved over closer to the man to protect him, but an arrow found its target in his neck. Surprise and fear flashed across his face for a split second, then he dropped to the floor. The ship finally found protection as it attached itself to the opposite side of the neglected ship; the arrows only hit the other ship. The Breath of Amun was safe for now. Sixteen men were suddenly dead and four were injured. The remaining sailors and army personnel gathered their dead comrades and piled the spent arrows. Narmer looked around at the devastation that had befallen his crew and boat. He remembered how he had wondered 'how could I doom them and let my army destroy them?' he soon lost his passion for these people.

"We are out of arrows to shoot back, Majesty!" Minnakht yelled as he shot the last one.

Narmer then devised a plan to move this little skirmish into his favor. As the arrows rained down, they pulled apart papyrus reeds from the side of the hull and quickly fashioned a square frame. They covered up the frame with the clothing of their dead comrades and stuffed it with any reeds they could pull up from the river. When the frame was finished they poled their ship out from behind Min's Wisdom and out in full sight of the opposing soldiers on the opposite bank. The arrows began being launched immediately landing safely in the piles of clothing and reeds.

"Hold on men," Narmer called to the sailors huddled behind the frame. "We will drain their supply of arrows soon," he said as he inwardly smiled at his sneaky plan.

After a short time the frame was covered with hundreds and hundreds of arrows. They could then hear screams to halt from someone on the bank.

"They are not being hit you imbeciles! You are just wasting arrows." A voice carried across the river. Hearing this statement of frustration made Narmer smirk.

Narmer then looked at Minnakht and whispered, "You said you needed arrows?" and then motioned with his chin to the bounty they had just collected. They carefully poled to the unexposed west side of the anchored ship again and set about collecting arrows off of the frame. More yelling erupted from the bank behind them. Narmer stood beside the commander and said, "We need to see what those men are up to. Find someone able to swim along this ship, and peer around the edge."

Minnakht singled out Re'hotpe and ordered him into the water. The man cautiously slipped in and guided himself around the anchored boat and right to the bow. As soon as he got there, more arrows were loosed barely missing the volunteered soldier. He made a hasty retreat back to the safety of Narmer's ship.

"What did you see?" Narmer excitedly asked after Re'hotpe was helped back on board.

"I think they are sending someone over. They are making a raft of some sort. That is all I could see."

"We just have to wait until they arrive . . . and shoot them down," Minnakht replied.

They relaxed briefly and tended any wounds they had received until they heard another set of arrows thud into the King's ship; then silence. A few minutes later a soft crackling sound could be heard. Narmer and Minnakht looked up apprehensively. A billow of smoke streamed into the sky at an alarming rate from their perceived hide out – their aggressors had set the boat ablaze. They heard yelling again, along with the splashes of people entering the water. As the commotion got louder and louder, the boat's fire got hotter and the smoke thickened, forcing Narmer to abandon their shelter. Luckily their ship was moved just in time, because within minutes the derelict was fully engulfed in flame and smoke. As they poled to the western bank, they no longer could see the army on the eastern bank due to the heavy smoke. Movement on the far bank to the left side attracted Minnakht's attention. Two boats were being launched into the river; heading their way.

"How many arrows do we have, Commander?" Narmer asked.

Minnakht looked at the pile and did a quick calculation. "The enemy has provided us with four hundred and fifty-seven arrows, Majesty, the remaining ones they shot are damaged . . . fifty-eight," he replied as he pulled another one more from the frame.

"Very good. Set up here," he said pointing to the bow of the boat. "Shoot this boat if they get within range," he commanded.

The flames from the anchored boat stopped in an instant, just as one of the hull's flaming boards gave way and allowed water to gush in and sink the derelict. Now they could see the enemy on the eastern shore. It appeared they were in the middle of their own fight. Re'hotpe placed an arrow on a bow and aimed at the oncoming boats. He noticed the approaching men were flailing their arms – hands open and unarmed. He lowered the bow and was then joined by the King and the captain.

Yelling intensified on the eastern bank as all-out fighting continued. Still, the boats approached. By their clothing and beards they seemed to be a part of the enemies group, but they were making no aggressive moves.

"What are your intentions?" Minnakht shouted to them.

The man that was frantically waving answered back. "We come in peace and do not want to fight."

Narmer stepped to the bow and waved them forward. As the boats met, a man stepped forward out of the group. "My name is Teremun. We have escaped from Lahun's prison. I assume you have come from the south?" he said with hope in his words.

Narmer and his men were quick to notice the difference in accent of these northern men – it wasn't too bad as they understood him very well.

Narmer looked at Minnakht in disbelief at the boldness of the man. "Yes, we come from the south," Minnakht replied not sure of this man. "You are addressing the **King**, so on your faces and show the due respect!"

Teremun and his men immediately bowed to the floor of their boats and waited for a bid to rise.

"You said you escaped from prison . . ." Narmer said. "My father came from the south, wanting to join with you, yet you drove him away. Why should we pay heed to what you have to say?"

"I tried to encourage our chief to accept your King's offer, but I along with my supporters," he said motioning to the men standing beside him, "were thrown into jail. We tried to appeal to Thesh, our King, but that failed and our wives were put to death in retaliation. So you see . . ." he shrugged his shoulders and lifted his hands, "we have nothing to lose, but beg leniency from you."

"How can I know if I should trust you?" Narmer asked bluntly.

Teremun looked at the other men, whispered a few words and turned back to face him. "We have nothing to hide, Majesty . . ." he said.

"Are you willing to turn away from Thesh and pledge yourselves wholly to me?"

The fighting on the eastern bank slowed considerably until it was no longer there. Narmer saw that there was only one army still standing and what appeared to be the other remaining men bound and on their knees.

"Majesty . . ." the captain called to him.

Narmer raised a finger silencing Minnakht, but still intently looking at Teremun.

"We will pledge ourselves to you, my King," the men said in broken unison.

Narmer looked back at Minnakht. "Majesty look, the army is flying your colors!"

On the eastern bank, the standing army now was standing behind a pale blue and white banner that was fluttering in the breeze.

"You will give me all the information I ask," Narmer pointed the statement at Teremun. "Cast off and head for the bank."

O N THE EASTERN BANK, two hundred bound men sat kneeling on the ground with their elbows tied behind their backs. The smell of burnt wood still hung in the dead air like a smitten mistress reluctant to leave her lover's side. Menes stood with his men, triumphantly holding a blood soaked spear at his side. He was dripping in sweat and covered in dirt.

"You don't look too worse for wear, Brother," Menes said as soon as he saw Narmer.

"It did get pretty warm there for a minute. I have been troubled though," he said. "I need to sail south shortly to see Eshe and Mother. We should go south as well to take part in the Wag festival. On other matters, how did you conquer this army?"

"Well I was fortunate to break through their lines on the east, but it was no easy task. These men gave us a scare when we first came upon them. We did lose a few men though," Menes said.

Narmer shrugged his shoulders sadly. *More death, when will I be free from those words?* he questioned. *I must get used to this; it is the responsibility of a King.* Menes then motioned with his finger for Narmer to follow him.

"Stand up," Menes ordered a captive that was kneeling on the ground.

The man stood. He had a thick black beard that matched his long dark hair, hard facial features and piercing brown eyes, but what was immediately noticeable was a hole in his face where a nose once was. The next man was ordered to stand as well – he too was nose-less. One by one the captives were ordered to stand, each one of them had some sort of mutilation or branding. Some mutilations, such as the lips and ears being removed, made Narmer feel sick to his stomach to look at. Some of the captives had painful branding marks all over their bodies. Others had scars from previous beatings covering their backs.

"Who are these men?" Narmer questioned Menes, aghast.

"These are the criminals of the north; they are rapists, thieves, liars and cheaters. This man had his tongue removed," he said pointing to an older man.

What will I do with them he asked himself? *I can't condemn these men for something I did not pass judgement over? They were judged by some sort of court though. I can't pass a second judgement on them and sentence them to death for following their commander's orders.* Narmer walked a little to the side, paused and thought deeply. *I think I know what to do,* he decided.

"Stand up all of you!" he commanded. Everyone obeyed. "I am the King. Hear what I have to say. In my studies of our old ways, my father Amun led me to this understanding: the great god Meretseger will forgive sins through repentance and atonement. All of you have sinned and have paid dearly for your misdeeds." He paused before he continued, "Do you repent and promise before the god to never repeat these actions again?"

There was a chorus of agreement that came from the criminals, but that was quickly silenced by Narmer's raised hand. "You must understand that this is a one-time pardon," he said as he pinched his face, thinking the men were just agreeing to anything to get out of their predicament. "If you return to your old ways and squander this gift, you will be put to death. You will be folded into this army and of course fight for me. Are each one of you willing to pledge their life to me and swear this sacred oath? Be careful when you answer," he warned.

Menes stepped closer to his brother and in a low voice spoke. "I do not trust these men, Narm."

"I must at least give them an opportunity," Narmer whispered back.

The men who could be mistaken for ghouls knelt down, their faces to the dirt and pledged themselves to Narmer – their new King. Narmer looked these men over; one in particular caught his attention. The man was missing his nose and ears, but he had a look of wisdom that shone through his calm brown eyes.

His name was Weren and his crime had been thievery and lying to officials. He had been spared his life if he would join this wicked northern army. Weren had been placed in the army eight years previously when Hsekui was King of the north. He excelled in his position under Thesh the new King and now was the leader of this fighting force. Weren was apologetic for his crimes, but he was sorrier for getting caught. He was a thief down to his core and still would take small things when it suited him.

Menes stood beside the captured army that his brother had now pardoned. *They have killed many of my soldiers in our latest contact. I will have trouble forgiving that,* he thought. *I will be watching these men closely, just one mistake . . .* he tightened his grip on his axe. *My brother the King . . . It is hard to think of that . . . hard to think of him like that,* he repeated in his mind. *I must follow Osiris-King-Scorpion's wishes, stand behind him and support him. I don't like it though. There must be a way that I can get my due credit seen and respected by others.*

* * * *

The hut was silent as Weneg leaned back on his stool and finished the story for the day. The feeling in the air was as if the old sage had physically taken his students on a wild ride and they had felt as though they had been right beside Narmer and Menes all the way along.

"Kah, will you open the window coverings?" Weneg asked.

Kah was snapped into reality and noticed that Ist had been tightly gripping his hand. He stood and walked to the window and opened it. A gust of cool air knifed into the room like a sharp blade cutting into ripe fruit – it was refreshing.

"Every person goes through hardships, even the King. It all depends on if you are going to fold under the pressure and not fulfill your responsibilities or stick to your promises. It is entirely up to you."

Anitka leaned back on his elbows thinking about his hardships and difficulties in life. *I guess it is true that even the great King Narmer had his share of problems. My mother died leaving me to fend for myself,* he thought begrudgingly. Anitka and his brother Hayki were not really left all alone. Asim, their father, had married quickly and his new wife Uadjit loved the boys like her own. *I just don't understand why I struggle so much in life – things like my possible relationships. I think Ist is beyond my reach – she has chosen,* he cursed as he saw her fingers interlaced with Kah's. As he thought about it he sunk into a deeper state of despair and could not wait to leave and go home.

Kah's thoughts were filled with his imaginings of his new life – a life with the girl who sat beside him. His mind was pulled in many directions. One was his home being built, but mainly his thoughts surrounded the life he was building with Ist.

Hayki just sat quietly – not absorbed with worries of life, he just watched. *I am well on my way to be what I want,* he thought pleased with himself. *I can already read and write – the two traits I must master to be a scribe. But the King . . .* he looked scornfully at his brother Anitka and smirked inwardly.

Weneg could almost see a cloud of hopelessness cover Anitka's eyes. *This boy needs to ground himself before he slips and does something regrettable,* Weneg thought. "Tomorrow I will tell you about the tragedy of Queen Eshe, so be here early."

Kah, Ist, Hayki and Anitka stood in unison, individually thanked Weneg and left the hut. Ist walked beside Kah on the way to her home. Enjoying the quiet cool sunset, they heard the insects coming to life and the coo of doves that pecked on the path. A crow screamed out and landed on the dry yellow reeds, perched there like a living gargoyle and kept watch.

* * *

Anitka and Hayki walked farther ahead arguing in short spurts all the time they were on the trail. At one time the older boy pushed the younger one into the scrub brush, yelling obscenities at him. Kah looked at Ist and shrugged his shoulders.

"Are you two alright up there?" Kah asked.

"Stay out of it, Kah!" was the reply from the older boy.

"I was just asking . . ."

"Well don't!" Anitka spat back.

Kah looked at Ist with raised eye brows, shrugged, reached for her hand and then walked hand-in-hand to her home.

"My father has written a marriage contract for us," Ist blurted out as she handed Kah the document.

Kah received and looked at the carved tablet in his hand; he read its contents.

I Prehirwennef, Chief Scribe of the workmen of Hor-Aha, give my first born daughter Ist to Kah; son of Bakenkhons High Priest of the temple of Amun.

As Amun lives, as the Ruler lives, I Kah, swear an oath to never depart from Ist, first born daughter of Prehirwennef. She brings: one comb made of gold and ivory, one bed made of wood, one wig, one kettle, two cups, one shenti, five hekats of grain, two goats and ten loaves of bread to this union. Upon my death, your household will care for Ist's mother Meretseger.

Kah's walk home brought him thoughts of trepidation for his future – *will Ist be a good wife? I, a good husband? Will we be successful in producing children?* He turned the tablet over in his hand, *well it is done now. Ist will be joined to me* – he saw Ist's smiling face flash in his mind's eye. *I can do this,* he thought. Kah then thought about the lesson that he had received from Weneg, *how can King Narmer trust these men who were obviously known for their crimes? Even I would have troubles with that,* he confessed to himself.

E SHE SAT SURROUNDED WITH her servant's doting on her and dressing her in a shear, off-white, full-length dress. They adorned her dainty neck and fragile wrists with her favored jewels and placed a long curly wig on her head. Her mind was far away from her daily life that had been filled with responsibilities – responsibilities that seemed to choke her life out. Her deep yearning for a child always challenged her emotions every time she left the security of the palace and saw a young mother doting on her new baby. As time went, on she became a shut-in and never left her rooms unless her presence was imperative.

"Your Majesty . . . a boat has been spotted," Betresh said excitedly as she entered the Queen's room.

"If the boat is flying the royal colors, that surly will mean that the King is back?" Eshe said stoically. "Other than that, I don't want to hear about it."

"Yes, a boat flying the royal colors has been seen sailing just a day's trip away. They are travelling light and quick."

"Do you think the King is injured?" Eshe gasped in concern.

"No, the reports say the King and his brother are standing in plain view on the deck of the boat."

Eshe straightened up, walked to the copper mirror and ran her hands down the front of her dress to smooth it. She looked at her makeup and touched up a small black line of kohl that had smeared on the corner of her left eye.

"Majesty . . . they will not be here until tomorrow. You do not need to worry until morning.

"I know, I know Betresh . . . I am just nervous and excited all at the same time!" Eshe said wringing her hands.

"Come out to the kitchen and have a little to eat to calm your nerves," Betresh said, heading towards the door with a beckoning outstretched hand.

Eshe considered the offer and looked at her Naos shrine that held Hathor, she walked over to the shrine and lit a small piece of incense, then followed her servant to the kitchen.

"What can I prepare for you, Majesty – I can prepare anything you would desire?"

The kitchen felt strange to Eshe since she was used to being served and not entering the servant's workstations. In some way though, it was comforting and she was determined to visit more often. A plate of cold meat, fruit and bread was prepared and the Queen started eating it with renewed relish.

"Let us go outside Majesty, we could use some fresh air – it will do you some good," Eshe's body servant encouraged.

Eshe stopped mid-bite and considered the invitation; *I have secluded myself in my rooms for a long time.* Just at the thought of leaving the safety of the palace, her heart rate increased and she began to sweat. Thump thump thump her heart raced and she started to feel lightheaded. *What if I see young mothers and their children – I don't think I can handle that!* She screamed inwardly.

"Come outside, Majesty," Betresh said again heading towards the door.

Eshe stood warily and headed to the door, but as she got closer a pain gripped her chest and she felt nauseated. Betresh had turned around just in time to see her start shaking as tremors started in her legs. She reached out her hands to steady Eshe who felt inwardly embarrassed, but could not control her symptoms of what would be called agoraphobia in the future.

"Be at peace, Your Majesty," her body servant cooed. "You can't be like this when the King arrives. Let us take this one step at a time," she said as she stood alongside her with an arm around her waist.

The outside did not seem as scary now as they took their first step out into the cool breeze of the morning air. Relief enveloped Eshe as she raised her arms in celebration – it was a major victory in her mind. She walked out into the sunshine – free of the too familiar walls of her room. *I will live my life to the fullest,* she told herself. The citizens that walked by the palace were shocked to see the Queen freely walking around. They greeted her in reverence, bowing low to the ground. Eshe was almost giddy as she greeted the shop owners that had setup beside the temple of Amun. *Nothing can destroy this day,* she thought. *I will see my husband, we will make love, we will feast into the night; it is a great day.* Betresh who stood beside her could see the Queen's elation. She was very glad Eshe was fighting this mental taskmaster that chained them both inside. This moment of enjoyment was short-lived though, as a young teenager with a child walked up to her and bowed. Familiar waves of panic mixed with jealousy and anger washed over her. The young girl held on to her child as she bowed. Eshe was at a loss as to what to do; she just looked at the child and young mother on the ground for several minutes. Betresh's hand slipped into Eshe's.

"Majesty . . . you must let them go," Betresh whispered.

The words were lost as Eshe looked at the child – *I need a child* she thought, then turned and left. Eshe walked to the temple of Amun and Min, both of which had joined under Narmer's guiding, making the worship of a single god Amun-Min. Betresh calmly spoke encouraging words to the Queen which helped calm her nerves, but Eshe had one goal in her mind and she was going to do it.

At the outskirts of the temple there was a pen with cows, tended by a short bald priest that wore a spotless white shenti.

"How may I serve you, My Queen," he asked as he bowed at her feet placing his head to the ground.

"You may rise, Priest. I require an offering to the god," she answered holding her head high.

"The god thanks you," he said as he selected an animal and called for a We'eb priest to herd it to the back of the temple for sacrifice. "What is your request, Majesty?"

"I want the god's blessing for me to bear a child." She said confidently.

"I would suggest that you offer two cows," he encouraged, inwardly licking his lips knowing that he as well as the rest of the priests would dine on the animals.

"Very well," she said, touching him on the head.

* * *

Narmer stood on the deck of the light boat he had acquired in Lahun – it was a fast moving papyrus reed ship with a bright white sail. The flags that once adorned it had been removed and replaced by the royal blue and white colors of Narmer. After the brothers had conquered the criminal army and brought them into his own fighting force, using them as shock troops; Lahun fell without any difficulty. The leaders of the town refused to bow though. More than five hundred citizens had abandoned the city and camped beside Menes troops. Narmer remembered how he had given the order to his brother to swarm the city and wipe out the remaining people, so the town could start anew. Narmer remembered the words that Nefrusheri had said to him regarding Eshe and how she was to die. He remembered disregarding her words and then all of a sudden became frightened – he had to see her. The closer he got to Abydos, the more his soul – his Ka – felt wary of what he would find.

As the boat rounded the bend in the river, Narmer could hear cheers from the villagers that had gathered along the banks. Ahead, Narmer could see the edge of the training grounds that hugged the banks of the river. The closer he got, the more people he could see. Finally his boat was parallel to the grounds – it was full. They were waving blue and white flags, dancing and playing music. The stone water steps, where they would dock the boat, had the full contingent officials and priests that were expected. Narmer stood tall and proud as his boat docked. He looked over the greeters before he left the ship. He could see Nestuwan; Hor-Nu; Nakht and finally, dressed in a deep yellow, he saw Eshe – his Queen. She was thinner and paler then he had remembered, but she was never-the-less beautiful. She stepped forward and did an extravagant bow as if she were showing off; it brought a smile to Narmer's face. Menes stepped closer to Narmer and whispered in his ear.

"Look who is happy to see you!" he said as he lightly jabbed him in the side.

What a relief to see my Eshe! he thought. *I guess that white-haired oracle isn't that wise after all.* Narmer felt confident as he strode down the gang plank to the solid ground. As soon as his feet touched the earth, the entire crowd that had gathered, unanimously bowed to the ground. The only person who didn't show obeisance was Menes who stood beside him.

"Rise citizens of Abydos. I bring good news of this land I have conquered. Lahun has fallen and my army is growing. I will soon bring Thesh, the new King of the north, to his knees and then we will complete my glorious father's vision. We will make Ta-Shemau and Ta-Mehu one land!"

The crowd erupted into cheers and a clash of symbols sounded, followed by music. Hor-Nu and Nakht raised their copper braziers that were billowing steady streams of sharp smelling incense. The priests then read out a prayer:

HAIL to thee, Amun-Min, Lord of the thrones of the earth, the oldest existence, ancient of heaven, support of all things;

Chief of the gods, lord of truth; father of the gods, maker of men and beasts and herbs; maker of all things above and below;

Deliverer of the sufferer and oppressed, judging the poor;

We thank you for your wisdom and giving Lahun to us, continue to grant us your favor as your servant King Narmer presses north.

As soon as the prayer ended, Narmer and Menes walked towards the palace and were joined by Nestuwan – the King's Mother and Queen Eshe – the King's Great Wife. Since he had arrived, Eshe had been staring at Narmer the entire time. *Wenemon is at my husband's side, oh how I have missed that boy. He looks so much older now! My husband looks very content with a child at his side – a child that I should have given him myself. The King looks so different now as well; he is very lean; tanned dark; his face has the look of wisdom shining through; his eyes are clearer and stronger. I need to give him children in any way possible to make our family last for all time,* she concluded.

A meal was called for in the great hall and all officials attended. The hall had shoots of fragrant myrrh trees growing in waist-high, glazed red clay pots, that sat between decorative shoulder width black vases. The wide-mouth vases contained growing blue lotus flowers and small live fish that circled the stalks. In the corners of the hall, flaming sconces filled the room with light. At the base of the dais there were rows of pillows, each one was sat on by an official waiting for the meal. All grew silent in preparation for the King to arrive and begin the much anticipated meal – they did not have to wait long. The double doors opened and Jahi walked in.

"Honored guests . . . [Jahi the palace introducer called out] The King of Ta-Mehu, god and protector of this land of plenty, Horus of gold, Narmer – Striking Catfish." He stepped aside and Narmer walked in. The man that stood in the doorway was wearing a spotless white kilt, thick gold armbands with matching bracelets and three heavy gold necklaces, each holding a beautiful inscribed pendant. He was a handsome sight to behold on those merits, but what really set his authority off was the tall conical white crown he wore. Narmer walked with authority and strength – it almost literally dripped from him. He loved wearing the crown that was once his father's. As a child he was never allowed to touch it; but secretly he had, on one occasion – he even put it on his head, but the crown had been far too big at that time – now it fit perfectly. Over the years he had grown up, he knew what he wanted and was determined to get it. Narmer was followed into the room by Menes, Eshe, Nestuwan Hakht, Hor-Nu and much to everyone's surprise, a young boy – Wenemon. They all walked up to the dais and took their seats. Narmer sat in the center between Queen Eshe and Menes. Nestuwan was seated next to her younger son and Hor-Nu sat beside him. Nakht was seated next to them. Narmer watched as Eshe caught Wenemon's eye, who was seated on a small chair on the very left side of the dais; she smiled at the boy and winked. Servers filed into the room from a side entrance, holding succulent plates, stacked high with steaming vegetables and meats. Baskets of warm breads baked with various grains smelled enticing as they were placed on nearby tables. Khu glanced over proudly at his son, who for some reason had ingratiated himself to the King. *I must speak with him,* he thought.

The meal continued late into the night and only stopped when Narmer stood and dismissed them. He walked – surrounded by his guards to his own apartments. Ubaid pulled aside the zebra hide that served as a door to his bedroom and welcomed the King inside. The King's room was brightly lit by twenty tall freshly trimmed oil lamps – five at each corner. Narmer had not taken his father's old rooms, but re built them to meet his growing needs. On the left side of the room in front of a shuttered window sat a Naos shrine that held an image of Amun. The shrine sat between two glazed, flower filled red pots. Narmer walked over to his grand gold-leafed bed and sat.

"This was a good day, was it not?" Narmer asked, not really needing an answer.

"Yes, my King. It was a great day," Ubaid said.

Narmer then stood in the middle of the room and was methodically undressed by Ubaid – his body servant. Ubaid then massaged Narmer's tired muscles after he laid down on a bench that had been set up in an adjoining room. Using jasmine scented oils, Ubaid's hands worked smoothly and expertly gliding them over the royal's resting body. In the corner of the room a musician hummed and plucked the strings of a harp. Ubaid then let Narmer lay, relaxing, while he went to prepare the golden bed for the night.

Narmer was sitting naked on his bed when Eshe was announced, which she was immediately granted entrance. He saw her gracefully glide into his room and bow to floor.

"Rise my sweet Queen, I welcome you. You have no need to bow."

As she stood, he could see her alluring body, nearly unhidden, beneath her loose yet formed dress. Her body was very pleasing to him and he loved her, but he could not shake the oracle's warning from his mind. He reached his hand out and softly grasped hers.

"I love you, my sister," he said. "You bring warmth to my heart, and to my bed," he said with a smile. "I have been praying to Hathor and Amun for a child . . . have faith that they will answer our prayers."

"I have prayed and sacrificed as well, my dearest," *a lot of good that has done though,* she thought despairingly. "How is Wenemon fairing?" she questioned, unsure what his possible response would be.

"Khu's son has been a great help. I even had to save his life at one time," he laughed. "I became close with him during the time I have been gone. I thought he should spend time with you, so I brought him back with me."

She ran her hand up his naked thigh and gazed into his eyes. "Thank you for your consideration, Brother, but I would like my own child. Shall we try again?" she asked hoping for a better result.

He leaned forward and his mouth found hers, leading them to spend the evening together in his apartment. Their time together was uneasy though.

* * * *

Weneg abruptly stood up, thanked them and with as few words as he could, asked the students to go home and come back tomorrow – he then walked outside. Tears had left shiny track lines on his face, but he hid them.

"What is with our teacher? That was a different way to end the lesson," Hayki said.

"I think there is something he is not telling us," Ist concluded.

18

FIVE PORTERS WALKED UP to a modest new home in Qena that was bordering the Nile. It was a very pleasing home in everyone's eyes that saw it, but in some ways triggered a seed of jealousy to those who were not as fortunate. Ist was in shock looking at the new home as she stood in front of her boxes of belongings. *I have never seen such a beautiful home,* she thought. She gazed at the structure she could call her own if she desired, but she had to make that first step and claim it. There was no one there it seemed and her family and servants who had followed her there stood in anticipation. Ist grabbed a medium sized box – one that held her bedding and boldly walked up the ramp to the front door. *It is so clean and new . . . I am not used to this!* She paused at the entrance and looked in, not entering. *Am I ready for this?* she questioned. *Can I bind myself to this man? Kah treats me well. He does have desires to get ahead in life and he is easy on the eyes,* she smiled. Her family waited for her to accept the marriage proposal and bind herself to Kah – all she needed to do was to carry the box of her belongings through the door to make it so. Ist held onto the box and walked through the doorway. Cheers erupted outside. In front of her was a freshly painted scene of Kah and Ist growing crops, fishing and hunting that exploded on the wall. Ist turned to the left and walked deeper into the house. She saw a large open room that had four cushions encircling a short sandstone bench. There were two empty clay pots that seemed to beg for decoration of some kind, resting on each side of a door to another room. Ist walked into the side room, there in the middle was a modest sized bed covered with pale blankets. She placed her box on the floor beside two other boxes and then sat on the bed. *This is more comfortable then my bed at home,* she thought. She looked around the room and saw the beautifully painted art that covered the walls [she paused] *yes this is my home.* She then exited the house and walked along its back. On the right side of the door there was an un-used fire place dug into the ground, surrounded by square stones that sat like a neglected item at a store. Beside it was a whitewashed, dome shaped oven that was made for baking bread. On the left side of the door a set of steps hugged the wall leading to the second story and the roof. Ist climbed the stairs, but on the fifth step, half the step gave way and crashed to the ground. She did not lose her balance, but made a note that this would have to be fixed immediately. The new bride now descended the steps and walked into the back yard. She could hear and smell the river as she walked over its tree-lined bank. The river was alive with water fowl – the trees nested various birds. A Grey Heron slowly stepped through water and searched for small fish as its next meal, at the same time as an Osprey stood guard at the top of the palm trees. Loud mouthed gulls screamed and called out to each other in an annoying chorus, while Ist walked along the moist banks. After walking a short distance she turned around and returned back to the house; now her home. The porters had now gone and moved her boxes and were storing them away in her room. Her family had also left – suddenly she felt alone. Inside the house Ist walked into the bedroom and exhaled – her things had been stored away and her new life as a wife had begun.

"Do you like the home I built for you?" Kah's deep voice asked, startling her.

She nodded, not turning around, but she could feel that he was right behind her and could feel his breath on her neck. Leaning back into him, she rested against him and felt her heart skip a beat. She could feel the heat rise, starting in her neck, moving up to her face, as he encircled her with his arms. She had never felt this way before, since she had never been with a man. He kissed her neck and she bent her head to the side, relaxed, wanting more. Kah continued kissing her; she reached her hand up and rested it on the back of his head drawing him closer. She drew in a breath as he slid his hands up her torso and cupped her breasts – no one had ever touched her before and it was a strange yet exhilarating experience.

"You are beautiful, Ist," he whispered in her ear. "We will make a wonderful life together . . . I'm so glad we found one another."

She let go of his head and turned around so they were facing each other. She placed her hands on both sides of his face, smiled and kissed him deeply. She embraced him – they stood unmoving for a long time. Their private moment together was only broken by the shrill wavering scream of the Black Kite warning other males to stay away. The horned ear tufts of the barrel shaped Eagle Owl, stood unwavering as the bird of prey stood watch in a nearby fig tree.

Kah backed away from Ist and grasped her hand leading her to the bed. She followed him. Kah then stood behind her and with trembling hands, lifted her shenti up over her head; leaving her naked. She covered herself as much as she could with her arms and hands, but by then Kah had backed away from her and began removing his shenti. Kah walked to the bed and sat. Ist had seen young naked boys before, but this was different – this was a man. In front of her was a man offering himself to her and all she needed to do was put down her shyness and accept. She squeezed her eyes shut, then opened them and reached out her hand, uncovering herself and accepted his offer. The rest of that day they enjoyed each other's bodies, then sat by the river, drank sweet beer and nibbled on fruits.

The well-trodden path to Weneg's hut was hard and dusty under Kah, Ist, Anitka and Hayki's feet as they walked together on their way to another lesson. Anitka seemed bitter as the couple tried to make small talk. Anitka pulled out his dagger and slashed the air as he walked and silently swore to himself. As the boy walked, Anitka flipped the weapon in the air. On one of the flips, he missed the handle; the blade fell to the ground and shattered.

"To Set with you," Anitka screamed as he saw his dagger broken into six pieces, lying on the path.

"You can always trade for another one Anitka, don't be troubled," Kah offered.

"Do you think a knife is my problem? Think again, oh great rich boy!" Anitka snarled.

The only answer Kah could come up with was his marriage to Ist that had taken place two days previous, but said nothing.

Look at those two – everything is going their way. Now it seems they are married! Where does that leave me? Nowhere. Nothing has changed and I still have to put up with this annoying brat, he thought looking over at Hayki. They continued to walk to Weneg's. Kah and Ist were reveling in their new found passion; Anitka and Hayki each in their own glum and bitter temperament. They arrived at the hut and they noticed the scrub brush had been neatly trimmed around the edges – the old branches piled to the side.

"I never knew the teacher needed to have these bushes trimmed. He could have asked me and I would have done that for him," Kah said to Ist, but Anitka had heard him.

"You trim his bushes? Don't you have **other** things to do . . ." he said bitterly.

"What is your problem Anitka, can you not just be happy for us?" Kah asked as he shook his head.

Anitka did not answer, he just entered the hut. Hayki looked back at Kah and Ist, shrugged and also entered the hut. Weneg was sitting on a short stool and looking through the basket of clay tablets, he seemed to give up as he replaced the ones he had taken out. Weneg pushed the basket away and sat back on the seat.

"I hear congratulations are in order for you Kah and you as well, Ist," Weneg said with a smile. As a lifelong bachelor, he did have an inner turmoil when he was around people who were in the stage of young love.

Ist's face was beaming and Kah could barely contain his joy – it looked as though he had a secret that he could not reveal.

"Thank you, Teacher. We are very happy," he said as he glanced towards Ist, lovingly.

"Thank you, Teacher," Ist repeated. "My dreams are slowly coming true."

Oh perfect for you! Anitka thought.

Weneg gave them a knowing nod. "Have you all been studying the tablets I asked you to study?"

"Ist and I have, I found the part about the founding gods most interesting. The part about Atum creating himself from nothing is almost unbelievable," Kah said.

"Hmmp, well that is where faith comes into play, Kah," the teacher said. "In this life, you are on a new path just like my old bushes outside. They too are now on a new path of growth. Anitka and Hayki, how about you? Have you been studying . . . are you on a new path?"

"Yes, we looked it over," Anitka lied for himself, not really answering the question, but still seething over Ist's marriage.

I don't know about you, but I did. I will be on a new path, Hayki thought as he glanced at his brother.

"Hmmp," Weneg thought. "I will continue my story then."

* * * *

It had been six months now since Narmer and Menes had returned to Abydos – Narmer knew that his progress with the northern towns was secure. He had left a large contingent camped just outside of Lahun and set up the town with loyal commanders to take charge. He also had charged the towns folk with general maintenance and cleanliness. Narmer spent his time with Eshe, most days being filled with private meals together and visits with their mothers. They hosted parties, made love with abandon, sacrificed to the gods and planned for the hopeful arrival of a child. Upon seeing no signs of pregnancy, Eshe slowly slipped into a state of depression once again and began pushing Narmer away. Narmer continued to be patient with her and doting her with love, even though she had become cold to him. But as the months wore on, he ached to get back to completing his sworn promise to his father.

Before he could leave and go north, Narmer realised that the Wag festival was quickly approaching and with him being home, he could celebrate it with Eshe. It was Thoth, the first month of the New Year. On day seventeen, the Wag festival would begin by a large celebration with boats, to the parade ground docks and then rejoicing would be held throughout the streets. They were celebrating their dead, offering them bread and other foods.

Narmer sat beside Eshe on the dais looking at the revelers dancing and yelling for joy.

"Don't you just love this?" Narmer asked his wife, who sat stoically at his side.

She did not answer, she just stared straight ahead. Nestuwan laughed as a jester who was doing flips across the path in front of them, deliberately crashed into his teammate. The jester stood up with a shocked expression and fake-slapped him.

"I think this is wonderful, Your Majesty," Nestuwan said to her son as she continued to laugh.

Eshe did not even crack a smile.

"Have some wine, this is a great year," Nestuwan said as she handed Eshe a cup.

Eshe took the cup and drank, asked for a second and then a third – she wanted to drown out her sorrows. The musicians assembled on the corners of the streets and played joyful tunes, while acrobatic dancers swung heavy balls around in large circles from their hair. There were colorful flags being spun around by midgets for everyone's enjoyment in the center of the parade ground. Large amounts of wine and beer were freely served to all in attendance until everyone was quite inebriated. In the center of the field, a large stage had been set up and everyone was waiting in anticipation for the myth that was about to be acted out.

"In the mysteries of the past we are told about Ra's daughter and how she was sent to destroy the evil men on Earth, but her blood lust got to be too much," Nakht yelled out with a loud voice for everyone to hear. "Let us celebrate and watch this story."

The crowd was silent as a man and woman stepped to the stage. The actress that was playing Sekhmet had a fierce lioness mask on and the man that was playing Ra, had gold paint that covered his body and wore a crown that had two large feathers.

Ra walked with Sekhmet to the middle of the stage as a group of actors and actresses crowded to one side and yelled at them. Ra pointed to the actors and pushed Sekhmet towards them.

"Kill those evil doers!" Ra ordered her.

Sekhmet ran towards them and pretended to kill them one at a time. More people crowded onto the stage. Sekhmet screamed out and began killing them as well. Ra called his daughter back to his side when he saw that she wasn't just killing the evil doers – she was killing everyone. She did not listen.

"This is so well done," Narmer whispered to Eshe, who continued to sit as if almost in a daze.

Why is this time in her life so hard, she knows I love her no matter what. I have always told her that, children or not.

Ra called to his daughter once more, but she ignored him – her blood lust had taken over. Some of the actors that were playing dead, revived themselves and stood back up just to be killed again. With the help of five costumed men, Ra brought a vat of wine onto the stage. With a lot of flamboyance, Ra took out a sack of red ochre powder and dumped it in the vat. He took a spear and started stirring until the wine looked like blood. Ra then took a large cup, filled it and began throwing it on the stage. Sekhmet stopped killing and began to pretend to drink the blood colored wine off the stage.

"What a waste of good wine," Narmer humorously said to Eshe.

Sekhmet then pretended to stumble around the stage that was representing the Earth until she passed out. An actor that was dressed up in mummy wrapping, representing the god Ptah, approached her sleeping form. When she awoke from her drunken slumber, she grabbed Ptah's hand and her blood thirst was suppressed. A loud cheer rose up from the onlookers. Sekhmet now had changed from a vicious lioness hunter into a calm and forgiving goddess.

"That was a beautiful story," Nestuwan said out loud so everyone on the dais could hear.

Narmer reached over lovingly, grabbed Eshe's hand and smiled at her. Her hand was still cold and stiff, but gradually she warmed up and even looked at him and smiled. A loud crash of symbols reverberated from the temple area. All revellers attention now focused on the double copper doors of the temple of Amun. There was a pause, but with a loud creak the doors slowly opened. Seven We'eb priests carrying a gilded barque slowly came to the stage. On the barque, a large Naos box that held the god, was covered with a flowing white linen sheet. The shrine would not be opened out in public, since it had already been opened in the privacy and protection of the temple. The god had been washed, clothed, fed and had new makeup applied. A slow methodical beat from handheld drums and sistrums began. Soon, lutes and guitars joined in and finally a priestess began to sing.

"Adoration of Ra, everliving, O Solar
God who creates by utterance. O
Lord of the Sky, giver of light, Lord of the
unplundered tomb, who gives life to
those who acknowledge him; O Heavenly
Father, may I enter your Kingdom of

Light, having been justified before the Tribunal.
"The birds in the trees exalt your name,
the bulls of the field dine on your
radiance that causes grasses to germinate.
Distant lands echo your intellect, and
are envious of your followers.
"O Ra, Lord of Light, Giver of Life and
taker of it, cast your light of peace
unto the world. *[2]*
[houseofanubis.webs.com/Selections%20of%20Ancient%20Egyptian%20Prayer1M701.pdf]

Narmer gently squeezed Eshe's hand to get her attention. "How are you faring, my beautiful Queen?"

Eshe smiled back at him and replied, "When this celebration is finished, I would desire to be taken to your bed so we can try for a child again."

Narmer was interested in that offer, but was surprised with her abrupt change in attitude. *Maybe this time together or this celebration has calmed her spirit. Oh my sister and light of my life, I pray that it is so.*

At the end of the day's festivities, Narmer and Eshe walked hand in hand to Narmer's royal apartment. They were too inebriated to do anything so they collapsed on the bed and slept. Early in the morning, Narmer fulfilled the request that Eshe had made the previous day. Both were satisfied with their renewed attempt to get pregnant, but Narmer still did not reveal his dream or interpretation to Eshe.

"My beautiful sister . . . I will be leaving Wenemon behind to serve you in my absence. Have faith my Queen, our desires will be answered in due time."

Narmer left with a small contingent early one morning. The King had said his good-byes to his family, he left Wenemon as company for Eshe and sacrificed to Amun-Min; then rode the current north.

Menes had stayed behind from the trip north as well, as he needed to complete the final touch-ups to his expanded apartment on the eastern side of the palace. He also had some construction plans for monuments that he had not put his final touches on yet and needed to finalize them with the workers. He then would be travelling north to the meet King. He also had a secondary desire – he wanted to enjoy the company of some local girls and visit his father's tomb.

Menes walked to the temple of Amun-Min and chose a large healthy bull as a sacrifice from the walled enclosure. As he stood waiting for the priest to finish, a temple prostitute dressed in a blue beaded mesh dress approached him.

"Would you like my services, Prince?" she asked with a twinkle in her eye.

He looked at her in consideration – she appeared only a few years younger than he was and very pleasing to the eye. She wore heavy blue eyeliner, red lipstick, had three rows of black lines tattooing her outer thighs and two double rows of beautification scars on her abdomen. He did not have to consider her offer too long and agreed.

"Come to my apartments at the palace and show this to the guards – they will not bar your way," he said and gave her a ring with his symbol on it.

The prostitute received the token, bowed low to the ground and whole-heartedly thanked him. Her name was Halima and this was her first time as a ghazye serving the god and besides the priests; Menes was her first client.

The burial place of King Scorpion was a quiet wind-swept place. His tomb – the short sand-filled, mud-bricked, roofless resting place seemed to be peaceful until Menes heard animals yipping sounds. The mistakable sound of jackals brought the prince to full attention. He tightened his grip on his spear and ran to the building. Three jackals were at work digging into the sand trying to dig up the corpse for a meal. Menes yelled and swung his spear, chasing the black-haired animals away. He was furious at the scavengers and chased them for a while, managing to kill two of them with a well-placed throw. After he had retrieved the spear, Menes observed the damage that the animals had done – it was disgraceful and he was glad that he had killed at least two of them.

Menes kneeled on the ground at the grave's entrance. "Father," he said speaking to his father's Ka. "I have tried to support Narmer the best way I can. Please guide me, make me satisfied with this path my life is on. I want more for my life. You know I will be faithful to him and to my promise to you. I am satisfied knowing I will never be King, how can I show my worth to you and the gods?" he cried out – baring his soul to the warm sand-filled wind. He had always inwardly cursed himself, though, asking: *Why did I make the promise to support my brother when I could have taken control myself?* As he cried out, vultures began circling; ready to feed on the dead jackals. As the scavengers circled, they slowly flew closer and closer to Menes as if they wanted to listen in on his prayer and renewed promise.

His way back to the palace was surprisingly peaceful even though the damage to the grave was extensive and hard to see. As Menes walked along the hard-packed path, he saw a familiar dark-ribbed coloring of an asp, at the base of the scrub brush that lined the trail. Menes stopped. He knew that the asp was very deadly and he did not want to disturb it. *That would just be my luck if I get bitten by Wadjit – the protector of the north.* The snake just sat, unmoving, but intently watching. Menes crowded the brush furthest from the reptile and slowly walked past it.

At the palace he saw Eshe sitting with Betresh playing Sennet on a carved ivory board. Menes stopped to watch them play for a short time and made a comment when a particularly good move was made. Eshe's sad eyes spoke of her defeated Ka that she held at bay inside.

"Do you find me beautiful, Prince?" Eshe asked as she stared at the ground.

The question caught Menes off-guard, but he carefully answered. "Yes, my Queen, you are like the morning sun – always a pleasure to see."

"Hmmp," she said.

He turned and walked back to the palace and into his apartments. He lit a small incense burner to refresh the stale air and sat at a small gilded table. Outside, workers were busy constructing the additions he had planned, so he pulled out a Sennet board and began to mindlessly play a game by himself. After a short time, a guard appeared at his door and asked for admittance.

"I have been asked to grant an audience with you by this woman," he said after he had bowed.

Halima stood nervously behind him. She wore a white dress that had openings stylishly cut into it, exposing her midriff.

"She may enter."

Halima walked in and stood in front of the prince. Menes couldn't help but smile seeing the woman and extended his hand to her which she softly grasped. She was quite beautiful in his eyes as he scanned her light brown complexion.

"You may go," he said to the guard.

He turned his attention back to Halima and ran his fingertips across her beautification scars. "Come sit with me," he requested, pointing to a short gilded chair.

WENEMON WALKED UP TO the palace and was immediately confronted by a palace guard. "Where are you going, runt?" the guard spat as he roughly grabbed the boy's arm.

The thick calloused hand squeezed, causing a wave of pain searing through Wenemon's arm. After the boy cried out, he was pushed to the ground. Even after being around hundreds of soldiers, he was not used to the rough demeanor of this security guard.

"What do you want, young one? You do not belong here. Be gone with you!"

Wenemon cowered on the ground, feeling the bruise that would begin on his upper arm, start to ache. *What did I do wrong?* he cried out, but never verbalized.

"I . . . I . . . was asked to . . . to attend the Queen," he stuttered, ashamed and powerless that he had begun stammering again.

"Who asked this of you? . . . It is not your place to pester the Queen," the guard barked. *This young stuttering annoyance will soon be gone,* the guard muttered under his breath.

"The King asked me t . . . to."

With just those words, all feelings of authority disappeared and he felt chastened by the boy. The guard stepped back regretful that he had laid a hand on him.

"My mistake lad . . . Your name?"

That apology gave Wenemon his confidence back; he boldly stood up straight and quickly rubbed his arm. "My name is Wenemon . . . Khu's son. I traveled north with the King and sailed with his ship south."

That is why I do not know him, he thought, *since I just arrived here one day ago I had no chance of being familiar with him. However, I do know Khu.* The guard stepped aside and allowed him access.

The front entrance of the palace had not changed that overly much in the last two years – it still boasted a large cedar door between twin granite statues of Narmer. Delicate red flowers in wide unpainted urns had been added giving the entrance an inviting feel. Wenemon entered the open doors and was greeted by a palace servant.

"Greetings, my name is Anat. I am in charge of all the happenings in the palace. The King has instructed me to bring you to Queen Eshe – follow me. Even at a young age, Wenemon could see this woman was beautiful. She wore only a plain pleated dress that was held up by two wide black straps that covered her breasts. She had papyrus reed sandals on and thick kohl eye liner. She wore no jewelry – she didn't need to. Her hair was cut short and was no lower than her earlobes. Anat wove through the maze of palace hallways making sure that Wenemon kept up and did not get lost. At the end of one hall, Anat stopped and turned to the left. The door she stood in front of had a wide blue linen sheet that had been split in two, framing the entrance. Anat entered the room. Queen Eshe was sitting in the middle of the dimly lit room having her makeup applied by whom Wenemon would later know as Betresh. The room had the exotic smell of kyphi that seemed to permeate everything. Wenemon was used to this scent since he knew too well the priests regiment of incense to the sun god Re. He remembered that the priests would burn frankincense at dawn to celebrate his birth, they burned myrrh at noon and his favorite – kyphi was burned at sunset. He was not used to smelling this – in his view, this beautiful mysterious smell anywhere other than around the temples, seemed strange. *I could get used to this,* he thought excitedly.

"Come in young one," Eshe's soothing voice floated to Wenemon.

Wenemon timidly obeyed and stepped onto the large blue reed mat – it felt soft under his bare feet. He saw the body servant expertly applying black kohl over the Queen's eyes with a wooden stick and green malachite eye paint underneath them. Betresh then painted red henna on the Queen's palms and the souls of her feet. Wenemon knew this was only done to the royalty as a display of power and authority. He was surprised that he was allowed to view Eshe getting prepared like this, but he did not mind; besides he was very comfortable with her.

In the corner he saw a rectangular box with square boxes cut into the top – that intrigued him. After he walked over to it, he recognised that it was the same game he had seen the soldiers playing. This one, though, was very high quality and not just scratched into a broken board like in the army camp. Wenemon took a closer look at this majestic game board. The black ebony board had three rows of ten squares; totaling thirty squares. He noticed each square was outlined with inlayed gold. At the end of the game box there was a drawer that when opened, were fourteen game pieces. Half were white and cone shaped – the others black and spool shaped. He knew that this game mirrored the path a soul would travel through the netherworld, but he did not understand it completely.

"Do you like it?"

Wenemon quickly looked towards the voice – it was Eshe who was now standing beside him.

"You startled me, Majesty!" Wenemon said. He remembered Eshe from when he was much younger and he used to even call her 'Mother' at times, as that figure in his life had died when he was young. He needed someone.

Eshe grinned. "It has been a long time. Are you hungry, Wenemon? I'm sure Betresh can find something for us in the kitchen."

The boy nodded. Eshe then called her servant and asked her to bring some cold chicken pieces and fruit slices. Wenemon smiled and thanked her again, finishing off by bowing low to the floor. Eshe waved the bow off like it was nothing. Betresh returned to the room carrying a platter of food and placed it on a table that sat between two brown cushions. The servant kicked the one cushion out of the way and placed a gold leafed stool in its place. Wenemon quickly sat on the soft pillow and Eshe sat on the chair. They picked at the food the remainder of the afternoon and shared some small talk.

"Wenemon, today you will meet Jandayi – my mother. I expect you to be on your best behaviour." He nodded.

I wonder what Eshe's . . . I mean the Queen's mother is like, he questioned. After a short while an older lady appeared at the door. She was dark skinned, short and wore a long wig that touched her backside. She wore heavy makeup and a colorful dress cut to her ankles, her sandal thongs had been painted red as if she was wanting to show authority. Wenemon bowed and then retreated to the side table that had the sennet game board. Jandayi looked down at the young man realizing who he was, but was too self-absorbed in her own status to show any grace.

"I see you have Khu's son trailing after you again," Eshe's mother said skeptically.

"Yes, the King sent him by to spend time with me while he is gone to war."

Wenemon sat by the game board within earshot, setting up the game and playing against an imaginary foe. He loved this ornate board – the pieces were so beautiful he imagined that this was the quality the gods used in the afterlife. Jandayi leaned forward and whispered something to her daughter which made Eshe sit up straighter in her chair.

"Mother!"

Jandayi put her finger to her mouth trying to silence her. "I just think the King has the problem and Menes is better suited," she whispered.

Even though she tried to speak quietly, Wenemon's keen ears heard what was said. He knew that what they were talking about was wrong and he did not like it. Wenemon picked up the counting sticks and rattled them between his palms, cast them on the floor and moved the corresponding number of spaces.

"They are twins, so what is the problem?"

"They may be twins, but I do not like Menes that way, Mother!" Eshe said in a hushed tone.

"That does not matter!" Jandayi almost shouted, startling Wenemon and making him knock some pieces to the floor.

The boy quickly picked the pieces up and put them back on the board.

"Like I said, Daughter," Jandayi strongly whispered. "The thing that matters is; Menes is of the same bloodline. Trust me, the King would never know."

Wenemon rattled the sticks again and cast them on the floor which seemed to break the tension.

"I do not know, Mother . . . if anyone found out . . . how could I live with myself!" her voice cracking as she whispered.

"Get a grip, Daughter. Your life is going nowhere," she said under her breath, but loud enough that Eshe heard her. She turned to her daughter and said to her evenly, "You don't want to be worthless do you?" this cut Eshe to the core.

Wenemon stayed silent knowing he should not have heard the things he did. Eshe stood up and tears streaming down her face, walked to the door, looked at her mother and pulled back the flap encouraging her to leave. As soon as Jandayi left, Wenemon was alone with the Queen.

"You know Jandayi was just joking right?

"What she said was wrong," he said, but that did little to help her mood.

* * * *

Weneg looked at the students that were sitting in front of him. *Are they learning anything,* he questioned – he thought they were.

"What do you think Wenemon should do?"

"I think Wenemon should keep his own council, Ist said. What could he possibly do? It is the Queen, remember?"

"Yes it is the Queen, but isn't it the Queen's mother who is to blame?" Weneg asked, noticing Anitka was not even listening or paying attention. "Think on those things and come back tomorrow. Today's lesson is over. Tomorrow I will reveal more."

20

BETRESH SAT WITH ESHE in the royal's apartment trying to engage the Queen in any type of calm conversation.

"What can I do to ease your pain?" Betresh asked.

"I need time by myself to sort things out," Eshe said.

"I will wait for your call, Your Majesty. Will you need anything at all tonight?"

Eshe loudly sighed and shook her head. She walked to the back of her apartment looking for nothing at all.

"I will be alright Betresh. You may leave for the night."

Betresh stared back at the Queen not entirely convinced.

"Shall I sleep outside your door tonight?"

"No not tonight. Go home to your family . . . I will be fine," Eshe instructed.

Eshe tried to rest, but alas she had a very troubled night. Later, she sat in front of her cosmetic table and stared at her reflection in the copper mirror. Her shoulder-length hair was black as midnight and expertly trimmed. She still wore all her gold rings and her gold necklaces at this time of night, just to feel worthy. Even though she wore all the trappings of importance and her status was beyond reproach, her eyes broadcasted sorrow and worthlessness. She considered her life and thought about where it was going. *All my life I have wanted just one thing, but the gods have barred my way. Why have they done this? Even Menes turns me away like a disease. Have the gods cursed me? If the gods have cursed me, there is no hope to ever having a child.* On the table, she scanned the bottles in front of her. The dishes of makeup that helped to make her beautiful did nothing to interest her and the vials of exquisite perfume repulsed her. There, hidden behind some moisturizing oil, was a small bottle of poison. She picked it up and looked at it for a long time and finally opened it and brought it to her nose. It smelled deceivingly sweet. *Will I do this?* she asked herself. She then touched her tongue to the bottle's spout. Immediately she felt a buzzing and numbing sensation where the bottle touched. "You are worthless," she heard Hor-Nu say again and again in her mind. Her mind flew to Narmer's smiling face. *He deserves better than a worthless woman,* she told herself. *I will never beat the gods . . .* as a tear rolled down her cheek, she tipped the bottle's contents into her mouth. The poison slid down her throat easily, but an uncomfortable burning sensation was left in its wake.

Eshe dropped to her knees and convulsed uncontrollably and flopped over onto her side. She could feel and taste the bile come up her throat and touch the back of her tongue. She heaved uncontrollably as she vomited on the floor. Eshe's stomach felt as though it was on fire as she vomited a second and third time. "Oh, why did I do this?" she cried softly to herself between convulsions. Eshe lay on the floor alone as her insides revolted in searing painful cramps for one hour, but when Ako the cat jumped up on the window ledge and meowed, Eshe breathed out slowly and stopped fighting the poison. Two minutes later she was gone.

* * *

Narmer stood on the deck of The Amun Breathes and looked out at the town of Meydum. It was slightly easier to conquer than Lahun since its army was not as numerous. Narmer's mind constantly went back to Abydos and Eshe. He knew that he should have children to continue his family line and so far a pregnancy had not happened, but he was confident it would. *Oh how I miss my brother,* he thought as he looked out across the water. Narmer had felt twinges in his Ka during his brother's time south, but didn't know what it was. He wondered if something had happened to him or to the young boy he had left behind at Abydos to be with Eshe. Leaving the boy with the Queen as a distraction was all he could think of to sooth Eshe's tortured Ka and he hoped it had worked. *Should I marry a second wife? Maybe I will get blessed with a child with a different woman – all these questions will have to wait until Menes returns.* Narmer relaxed on his boat at night listening to the gurgling sounds of the river and humming insects. He looked up at the salting of stars that coated the sky and thought about how the citizens of Abydos were enjoying the same visual as he was. An owl hooted as he saw quick flits of movement overhead, as small bats dashed through the air gobbling up hundreds of mosquitos throughout the night. He heard a splash close to the boat, *probably just a fish,* he thought, trying to put his mind at ease. He knew that crocodiles hunted at night and that realization was always on his mind. Narmer closed his eyes and said a quick prayer to the crocodile god Sobek for protection and retired to the mid-ship cabin. He lay down on his cot after he had lit a small oil lamp and tried to sleep. His mind tumbled over and over the week's events, but came to rest on his brother and the odd feeling he had experienced concerned him. He thought about the criminal army and how they had shown their worth. Only once, so far, had he had to follow through with his pledge to kill a criminal who did not abide by their promises. The soldier had stolen two loaves of bread and a copper cup – both of which he did not need. *What a loss – to throw away your life for bread and a cup.* His thoughts now turned to Eshe and Nefrusheri proclamation about her being barren. *Should I have told my sweet Eshe about that? Maybe then she would not be so concerned about her inability to bare a child if it is not in the god's will. Maybe I should marry a second woman –* these thoughts rotated and plagued his mind on a consistent basis and he could not decide the best action. *Will Menes have a child and the future of this land grow from him?* The rocking of the boat and lapping of water lulled him into a restful sleep, only to be awoken by the calls of sailors as they began their morning routine.

"Majesty?" Ubaid called.

Narmer squeezed his eyes shut, then opened them. Light was creeping through cracks in the walls – it was morning and Narmer had slept in. The lamp was trimmed and a steaming basin of water sat on the floor ready for Ubain to wash him. He saw a folded white kilt and his golden armbands sitting neatly on a short stool by a small tiring box.

"How was your night, Majesty? Was it restful?"

"No, it was not," was the answer as the King swung his legs out of bed and stood up. "My mind would not quit . . . being King is not all that it seems," he confessed.

Ubain kept silent, but nodded trying to understand. Narmer waited while he was undressed and washed. The scented warm water felt good to him but he missed the washing slab at the palace. He missed hot meals in the dining hall and he missed his mother's humor. Most of all he missed his wife, even though she struggled emotionally; he did love her.

During the day he walked with Minnakt on the bank of the river and into Meydum. The town was cleaner than the other towns he had come across – the trees were well kept and trash was picked up. Gutters that drained into the river that were once clear, now flowed sluggishly with black ash. The fires that had been set to the government buildings were almost out, but the smell of burnt wood and reeds still hung in the air. He had only lost one of his soldiers in the fight, but that particular man had been suffering from a previous injury that had hampered his abilities. As the King and

Minnakt walked into the town – now his town – the citizens bowed in supplication as he passed them. They asked for his blessing and offered him small trinkets thinking that that would in some way bring them blessings. They continued walking through the town, the buildings in this city were not as pressed together as in the other towns.

"It appears as though this town is more 'upper-class' then others that we have seen."

"That is true, Majesty."

Narmer considered the higher quality of housing here in Meydum and decided that all future building projects should be like these.

"Do you think the next city will put up much of a struggle for us?" Minnakt asked. "I hope that it will not be like Lahun."

Narmer thought briefly and said, "The next town is called Dashur – it is a large town but I have not been told of its strength. I hope as well that it will not be a difficult fight. I would hope the places we come to would bow in submission and want to be part of this great plan."

Minnakt rolled his eyes and shook his head. "That is as likely to happen as playing fetch with Ammit, before she eats your heart when you fail in the Judgment Hall."

"That is true, but I can always hope. I do not like killing my own countrymen."

"They are not your countrymen yet, Majesty," Minnakt said trying to sympathize with Narmer's thinking, but he could not. He thought – *give them one chance to change, then kill them if they do not.*

"No, they are not Minnakt, but I have to give them a chance."

Narmer and Minnakt walked to a large temple sitting in the middle of town that had many Ficus trees growing around it. The trees' wild whitish limbs spread out like upraised palms that looked like they were worshiping their makers. These trees had an abundance of purple colored figs that were free for the taking, so they each took one and bit into them. The temple had smooth whitewashed walls with red potted flowers that had been placed on each side of its large double copper and gold doors. There was a myrrh tree that grew from a single wide decorative pot that was half buried in front of the grand entrance. A pool sat in the center of an ornate garden that had three sacred white ibis' and leisurely walked around blue lotus flowers scrounging for any small fish they could find. Narmer then walked into the temple alone – Minnakt waited outside. The temple was filled with the remnants of incense smoke that seemed to cling to the air like a stain on a well-used sheet. It was a pleasant smell though, and he enjoyed it as it reminded him of the temple of Amun at home. Even though he had not been gone for too long, the soothing words of Nakht always seemed to calm him. A young priest approached him carrying a long censer that smoldered with myrrh incense. He had been completely shaved bald, wore a linen kilt and papyrus sandals. Dark kohl liner circled the priest's eyes, protecting him from the sun's glare. He was only sixteen, but exuded a look of wisdom beyond his years.

"Is the high priest available?" Narmer asked.

"Meresamun is our high priestess, but right now she is currently servicing the god. She will be out to talk with you after she sings praises to Isis. I have to ask you to wait here until she is finished," he said, pointing to a spot beside an upraised level of the room.

Narmer stood where he was asked to and waited. As he stood there, a beautiful voice began singing in the deep recesses of the temple. *What a lovely voice,* he thought. The walls of the temple of Isis were ornately painted in bright colors – something he loved. They depicted scenes of the goddess standing with Ma'at – the goddess of divine order serving Osiris. The inside of the temple was much like the outside – filled with flowers. Narmer paid close attention to the beautiful voice that floated out of the sanctuary, the song was now being joined by the shaking of a sistrum and was very pleasing to Narmer's ears. The song ended and he waited on bated breath for the priestess to come out. After a short wait, a middle-aged woman appeared from the sanctuary. She was shaved bald just like the other priest, but she wore a leopard skin, draped over her shoulder that covered her right breast.

"You have a very beautiful voice priestess," Narmer complimented.

Meresamun smiled and bowed. "I am pleased that you enjoyed it . . . I believe Isis likes it as well."

"I'm sure she does. I would like to give an offering to Isis and ask for her blessing."

She hesitated and placed her sistrum on a nearby table. "I will pray to her on your behalf, but you do realize that we are used to the old ways and were comfortable with our King. Maybe it will take some time before we will be open to your new ways."

Narmer thought about what she just said, and then replied. "I am fulfilling the promise I have made to my father Osiris-King-Scorpion," he said a bit perturbed. "I do not need to answer to you priestess! I will join these two lands – I will give anyone a chance to be a part of this dream, but if they choose not to follow my vision, then they will not be a part of this great land."

Meresamun could see the passion in the words he spoke just by his demeanor and how his face was now flushed.

"I apologize, great one," she said as she kneeled to the ground. "I misspoke."

Narmer wondered if these plans for the north would stir up a deep resentment in the citizens, but soon disregarded the thought. *I will be faithful to my promise,* he commanded himself.

"Can I count on your loyalty, Priestess?"

"Yes you can, Majesty," she replied without pause.

"Tell me about the next town," he asked.

Right away he could see fear in her eyes and what seemed like sorrow emulating from her brown eyes. "Please do not lay waste to that city, Majesty!" she said as she bowed again and kissed his feet. By now she was openly sobbing between kisses.

Narmer stepped back, *what is this?* he thought. "If they do not accept my offer of unity and accept me as their King, they will perish. Why do you care so much that you would embarrass yourself like this?"

She took a minute to compose herself and tried to wipe off her dirt-streaked face. "Dashur is the next town."

"I know this, Priestess. Tell me about their strengths or weaknesses. What are they like?"

Meresamun was now put to the test; would she mislead Narmer and try to save the town folk and incur Narmer's wrath? Or would she be honest? "It is a large town and very loyal to Thesh, but [she paused] the King's sister serves in the temple of Hathor in that town. She is my best friend. Please save her," she begged.

"If she will not accept my rule as her King then I will not save her. I cannot play favorites and grant favors to anyone. Tell me about her though."

"Her name is Neithotep, she is a twenty year old, pure-singer. We have been friends since we were very young. Her voice is more beautiful than mine," she said trying to boost her friend's value in Narmer's eyes.

Narmer could sense that this priestess was truthful. He thought about her request, but knew he could not promise anything. Outside the temple, Minnakht who had been patiently waiting, told him of the exciting news.

"Menes has returned from the south!" he said excitedly.

Narmer walked to the docks and saw his brother's small, light boat docked beside the Amun Breathes, slowly bumping it with the calm rise and fall of the waves. Narmer suddenly had a quick, sharp feeling of sickness that gripped his stomach; he, never-the-less, walked to the boat and greeted his brother. Right away he could sense there was a problem. Menes bowed to his knees.

"Majesty . . . my brother. I am the barer of sad news for you. Can we go to a private place?" he said, noticing the gathering throng of soldiers.

Narmer bent low to the ground and touched his kneeling brother's head.

"Let us retire to my ship then – we can talk privately there."

As soon as they were in the mid-ship cabin, Menes once again kneeled at Narmer's feet.

"What is troubling you, my brother?" Narmer asked.

Menes looked up at the King and responded, "The Queen is dead . . . Eshe is dead. I think I am to blame,"

"What?! Explain yourself!" he yelled as he drew a dagger, ready to strike his brother down in a fury.

"A woman came to me one night – she was dressed up like the ghazye I was seeing, it was dark. After she crawled into bed with me and I lit a lamp, I saw those three moles Eshe had on her neck and I pushed her away. I asked her what she was doing. She said that her mother had suggested that the reason she could not bare children was probably because you were the sterile one. She said that if I could give her a child, she would be spared the shame and the child would still be of your blood."

By now the rage he felt was replaced by sorrow.

"What did you say, Brother?"

"I told her that I will not ever touch her in that way and I told her to get out."

"How did she die then?" he asked as the memory of the oracle's words of her death played again in his head. Tightness in his chest and neck gave way to sobs; he tried unsuccessfully to hold back.

"That little stuttering runt found her lifeless body. He was found crying and hugging her corpse. I demanded to know what had taken place and the boy stated that he had found her on the ground with an empty vial of poison clutched in her hand. She had obviously drank it. Since I feared for her Ka, I talked to Nakht, but he eased my fears. He said that 'suicide was not a violation of the spiritual code. The gods saw it as a just way to die if one was faced with unendurable suffering – be it physical or emotional.'"

Narmer burst into uncontrollable sobs as he slowly sank to the floor, gripping bundles of fabric from his kilt in his fists. *He will lose his wits over this, maybe this will be my opportunity to gain control,* Menes thought mischievously. Narmer cleared his throat, raised his hand and shook his head; tears still slowly rolled down his face leaving shiny opaque streaks in their wake. A cicada buzzed its mating call, giving the river a weak ambiance of loneliness.

"I talked to an oracle in Beni Hasan and asked her to interpret a dream I had. This dream revealed that Eshe was barren. I know now that it did not matter how many sacrifices I offered, her path was predetermined. I just could not bring myself to tell her that, so it is my fault."

Menes eyes narrowed. "You could have adopted a child. That would have saved her!" Menes scolded.

Narmer shook his head. "The dream also revealed that she would die."

Just then a flock of ducks flew overhead, quacking a loud chorus and letting everyone know of their presence – it was a much needed break in their heavy conversation. After they flew by, the calming sounds of cicadas and croaking of frogs returned to the gurgling river. *The dream of being King is slipping from my hands!* Menes thought sadly.

* * * *

Weneg stopped the story there, leaving the students perched precariously on the edge of the tale of mental anguish. He cleared his throat several times – this time, though, he could not hide his tear-streaked face. He stood up and grabbed a stone adze and a short flint knife and walked outside. The students looked at each other and one-by-one they stood up and headed towards the door. Kah was the first to push the leather flap that hung in the door frame, aside. It was dark outside, but the full moon and silver peppering of stars was adequate light. Weneg was using the adze he had taken and chopping at the scrub brush that still stood by the hut.

"Hmmpf . . . An old man like you should hire someone to do this for you," Anitka said in a snarky tone. "Why waste your remaining days trimming ratty old shrubs?"

"This is a task that I need to do myself," Weneg replied, answering the deeper reason honestly.

Not happy with the answer he was given and unwilling to ask any further reason, Anitka shook his head and left, obviously annoyed.

"Why are you doing that, Master?" Kah asked as Anitka quickly ran down the path to his home.

Weneg stood back and in an almost frustrated tone said, "There are times in everyone's life that you need to trim things out whether it is friends, responsibilities or un-needed jobs. These," he said, pointing to the pile of cut branches, "were unneeded and were crowding my life and my home. I must do this trimming myself, just like with your own life, you must trim things yourself. I am trying to help and teach every one of you to take responsibility for your own lives."

Kah's hand found Ist's and gave it a gentle squeeze.

"Come back tomorrow and I will continue the lesson."

"We will be here!" Kah said with a quick nod of his head and a smile.

21

A T THEIR HOME KAH quickly viewed the latest building addition to the second story that had been completed during his time away. The short entranceway bricks had been completed, the broken step had been repaired and new walls were slowly being erected. *I am very pleased with my workers. I must reward their diligence.* After talking with Ist, they spent the last few hours before they slept, on making extra loaves of bread. The workers could be paid over and above the agreed two loaves a day payment this time.

"What shall we trim in our lives, my sister?" Kah asked as he held her close in their bed.

"Hmm?" she asked.

"I said 'what should we trim in our lives.'"

"I do not know," Ist answered sleepily. "We should rest."

The next day Ist and Kah sat in the hut in front of Weneg. They looked around at the now seemingly empty room. Weneg had a disappointed look in his brown eyes. *What did I say to drive students away?*

"I see that we are missing some people today," Weneg observed sadly. "Shall I continue?"

Just as he said that, Hayki rushed into the room.

"Sorry I am late, Master!"

Weneg acknowledged him with a nod and motioned to a place on the floor for the boy to occupy.

"I will continue."

* * * *

Over the next several months of travel, Narmer and Menes unfortunately missed the burial of the Queen, but they still returned home to pay their respects. A place in the desert was hurriedly chosen as the site for her remains since she had not previously prepared her own tomb. As Narmer spent time sitting beside Eshe's brick encased, wooden coffin that now lay under a large amount of sand, he inwardly cried out, *why did you go to such a drastic measure and end your life? Did you not know I loved you no matter what? Yes you were barren, but that did not matter to me,* he sobbed. *Adoption could have been an answer, but you knew that, didn't you?* he thought angrily. He then thought about Jandayi and how she encouraged Eshe to try to get pregnant by someone other than himself. *That is a crime,* he thought as his anger seethed. *It pains me to do this, but as King*

I must uphold the law of Ma'at and punish the crime.
He considered the next steps he should take. He could
not excuse Jandayi's actions. *Before I pass judgement
though, I must talk with Wenemon and ask him his side
of the story.*

Hidden a short distance away Wenemon crouched at
the base of a Ficus tree and bitterly poured out his tears.
As he had done many times before, through tear filled
eyes, he looked up at the half dead tree and counted the
maturing figs it had produced.

"Oh Eshe you were just like this tree, weren't you;
sweet and beautiful, but half dead inside. You could
never die in my heart. You were the only mother I had
known."

* * *

Narmer walked with Wenemon along the Nile, far
into the wild looking trees that grew haphazardly along
the great river. The tree's trunks were a little more
than a man's arm width wide and they grew twice as
tall as a man. On the opposite side of the river, large
swath of dense papyrus plants grew into the sky – some
individual plants were as wide as a man's waist. The
papyrus plants had yellow fan-like flowers jutting from
their pinnacles that slowly swayed in the breeze. As
the wind agitated their flowers, a yellow haze of pollen
danced from flower to flower, pollenating every stalk.
Bees danced in the air making loud buzzing sounds
and gathered precious pollen for their hives. Narmer
watched the bees hoping to locate their hive and gather
some honey, but he was unsuccessful. Just as they

were about to continue, a lone bee landed on Narmer's shoulder and stung him.

"Ouch!" he complained and flicked the offending bee off his sinewy shoulder. *That is going to hurt later,* he thought annoyed.

They passed snorting hippopotami lazing on the muddy banks and resting mother alligators who kept a wary look out on their precious nests. Crows cawed from the tops of the thin trees as Narmer and Wenemon walked further and further from the safety of the palace and its guards. They talked and laughed and shared their feelings until they were free from the secrets they held from each other.

"Where are we going, Majesty? I'm nervous." Wenemon asked as he looked at the hippos through the trees.

A pleasant smile spread across Narmer's face. "We are just travelling a bit further, do not worry, you are in safe hands. I will give you this though, if it will make you feel safer," he said as he handed him a gold-handled obsidian dagger.

Wenemon cautiously took the weapon and held it in his hands. The golden handle had varying red, yellow and black lines between strips of brown leather – the majority was yellow gold.

After traveling another short distance, Wenemon saw something. "A door frame, Majesty!?"

There nestled between the scraggily trees, two sides of a building stood in terrible disrepair. The building's entrance and left side remained intact, but its rear and right side had collapsed. The mud bricks strewn on the ground had now deteriorated into little more than mounds of dirt.

"This was the temple of Amun at one time," Narmer said. "I came here as a young boy with my friend," he said despondently, remembering the time with Eshe.

"What were you doing here, Majesty?"

"We were just discovering things . . . it was just an adventure we went on."

"Did you find anything?"

"Yes, we found an important image of Amun."

"Wow, do you still have it?"

"No, I brought it to the High Priest of Amun in town."

"Hmmp," Wenemon said.

Wenemon walked towards the building and stepped inside. He saw a rotted frame of the roof in the middle of the floor – it looked interesting. There were swirls of dead leaves piled up in many places that covered most of the floor. Narmer followed Wenemon inside. Once inside, memories of his young wife flooded into Narmer's mind – she was so innocent and caring, but she had a tortured Ka later in her life. *How I miss her,* he said to himself. Wenemon could sense the drop in the King's mood.

"I really liked the Queen," he blurted out. "She was really nice to me."

Narmer did not doubt that for a minute, he smiled and nodded his head. "What do you want from your life, Wenemon? Everyone has a plan . . . my plan, [he paused] no my **goal**, has always been to please my father, Osiris-King-Scorpion."

"I want more than anything to please you, my King," Wenemon said in all seriousness.

"Hmmpf. I have a job for you then. Over there," he said pointing to the left hand wall, "is a small door which you will be able to fit in."

Wenemon glanced over and sure enough there was a small door half buried by rotted debris.

"I would like you to retrieve something from inside there that I left in there many years ago. I want to complete the task that Queen Eshe and I started as children – it has plagued my mind," *well it hasn't plagued my mind, I'm just really curious,* he thought.

"What is in there, Majesty?" Wenemon questioned.

"A box," Narmer answered point blank.

Wenemon thought for a second and walked over to the door and started digging. As the boy cleared away the door, Narmer looked around at the remaining walls. There - just where he remembered – his name was scratched into the wall. It was not as crisp as it was originally, but it was still there. He walked over to the inscription and re-etched his name – this time deeper. In a rush of emotion, he scratched Eshe's name beside his. *There my sister, now the gods will remember you and find you in the netherworld.* He placed his hand on the wall and traced her name with his finger.

"I found it!" Wenemon cried out.

"Good, good now bring it out here."

Wenemon emerged carrying a black box that was covered with a thick layer of dirt. He placed it on the floor and cleaned it off.

"What do you think is in there?" Wenemon asked excitedly

"We will find that out," Narmer said as he pulled the top off the black wooden box.

Inside, there were coils of linen cloth and a clay jar stopped with a wax covered wooden plug. There was a second jar, this one though had long ago been broken, but it obviously had held black ink. Under the jars there was a second smaller box; it was green, the length of a man's hand and three fingers wide. Narmer picked it up and turned it over in his hand. The back of the box displayed golden drawings of scorpions. He held the bottom of the box and lifted its lid off. Wenemon leaned forward in anticipation, but soon jerked back as he saw a scorpion stretched out in the elongated box. Wenemon kept a wary eye on the wicked arachnid. At the tip of its tail was an oversized sharp black stinger that was very scary looking. Wenemon noticed that the scorpion had never moved – that did bring a small bit of peace to the boy.

"This is made out of brass," Narmer said as he picked it up and tapped it in his hand. He looked at it and then at Wenemon. "Do you want to swear your life to me, Wenemon?"

"Yes I do, Majesty, what can I do?!"

"If you are sure, then come and sit in front of me and give me your arm."

After the boy joined him, Narmer opened the ink jar, picked up the scorpion and held out his left hand. Wenemon sat and offered his arm.

"This will hurt," the King warned, quietly.

Wenemon looked pensively at his King and then at the metal scorpion. Narmer tipped the scorpion's stinger in the jar of ink and tightened his grip on the boy. Wenemon did not know what to expect – he just squeezed his eyes shut. The ink-coated needle pierced Wenemon's skin with a sharp painful jab. The boy's eyes flew open and he jerked his arm back, but it would not move from Narmer's grip.

"Will you swear your life to my service?" Narmer asked.

Wenemon nodded. "Relax your arm and do not move," he commanded.

It was all he could do to relax, but he did. The stinger was dipped again and Narmer used the ink-soaked needle to repeatedly jab a design into the boy's forearm. The pain was like a hundred bees stinging in succession. Tears streamed down young Wenemon's face as the tattooing session continued on into the afternoon. When it was done, Narmer wiped up the blood and ink, wrapped his arm in one of the old linen cloths they had found and patted the boy's shoulder. Wenemon was now very pale and in no mood to continue discovering.

"You were very strong Wenemon. You held your emotions and pain together and did not let it overwhelm you. You are like Weneg, the ancient son of Ra that keeps chaos from crashing down to earth."

Wenemon half smiled to himself, not really listening, as he was continuing to feel the throbbing pain radiating from his arm.

"You will be known from henceforth as Weneg, Judge-of-all-gods and Tamer-of-chaos."

* * *

A dais was set up just outside the palace's main entrance on a warm afternoon, for the public trial of Jandayi. Murmuring was kept to a dull roar as the King climbed the three steps and sat on the scorpion throne. He was flanked on each side by the priests of Amun-Min, Nestuwan, Menes and several court officials. After a brief moment, Narmer stood and raised his hand silencing the crowd.

"Bring the accused forward!" he called out.

From the back of the crowd, Khu led an older woman who was covered completely by a tattered grey shawl. She had no sandals on and wore no jewelry. A second man – her husband who was also unadorned, held on to her hand and walked beside her. Nestuwan sat higher in her seat as if she wanted to show authority, as Jandayi was ushered in front of the judges.

"I am here to pass judgement on the Queen's mother – Jandayi. These crimes include encouraging her daughter to seek out Menes and commit adultery. This was substantiated by the fact that she approached my brother and asked him to give her a son."

Gasps rippled through the crowd. Narmer raised his hand again, silencing them.

"Weneg, my trusted friend, was sent here to comfort the Queen in her times of heartache and was witness to Jandayi's repeated encouragements to the Queen to seek out other men."

Jandayi swivelled around and glared at Wenemon. "You bastard!" she yelled out, but was silenced by a strong slap from Khu.

"Narmer looked at me – I was standing at the bottom of the dais. 'Is what I said true? Were you witness to Jandayi encouraging the Queen to ask Menes to give her a son? Remember this is a serious charge.' he said.

I looked around and absentmindedly held onto the dagger that the King had gave me, for some reason I was given inner strength – I was nervous. 'It . . . it is as you say, my King,' I replied after there was a short giggle from Jandayi.

Narmer snapped his fingers and pointed at the woman, silencing her. He called the oracle up to the dais and talked to him.

'I have decided on my sentence: you will be banished to the southernmost parts of my empire and be under King Alafin's command. You will never be welcome inside the boarders of this county again. Your family now will carry the shame of your deeds and your properties are now repossessed and belong to the temple.' Jandayi let out a short high-pitched gasp and crumpled to the ground. 'Furthermore, any person helping you return to this land will be subject to the same judgement towards their family.' [He paused] 'Do you have anything to say for yourself?" Jandayi and her husband said nothing. 'In that case, you will be given safe passage to our furthest southern border and released into the Nubian Chief's care.'

Visually distraught, Narmer paced back and forth unwilling to make his last judgement that he knew he must make. The oracle whispered to Menes. Menes whispered back, but the oracle shook his head. Finally Menes approached his brother and placed a hand on his shoulder.

'You must command it, Brother.'

Narmer now looked empty as he let out a sigh and looked at the oracle who nodded his agreement. 'Let the Queen's name be stricken off of every tablet and every shrine. Let her name be gouged out from her burial mound so that the gods will never find her. She will traverse the underworld unseeing. There will be no knowledge of where she is,' he said shakily and full of emotion. There is one hope for her though, as he thought about her name he had inscribed in the wall.

Narmer then turned and stepped off the dais and left."

* * * *

Weneg leaned forward on his stool, placed his elbows on his knees and stared remorsefully at his students. Tears were freely flowing down his face. The only mother figure in my life was damned," he said. Weneg stayed like that until he had gathered his emotions together.

"Why did the King banish Eshe's parents?"

Kah was the first to speak, "It was the law since their daughter committed such a treason; it brought disgrace on her whole family."

"Yes, but that is not all. Narmer had to trim the unneeded and potentially harmful relationships from his life. This way he could start fresh and let relationships grow anew. It is just like how I trimmed the dead and encroaching bushes the previous days. The reason he sent them to Nubia was just like the pile of dead branches that were outside; if I hadn't removed them, they would have been a haven for snakes and scorpions."

Ist wondered where the pile of branches had disappeared to, but never asked. "Over time they would have become hazardous to the King," Ist said, when she realized the message that was conveyed.

"You can see now, if Jandayi and her husband were allowed to stay, their presence would be a constant weight on the King's reign and it would soon lead to his destruction."

"What ever happened to them?" Hayki asked.

Weneg opened his palms and shrugged. "No one ever saw them again. It was up to the gods, we have no way of knowing what happened."

Hayki shifted on the floor several times and finally locked eyes with the teacher. "Are we going to learn about our Ka?"

Weneg smiled. "Yes we are Hayki; that was the next lesson I was going to talk about right now."

Immediately, Hayki had a sad expression sweep across his face. "Oh . . . I had hoped Anitka would have been here for this," he said glumly.

"If you take notes on what I have to say; he will not miss anything."

The boy nodded.

"As you know, we are made up of many things: a person is made up of their Ka – their living essence; their Ba – their body; their Ren – which is their name and finally their Ib – their heart. These things make up our soul. Protect them well."

22

KAH WALKED HAND IN hand with Ist on their way back home with Hayki staying a few steps ahead of them. As they approached the first split in the trail, Kah and Ist called out their farewell to the boy. Hayki stopped and waited for the couple to catch up. He had a concerned look in his face.

"Something is wrong with Anitka," Hayki blurted out.

"What is it that is bothering you?" Ist asked with a troubled voice.

"Anitka is being increasingly volatile when I am around him. He also has not come home to sleep for the last three nights and my father does not know where he has been spending the time. I am concerned about him."

"I am starting my three month long role as a Hem netjer in the temple of Osiris. I will ask there if anyone can help your brother," Kah said.

"Thank you, Kah."

Hayki took the split in the path towards his home which then left Kah and Ist alone on the increasingly darkening night.

The walk home along the edge of the river progressed and the croaking of frogs began – first, one started, then another, until it turned into a constant unrelenting sound. This was cut short by a large splash when a crocodile snapped up a frog as a meal. The night became darker and darker until Kah was forced to look up at the moon to see what was amiss. There was only a sliver of the moon still visible, as a full lunar eclipse happened before their eyes. The orb of light was blotted out and then turned red. Birds stopped chattering as if in anticipation for the moon to reappear – it was deathly silent. Kah and Ist stood in fear as the bad omen played out before their eyes. Ist hugged Kah's arm looking for any type of comfort. Kah held his ground unwavering. They watched for a moment, but then alas the moon turned from red to its normal color again, giving the couple a peaceful feeling of rejuvenation. Evening normalcy returned, as life resumed again; doves started cooing and frogs began croaking.

Before they walked down the path to their home, Kah placed his arm around Ist's shoulder and leaned close to her ear.

"I have a surprise for you, Darling," he whispered.

He grabbed her hand and led her through the twisting scrub brush and then to a small wooded area that opened in front of them. A mud-bricked structure sat unassuming between two short palm trees. A small stone statue of Osiris stood beside the building's door. Above the doorframe was Bakenkhons – Kah's father – hand in hand with Anubis. The god of embalming seemed to be guiding him into the afterlife. *Is this Kah's family tomb?* Ist thought. *What an honor if this will this be my resting place as well!* Kah walked into the structure. Ist cautiously followed him. There was a wooden table just inside the entrance with a small meal of wilted lettuce, fruit and meat beside a cup of beer. To the left Ist saw a wooden plow and a garden hoe that sat beside five reed baskets. There were three stacks of folded white blankets and twenty jars of wine. Ten dust covered clay cups sat on the dirt floor seemingly waiting to be filled. Ist saw that some of the cups were ornately painted in red and black, others were gilded with golden repeating antelopes. Kah walked in a little further and stood beside a wrapped body. Ist looked around the room – she saw three other linen wrapped figures.

"This is my family." Kah said as he swept his hand towards the bodies. "This is my family tomb," he bragged. "We will be buried here. I hope you like it."

Kah reached into his shenti and retrieved a shell necklace and placed it by a body.

"This is my grandmother," Kah said as he gently placed his hand on the figure. Kah then turned and left.

They soon approached the entrance to their home, walked up the ramp and entered their house. Right away they saw a problem. A small piece of plaster had cracked and fallen from the painting at the entrance, but it wasn't disastrous. *I will have to get Kwab to repair this,* Kah thought.

As they lay beside each other on their bed, Kah's mind raced. *In one more week I will be leaving and beginning my duty as a priest of Osiris! I wonder what my responsibilities will be and how much time I will be away from Ist? Well, at least I am on my way to become wise like Weneg. My father was a priest of Osiris a long time ago, maybe I should ask his advice. I wonder where Anitka is in his life?* he thought in quick-fire succession. *I need to get some sleep!* Kah finally fell into a restful slumber.

Loud chattering birds woke the sleeping couple early the next morning. They were still groggy, but fitfully rested. Kah laid in bed as Ist stood up at the end of the bed and chose her clothes for the day. He touched Ra's eye – the black pendant that he had handmade and was attached by a thin red cord. Kah watched his wife undress – she also wore a black handmade eye of Ra pendant; hers was slightly smaller though. He watched his wife go about her morning routine and confirmed to himself that this was the best part of his day. Ist was letting her hair grow and was beginning to wear a small amount of makeup.

"I am glad that the teacher revealed so many things to us yesterday," Ist commented.

"I enjoyed that as well, my sister," he replied lovingly to Ist.

She smiled. "I made some special bread for us yesterday . . . would you like some before we see Wenemon . . . I mean Weneg," she said, then giggled.

"Yes I would," he replied as he grinned.

Kah got out of bed, reached over and grasped the pendant that dangled between her breasts and used it to pull her head close to his, playfully kissing her. Ist closed her eyes enjoying the moment.

"You have not told me one of your poems for a long time. Tell me one!" she said as she smiled.

Kah thought for a moment as he tied on a loin cloth.

"I'm waiting . . ." she said in a sing song voice as she slipped on a cream colored shenti.

"Ok I have one." He said.

"I wish that I was your mirror,
So that you always looked at me.
I wish that I was your garment,
So that you would always wear me.
I wish I were the water that washes your body.
I wish the unguent, O Women,
That I could anoint you.
And the band around your breasts,
And the beads around your neck.
I wish I were your sandal,
That you would step on me."
[http://allthingswildlyconsidered.blogspot.ca/2010/09/i-am-not-beside-you-where-will-set-your.html]

"That was beautiful, my brother," she replied, moved.

Kah stopped and fixed his eyes on Ist and sucked in a breath. "You are my comfort when I am in need, my darling. You are my lover. You are my wife, my sister. If I were a sentence, you would be the words that construct its meaning. My body is yours to command. I will be loyal to you forever in this world and the next. I love you so much, darling."

Ist had no words to say to him that would relate her feelings back to him, she just melted into his arms as tears of happiness rolled down her cheeks. They embraced each other and deeply kissed until they had to leave for the next lesson at the hut.

As they walked towards Weneg's, they met Hayki who had been waiting at the end of his laneway. Kah noticed that Hayki looked dispirited.

"Greetings, Hayki!"

The boy just lifted his hand in acknowledgement and then looked away.

"What is wrong?" Ist asked.

"Anitka came home last night," he stated.

"That is great!" Kah responded.

Hayki looked at him with upraised brows and slowly shook his head. "It was not great. He yelled at our parents late into the night. My father beat him for his disobedience and would not feed him. It was a rough night."

"I am sorry to hear that Hayki, is there anything I can do?" Kah asked.

"I don't think you can as he left again, anyways," he answered.

They entered Weneg's hut and found a place on the floor to sit.

"Greetings, Wenemon," Ist said with a smile.

"Today we will talk about the soul," Weneg said, smiling at Ist with acknowledgement. "Your soul is something you must protect at all costs. When you meet Osiris in the Judgement Hall and your heart is weighed against Ma'at's feather; you cannot ask to be forgiven at that point when your heart fails you. Live properly because your deeds of your life will be weighed. This is why I was not concerned about Rayu – he was very young and a good boy. I talked to his family after he was taken; he did not curse the gods or cheat or steal from others. He tried very hard – he obeyed and took instruction. He was a model that each one," he said as he pointed at each of the students, "of you could learn from."

The students sat up straighter. "Protect your Ka – your soul. Yes your Ka has many parts, but you only have one Ka."

"What can we do to protect this great thing?" Hayki asked

"Remember what I told you to do just a short while ago?"

"Yes, I do. You basically told us to trim the things out of our lives that hold us back," Ist replied.

"Yes. And what has been the one thing that has consistently brought our class down?"

"My brother," Hayki admitted sullenly.

"Do not let his actions affect your lives. He is an adult and he alone will answer for his actions, just like Queen Eshe had to answer for her actions. Keep in mind, at any time you may look over my tablets and ask questions. Do not be dismayed as you're still young and your life choices can and will change."

"Anitka is going through some major problems, I think. We should be supportive of him if he reaches out to us."

"That is correct Hayki."

I do not know if I can support him if I am honest with myself. I hope he never comes back to our lessons, Kah thought, disappointed with his thinking.

The fog of sadness soon dissipated when Weneg stood up and walked over to the sputtering oil lamp that sat in the corner. He added more oil from a red clay jar and trimmed the wick, eliminating the small amount of smoke it was releasing.

* * * *

"Back on board the ship; Narmer, Menes and I rode the current north for several days to Meydum where we disembarked. Minnakt had been drilling the soldiers for their next clash that would happen when they met Dashur's army. I was given the responsibility of being the King's ears in the army and learning about the men's morals and overall happiness. I did learn that a great deal of them were satisfied with their job that they had been commissioned to be a part of, but there were others like the criminal army, that were overly unsatisfied.

As we arrived at Dashur, the river was blocked by large wooden frames which had sharp poles that jutted out from them, ready to snare any boat wanting to bypass the town. On the banks of the east side of the river, their archers were set up with their bows drawn. They shot some arrows as a warning – one arrow did land **very** close to me. I remember being extremely afraid so I hid myself in the mid-ship cabin. It took me a while to live that down, let me tell you! I was called 'the spineless one' for a long time afterwards. Narmer retreated the ships and decided on a different approach. He pulled to the side at a safe distance and spoke with Menes.

'We should silently bring the military around and flank them on the right and also attack at the rear of their position, Majesty,' Menes offered – still feeling awkward calling his brother Majesty.

Menes looked out towards the army – the regular soldiers were sitting on the grass cleaning their weapons and retying any broken sandals that they had. The King saw Weren sitting stoically beside the criminal soldiers. A White Stork gracefully glided inches above the water and landed beside the brown bank, oblivious to any possible danger.

'Ask your new recruits if they are familiar with the area,' Narmer said, motioning to the shock troops, 'and use their experience to develop a plan of attack.'

'It will be done,' Menes replied."

Far to the east the military circled around the backside of Dashur and staked out a plan of attack. Previously Narmer had sent an emissary to ask if the ruler of the town would visit with him, the man had been decapitated and his body had been sent back. One hundred and fifty criminal army shock troop soldiers were the first to attack at the back of Dashur's ranks. While that was happening, Narmer's navy tore down the wooden snares that clogged the river. Menes main military force supported his shock troops from behind and overran Dashur's army. When the last of the blockages were destroyed; Narmer's ships filled the river beside the town. The town was burned and the officials were brought into the main square.

"What is this?" the major of the town yelled out. "Do you not know that we are loyal to Thesh – the true King? We will never submit to you," he said as he spat on the ground.

"You will help drag the bodies to the outskirts of town and you yourself will help dig the graves."

* * * *

"I noticed that the mayor was not too pleased with the proclamation and threw the shovel that had been pushed in his hands to the ground," Weneg said.

"That was an insolent thing to say to the King," muttered Hayki.

Weneg gave an agreeing nod, "Remember, the mayor did not know him as **His King**, he just saw Narmer as a man who had destroyed everything in his world," Weneg said continuing on with the story. "I will continue then."

* * * *

"We will bury these bodies so they can proceed to live with Osiris in the Field of Reeds," the King said. "Will you deny them this right? Be careful how you answer this."

"I did not know what was going to happen, but the answer was quick."

The mayor kicked the shovel over to the King and replied. "Bury them yourself, pretend King."

Narmer dropped his head and shook it from side to side. "Every citizen of this great land deserves a burial . . . you do not. You will be left out in the fields for the jackals and vultures."

Then Narmer took a spear and thrust it into the man and killed him on the spot. His body was left like refuse in the middle of the town. The King stood and looked at the devastation in this town. *I did not want this type of fighting to happen!* He was saddened that he had to gain control by these brutal means.

"What would you have me do, Father? Should I just kill the people that do not follow me?" Narmer cried out.

Be at peace my son, Narmer could hear his father whisper to his Ka. *You have given these people the choice to follow this great plan, it is up to them now. What you are creating is so much bigger than they can ever imagine.*

Narmer felt revitalized when he heard those words as he watched the soldiers gather the bodies of the dead. After a short time, a place was chosen outside of town for the burial mound. The King himself helped dig a large memorial grave, for the citizens to remember their loved ones.

"While this was going on I walked around the spacious town, it seemed so quiet now – the people that were left seemed to slowly be trying to put their lives back together. I walked to the large temple of Hathor. There were two large palm trees that grew on each side of the entrance and a stone encircled pond that had lotus' growing. On the whitewashed walls of the detailed temple, there was an image of Hathor standing hand-in-hand with the King. The god was portrayed as a woman and the mother of the King. I knew it was not my place, but I could not resist entering the temple. There was a large door that was open and one step up to get in. Inside I saw seven brass censors that smoked with incense, standing around a low lying table. At this point I was wondering why there were no priests anywhere, but I kept going. In the next room there another step up to enter. Again I pressed on, but as I entered this new room, I noticed that the inside of this room was much smaller. I do not know what it was, but I knew I was not welcomed there, and I felt a strange heaviness. I could no longer hear any sounds from outside and it seemed like the walls swallowed every noise I made. I pushed on and stepped up into an even smaller room. The room I entered seemed to have even more weight in the air then the rest of them. I felt like I was carrying a large man on my shoulders – I did not belong there. At the far end of the room which was not that far away, stood a beautiful woman. She had the ears of a cow and large headdress that contained a red disk between two cow horns. She had bare feet and wore a red, tight, fitting dress. As I stood there, the weight of the room seemed to be trying to smoother me. I then realized that the lady in the red dress was made of stone – it was the image of the god. I saw another smaller door with another step up, beside the image. I could not imagine how that would feel, being in that room – I knew it was Hathor's Holy of Holies. I began having a splitting headache so I commanded myself to leave immediately. All of a sudden, a woman stepped out from behind the god. It was too much for me and I collapsed to the floor."

23

"I AWOKE TO A cool breeze blowing across my face and the normal sounds of a town filling my ears. I could see four gulls lazily flying overhead and could smell burnt reeds and wood from the smoking embers of the roofs that had been torched. 'You're awake,' a woman said who had been staring down at me. 'You should not have been in there. That was only for the King and the priests you know.' I could barely understand what the woman in white was saying; all I knew was that her soft voice was the most beautiful one I had ever heard. She smelled of sweet lavender and myrrh. I was very relaxed.

'It is time to get up, Weneg,' Menes said.

My eyes flew open – it seemed my head had been laying in the woman's lap all this time. I stood up. 'How long have I been here?' I asked.

'Not for very long Weneg, not for very long at all,' she said with a smile.

'You will not tell anyone where I was, will you?' I asked.

'No I will not,' she said, continuing to smile.

I quickly looked at her; she was tall, thin and had long dark hair. Her eyes were framed in kohl, but she wore no jewelry. She also wore a spotless white dress that was held up by two straps that covered her breasts. She had immaculately clean papyrus sandals on. I just stood there almost in a daze.

'I am a priestess of Hathor in this temple,' she offered, pointing back at the beautiful structure. 'It was nice to meet you,' she said, heading back towards the temple.

'Stop lying there Weneg and come to the ships!' Menes, who had been standing a short distance away called.

I looked over at the prince, he had blood splattered on his arms, stone mace and kilt. Even though I had seen the travesties of war; that visual made it all very real. I was only a young boy at that point, but the tough world of conflict and pain had reared its ugly head. Surviving citizens were gathered and made to appear before King Narmer in the center of town. I could see that the King was getting more confident as the days blended together. Within the hour, I was in the mid-ship's cabin cleaning the King's armor and washing his clothes. This was a great honor; to be given complete access to all of the royal's personal items and I knew it.

As I scrubbed his belongings, I noticed the small Naos shrine that sat in the corner. There was a makeshift makeup pestle on the right side that was used to grind and mix the god's cosmetics during morning adulations. I walked down to the river to wash out the basin that held the dirty water I had been using to clean the King's soiled clothing. As I cleaned I thought about Hathor's temple. *What had I seen in there and why had I felt the way I did? Who was that woman in white – I know she was a priestess, but why did she save me, when I was in a place where I was not supposed to be?* As I cleaned, a flat piece of dark, grey-green siltstone came into view on the water's edge. It was two arms-length long and a little over an arm-length wide. *This is odd* I thought, so I dug it out of the bank and took it to the ship. After I was there for a short time cleaning and organizing; the King entered the cabin. He didn't say anything – he just laid down on his bed and dismissed me.

On the deck, gulls screamed out a chorus of annoyance for everyone to hear. I thought about the King. *He has gone through so much more than I could handle. He lost his wife and now he must purge the north and put to death his fellow countrymen to complete the task Osirus-King-Scorpion had sent him to do. What about Menes. He feels that he will never have the glory his brother will have and he thinks he is owed it. Will the town folk accept Narmer as their new King . . . I wondered?*

Soldiers and citizens worked together cleaning up the town's streets and youths not much older than I was, swept the tight walkways with long, reed brooms made from papyrus. The dead bodies had all been collected and Sem priests were at work preparing the bodies for their respectful burials. I understood there was to be a mass grave dug on the west side of the river; I was not interested in seeing that so I did not go to watch. We stayed there for several days as the town slowly returned to normal. Shops opened up and the bakeries and beer stores reopened again.

One week had passed by now and Narmer pressed forward heading north. His fears then came to pass . . . As he was standing on the bow of his boat he saw approximately fifty smooth, grey boulders partially submerged in the river, completely blocking further travel.

"How will we pass this obstacle?" Menes asked Narmer.

Narmer did not have an answer at the present time; he just stared straight ahead in contemplation.

"We could possibly take the ship to the bank and drag the vessel over the stones."

Menes shot Narmer an annoyed glance. "That is by far the most stupid idea you have come up with Narm! First off, the ship's weight would cause the hull to break, secondly this ship does not have enough rope to even make that possible."

"Well what do you think we should do then?" Narmer asked.

Menes was caught off-guard since he had never been asked for his opinion about these sorts of things before.

"This is an impossible task. I think the gods are sending you a clear message. Be happy with what you have been given and go no further."

"No! I cannot accept that. I must fulfill my father's wishes."

"Do not forget, he was my father too, Narm," Menes said out of annoyance.

Narmer looked over at Menes and shook his head.

"Be careful how you address me, Brother."

Menes rolled his eyes and turned away.

As they argued, they heard a grunt. They turned towards the sound, it came from the boulders. Right then, a spray of mist shot up from the rocks. The stoic boulders were in fact a herd of hippos lazing in the river! Narmer came to complete attention. One-by-one the grey beasts started moving. A large hippopotamus coughed and blew out more mist from its large nostrils. He coughed again.

"Let us put archers along the banks for some protection as we move forward," Narmer said, as he kept a wary eye on the beasts.

No sooner did he say those words, when the big bull hippo of the pod started charging towards the boat. The river then turned into a living torrent of froth, water and hippos; like a water fall rushing towards them from a great height.

"Head towards the bank!" Narmer screamed.

The oars were quickly manned and the boat pulled into the thick papyrus that hugged the banks. The stampede of animals roared into them and sent the ship crashing into the reeds like a wayward leaf in rapids. Those that had stood on the ship and were not holding on to the sides for steadiness, were knocked into the water and trampled. Narmer, Menes and Minnakt were able to escape into the papyrus as The Breath of Amun was helplessly battered.

"Aim at the head bull!" Narmer commanded to his men.

Arrows began flying through the air in rapid succession as Narmer held tightly to his spear. The lead bull was singled out and arrows peppered his body. As though the bull was determined to seek the royal out, the bull stopped mid charge and faced Narmer. Pink mist shot into the air from its nostrils as the beast coughed again. The nearby hippos seemed to gang up and charge at Narmer, destroying the papyrus plants. In the charge, Narmer got separated from his brother and his military captain. Unfortunately, the spear he had held onto as a last remaining peace of safety, was knocked from his hands. Menes watched as Narmer floated in the water in front of the angry bull, secretly wishing that maybe this was what would be Narmer's end to his rise to power. Since Minnakt was not close enough, he threw Menes his spear so he could in turn throw it to Narmer. As the bull bore down on Narmer, Menes threw the spear just out of Narmer's reach.

"I'm sorry!" Menes lied.

A hippo that had several arrows protruding from its side, lumbered close to Narmer and he was pinned between the oncoming bull and its flank. Now he was stuck. On one side was the hippo's flank and on the opposite were a mixture of broken, thick papyrus stalks and thin green reeds; both of which impeded movement. Escape was now impossible. With difficulty, Narmer turned in the water and faced the animal's side. Narmer grabbed the protruding arrows that were sticking out and managed to crawl up onto the beasts back. The animal lowered itself into the water. Narmer remembered how he killed the large bull when he was with Wenemon. He searched the flotsam for a suitable papyrus stalk that could be used as a weapon. Just as the bull was a body-length away, his prayers were answered. A seven foot long piece of papyrus stalk that had a jagged end was in arm's reach. Narmer was able to grab it and pull it on to the submerged hippo's back. The fear of these animals had disappeared from the forefront of his mind, so he was able to act quickly. The bull rushed ahead and Narmer threw the pole into its gaping mouth. The beast shook his head to try to dislodge the pole, but it did not budge. There was a brief moment when the hippopotamus stared directly at Narmer and snorted.

"Try to swim to the bank, Majesty! He will follow and when he is close enough I can help you. I will try to kill him for you!" Minnahkt yelled as he edged ever closer to the beast.

Narmer wanted to face this demon in his life, personally.

"I am not scared of you, destroyer of my dreams! Now I will send you into the chaos where you belong!" Narmer screamed.

The beast tried to rush over to Narmer and trample him, but the King was too quick for the attack and swam to the animal's side. Narmer used the arrows that protruded from the hippo's side, like hand grips and crawled up onto its back. The animal tried to cough again, but all that came out of its mouth was pink foam. As Narmer crawled onto its head, the hippo submerged from the water. The displacement of water brought more broken papyrus stalks to the royal. Narmer grabbed a second stalk in preparation. The water exploded around him as the large head he had been kneeling on came out of the water. The jaws of the beast were opened wide, exposing long wicked fangs as the hippo swung his head from side to side.

"Amun guide me!" Narmer yelled as he took the hardened stalk he had and jammed it deep into the opened throat.

The hippo stopped thrashing as if it were stunned and slowly sank back into the water.

After Narmer swam to the shore and managed to stand on the bank, Minnahkt bowed to him and kissed his dirty feet. "I was so scared for your safety, Majesty!" Minnahkt exclaimed.

"I am glad to see you are in good health, my King. We almost lost you," Menes said.

One week later, they repaired the damaged ship using thick papyrus stalks and prepared to continue the journey. It was only then that a notice came ...

* * * *

"What notice? Tell us, please!" Ist begged

Weneg smiled and winked at them mysteriously. "You will have to wait for the conclusion tomorrow," Weneg said as groans of anticipation filled the room. "You will really enjoy what will be coming next!" Weneg continued to entice them. "Go home and think about everything I told you this last while and get ready for the story to answer many of your questions."

Weneg stood up and stretched his legs and then his back while motioning them to the door. Kah was the first to stand and walk outside, later to be joined by Ist and Hayki. It was a pleasant predawn temperature with many of the animals still awake and filling the air with their voices. On their way back home, Kah and Ist came to Rayu's laneway to his house. Again a tightness gripped their throats and sadness from the loss of the boy reared its head once again.

"We never really got to really know Rayu, did we?" Kah said aloud.

Ist slowly shook her head. "I lived closest to him and I never searched him out as a friend," she said sorrowfully. "Do you think that I will be held accountable for that before the gods?"

Kah did not think so. *If that will be something that she will have to answer for then I too will be judged for that! This will not do, I must make this right and I know just how to do it!*

During their walk together they stopped by Kah's family tomb. Kah and Ist said a prayer and entered the small structure. Once inside, Kah moved the furniture slightly so he could access one of the walls. Kah pulled out his dagger and then neatly inscribed Rayu's name on an inconspicuous place.

"There you go Rayu! Now the gods will remember you and find you. You will live forever in paradise." Kah felt a weight lift off of his shoulders as soon as he finished the name.

Ist also was relieved with what her husband had done for Rayu's Ka and also felt a weight lift.

"Husband, will your father have a problem with what you did to the tomb?" Ist asked.

"No he will not since he himself has done similar things before," he said as he pointed out other names that had been scratched into the walls.

Ist nodded her head and was relieved. Kah re adjusted the furniture and said another prayer before leaving.

At home the couple had a quick meal and then retired for the night. The next day they could not wait, so they hurriedly ate and went on their way to hear the remainder of Weneg's story. They rushed out of their house and almost ran to the teacher's. As they passed Rayu's home, the usual feeling of pain and loss mixed with guilt was no longer there and they were happy with that. At Hayki's laneway there was no one there waiting which was to be expected since they arrived earlier then what was normal. Kah and Ist stood waiting for Hayki's arrival, but after a long time they decided to retrieve him themselves. As they walked back along the lane they were met by the family dog. He was friendly enough, unlike the sour disposition of Anitka – his master. After the dog barked several times, Hayki came out of the house.

The youths then walked to the hut and sat on the floor in anticipation, ready to gobble up whatever Weneg would say next.

Weneg smiled at them and sensed their eagerness.

"The last time we spoke Narmer received a note, is that correct?" Weneg questioned.

24

A LETTER ARRIVED FROM Thesh. It came by way of an emissary dressed in white. He carried a black wooden box and was flanked by two tough looking imperial soldiers. The emissary had a long, black, curly beard that was gathered into two separate braids, held by pins in the shape of the cobra goddess – Wajet.

"Greeting, King of the south," he said – his accent was so thick it was hard to understand.

Narmer accepted the engraved box warily. Inside was a small clay tablet with tiny inscription scratched into it.

"Greetings usurper from the south. You have disturbed my mind too many times. I know of your plans that are the same as that of King Scorpion, who was turned away when my father was King. I am of the same mind – I am not interested in your plans. Leave now before I bring down my full army and wipe you off of my land. You will return to your southern place and return all lands back to me – the rightful King. You have one week to comply with my command, after that time I will personally rip the crown off your little head and your lands will be forfeit."

* * * *

Weneg leaned forward on his elbows and looked at his students, they of course were eagerly anticipating the next things Weneg was about to say.

"Even the King is subject to bullies and as you can see, Narmer was warned by Thesh. What do you think the best way to respond to this situation would be?

"I think that if he leaves now, he would be giving up everything he has worked for in the past. It would have been a difficult decision." Hayki replied.

"I think he should leave and not stir up a hornets nest," was Ist's reply.

"We all know that King Narmer conquered Thesh, let me tell you how it played out," Weneg stated.

* * * *

"Narmer sent spies north to view the strength of Thesh's army, but the first thing he did was visit the temple to say prayers. I tagged along with him when he went to the temple. I, of course, stayed outside as I was supposed to and watched the King enter Hathor's precincts alone. I was definitely nervous about the priest in white revealing my previous presence in the temple to the King. *Would she keep her word and not tell anyone?* I questioned. It was two long painstaking hours before the King emerged from the temple; this time with the priestess beside him. As I watched him I did not notice any anger towards me – she had kept her word. I did notice a hint of affection brewing between them though. I had definitely felt relieved.

I was in the back of the Breath of Amun's mid-ship hut which had now been changed into a war counsel room when the spies entered. The King, Menes, Minnakt and Weren were all there ready to hear the reports. As the ship slowly creaked and moved with every wave, the counsel was silent, anticipating the spies' reports.

'Thesh has a large military force that is camped at Saqqara, but there is a second army camped at their King's capital in Memphis,' Gahiji who was now one of the spies replied.

'Does this force still use the old weapons or has he upgraded like we have?' Minnakt asked.

'They still use the old style weapons, but Thesh has a champion as the head of his army. He seems to hide behind this man whenever there is a conflict that arises,' Gahiji said.

'Hmmpf' Narmer replied. 'Tell me about this Champion, why is he so great?'

'Well . . .' Gahiji said shrugging his shoulders, 'it's not that he is very tall; he is actually normal height, but he is quick like lightning . . . like Anubis' judgement in the final hall at the end of our lives.'

'What are the numbers we are looking at when we meet this Champion?' Menes asked.

'Setaten is the Champion's name, he is in control of three thousand men. He controls twenty five hundred in Saqqara and another five hundred in Memphis. He is also the High Priest of Seth,' he said, as he did the Hamsa symbol warding off the evil eye. 'He will overrun us . . . and we have only days before the time of Thesh's mercy will have run out, so I advise a speedy decision.'

Narmer thought for a short while and weighed the bleak options. 'Where are the forces right now?'

'The last I saw them, they were at the boundary of Saqqara. They seemed to be sitting there just waiting,' the spy offered.

'I believe that Amun has led us to this place in our life and we should not run! Let us be bold in this opportunity and at least try. If we die, then we will not be judged harshly at the scales, we will be judged for dying because of obedience and of keeping a promise! We shall cross the river and camp out in the western plains, then travel north and strike them in Memphis.'

Menes quickly stood up, 'I do not disagree with you often brother, but is this rash or am I missing something?'

'You are missing something . . . something of great importance. We are not rash, we have just begun. Remember our lessons from Khu in our youth? Starting tonight you must ferry your entire army across the river and proceed, undetected, north. I will retreat to the south as far as I feel is safe. Can I count on you, Brother?'

* * * *

"This caught my attention right away when he said my father's name. I knew my father had taught the King and his brother, but I did not know what they meant. I think that is enough for one day; how about I see you again tomorrow?"

Kah and Ist stood up, walked out and headed towards their home; by now the sun was getting low in the sky. The vultures had completely disappeared from their lazy spiraling flight as they looked for carrion. The frogs had also started their rendition of evening croaking along with the mosquitos and blackflies that were doing their best to make life uncomfortable. As they walked – closer to the river – Ist hugged Kah's arm when they were close to the place where crocodiles had always been spotted. They walked farther when they heard the haunting call of the Eagle Owl that fed on larger animals. They also heard the chirps of baby crocodiles who called out to their mothers. This time of self-reflection was soon cut short by a loud splash as a vulture took flight by the nearby riverbank. Out of pure curiosity, Kah walked over and peered at the bank. There, a limp rag quite tattered, lay discarded on the mud. He didn't pay it much attention until he recognised it as the shenti that Rayu wore. Kah closed his eyes as he remembered the young boy and his joyful demeanor. Ist, who had come up behind him, tightened her grip around his torso and rested her head on his shoulder.

"That was Rayu's wasn't it?" Ist whispered.

"Yes I believe it was," Kah answered. "Let's go home."

At their house Ist prepared a small meal of fish that had been previously salted along with bread sweetened with honey and stuffed with fruit – which was a real treat for Kah.

"I have something to tell you, Kah," Ist said as she gazed into his eyes.

Kah felt sick right away – *what was wrong?* he thought.

"You remember how Eshe always wanted a child?"

He remembered that story and how Eshe killed herself.

"I too have wanted a child," Ist said.

He didn't like where this was going. He felt flushed and could feel the sweat start on his forehead.

"Kah . . . I'm pregnant."

His worry and ill feelings disappeared in a flash – all was right in the world. He let out a sigh of relief. A smile spread across his face and he then rushed to her and scooped her up in his arms.

"I am so glad Tarewet blessed us, Sister. This child will be born into such a loving home."

They walked outside and down to the river where the ducks liked to congregate and took in the peaceful sounds of the slow moving river. Kah and Ist stared at the glistening, flowing water. They could imagine Narmer and Menes on the Amun Breathes, sailing by with the blue and white royal flags fluttering, as the white square sails caught the wind.

"You know I will be fulfilling my monthly duty as a priest of Osiris. Then we will be able to get some of the sacrificed food so we can really provide for our son," he said enunciating *son* as his hopeful desire.

Ist looked at Kah with a humorous expression and raised her one eyebrow, smiling teasingly. "Kah . . . Ist" Hayki called as he jogged up to them.

"Greetings Hayki," Kah said.

Kah grasped Hayki's hands in his as he arrived beside them. "Ist is pregnant," Kah blurted out, unable to contain his joy, nor his excitement.

Hayki smiled at the couple as he looked Ist up and down. Ist self-consciously put her hands on her stomach.

"Well, it is very early to show any signs," Ist said shyly.

"What are you doing here Hayki, shouldn't you be at home?" Kah asked cheerfully.

Hayki looked around silently. "Anitka came home again last night."

"That good isn't it?" Kah asked.

"I thought it was at first, but it quickly changed to a very bad situation. Anitka began accusing Uadjit of being a home wrecker and then he said she would never be welcome in the family. It went from bad to worse after that. I had to get out of there, which is why I am here."

Ist raised her eyebrows at this new information and then at Kah for possible suggestions for what they could do. Kah thought the situation through and then looked at his house – it was plenty big – almost too big for them.

"We have the upper level that you can stay in," he said pointing to the second story that was now completed.

Hayki looked up at the upper level and smiled. "I thank you; thinking of me. I will contribute as best I can to the household. You will not regret this."

The next day the three of them walked to Weneg's, but Kah kept an eye out on the river to see if Rayu's shenti was still there – it was gone.

* * *

Weneg was sitting by the basket, in the center of the hut, of clay tablets that he had brought once again and was thumbing through them.

"I have taught you about the beginnings of the gods and what you should avoid in life. I have taught you to look ahead for your future and how to trim unnecessary things in your life even though they are difficult. We have seen hardships together with the loss of Rayu and disappearance of Anitka. We also have had celebrations of a marriage between Kah and Ist. What more can I teach you? You must now go on, into the world and continue your life."

"I . . . we thank you teacher. Our lives are in your debt," Kah said but then added; "I have been told by Hayki that Anitka has returned, but because of continuing issues in his life, it has now become impossible for Hayki to safely stay at home. We are encouraged to have him stay with us," Kah said as he glanced at Ist and gave her hand a squeeze. "I must stay for a short while before I start my job as a priest of Osiris. Could you kindly finish the story?"

Weneg nodded, then smiled. "I will complete this story for you, Kah. I am happy that you have stepped up and supported Hayki in his time of need. The gods will be glad that you are not only following their laws, but living them."

* * *

Sails were cast and the Amun Breathes travelled south along the river taking a day to leave Dashur. They did, however, pull off to the western bank and disembark to set up camp. While this was occurring, Menes' army travelled deep into the west and then travelled north bypassing Saqqara – the next town. During the days away from his brother, the King, Menes was struggling with his own demons that made him question his loyalty.

Will I just be a support to him and let glory pass by and die in this suicide fight? Who will remember me? What have I done? Nothing. Halima will remember me, but I cannot marry a temple prostitute and make her my Queen, especially when I am dead. He remembered running his fingers across the beautification scars that lined her abdomen, which were very alluring to him. He remembered feeling for them in the dark when Eshe came to him, but when he could not find them, he knew it was not Halima – this was a detail he never revealed to his brother. *What am I thinking? I would have to be King first to make Halima Queen!* His mind dabbled on those thoughts briefly, but he then remembered his father's words to him and his promise to always support Narmer. He cursed himself. *I should have never made that promise; then I would not feel so guilty thinking the thoughts I have had.*

During their trek into the west, they camped at a small oasis that was full of many types of trees. Among them were figs, apple and pomegranate. Wild animals that could easily be caught, supplied a majority of nutritional requirements. It was quite swampy and there were many fresh water ponds which were also used for the soldier's needs. As they travelled, they did miss the dry heat of their home in the south since they were not used to the rashes that plagued them during the long marches and longed to return home.

As Menes sat beside a small pond with Weren, Menes could not help but look at the criminal's awful profile. *I cannot imagine the pain this man suffered as his nose was cut from his face. The torture he experienced; I do not know if I could handle that either. Now we are going to send him to his death. Has he not paid his debts in full? And, will this man be loyal to us in the end? Could I be? I honestly do not know.*

NESTUWAN PACED BACK AND forth in the palace hallway worrying about the safety of her sons. She typically was on edge for them whenever they were away since that was what led to her husband's injury and finally his death. She told herself repeatedly that they were in good hands and safe, but she still was not entirely confident. As the King's mother, she visited the priests of Amun-Min and sacrificed regularly for both her son's safety.

After she spent time at the temple; she walked to her shower slab and was undressed by Anat, her body servant. After she stepped behind the curtain, Anat slowly dumped hot scented water over the retired Queen's head to wash off the day's dirt and grime.

The servant took handfuls of natron and scrubbed Nestuwan's body to cleanse it. Anat then set up a gilded wooden massage table and rubbed her charges knots and aches away, as a royal lute player strummed a relaxing melody.

Feeling refreshed, Nestuwan and Anat took a small skiff across the river and walked into the encroaching desert. Even through the palace, two security guards were not far behind; she felt secure walking through the sands of the barren land. She desperately longed the hear word from Narmer and Menes and hoped to see Chisisi's boat sailing from the north.

A lion roared off in the distance, breaking the silence. *There is something unsettling about overbearing silence of this barren landscape,* she thought as she saw a mirage in the distance. A snake undulated across the drifting sand between two small sand dunes and she made a mental note to stay away from that area. The distant lion roared again which placed a nugget of fear in her mind. I do not want to be out here alone with Anat when this beast comes closer. In the distance Nestuwan saw the two security guards casually speaking to each other and signalled them over. For the next hour, the three assistants walked with her between the river and the bleak desert land. A mother crocodile watched her nest by the scrub brush, from the cool, relative safety of the water.

A small, but sleek craft with square white sails came into view from around a bend in the river and the mother crocodile submerged herself into the brown watery depths. Nestuwan raised her hand in greeting, not sure if Chisisi saw her and rushed towards her skiff. Within the hour she was poled across the slow moving, brown water towards the old docks. Chisisi had already docked his boat and was disembarked, but a few soldiers still guarded the boat. *I must talk with Chisisi as soon as possible and hear what news there is from the north,* she thought.

In the throne room, Nestuwan sat on the Scorpion throne and listened to the slow methodical swish of the peacock fans, held atop of tall poles by servant girls. Beside her sat Hor-Nu who in her opinion, had not been favored by time. Nakht sat next to him, who seemed to be untouched by the ravages of the years. He still had a full head of hair unlike the other priest and happy continence of youth. She remembered him when he was just the priest of Amun back when Amun and Min had not been joined together, but now Maya was a new priest that would be taking both of these men's responsibilities. He was seated next to them, Duaenre – a court official was next to him and then the previously retired soldiers Khu and Nakhti.

Chisisi, the dispatch runner who now looked very much worn out in life, approached the front of the room. He bowed with much struggle, low to the ground and waited for the King's mother to bid him rise.

"Greetings Chisisi, I trust you have brought word from the King's fight in the north."

"Indeed I have," he replied as he patted his brown leather satchel, tied to his waist.

After he stepped forward and handed her a tightly bound scroll, he motioned to her that he wished to speak.

"As you are well aware, I have travelled back and forth on the river for the King and the Osiris - one before him for many years," he said cautiously.

Nestuwan listened carefully to his words and made her judgement on her heart's urgings.

"I have brought the King's loyal servant Weneg with me and the Northern Princess, Neithotep, to be kept safe in the palace. I am old and tired. I would like to retire from this job set before me."

"Stand forth Princess, let me see you!" Nestuwan called out. A woman in a long white dress stepped forward. Her delicate features and natural long, black hair was like a ray of sunshine entering the room. She was mid-age, tall and fine featured. She had green malachite makeup on her eyelids and gold dust on her cheeks. Her lips were painted deep red. Nestuwan was shocked that she had not seen this woman of beauty upon entering the throne room.

"You have done a great work for this land Chisisi. I will indeed receive this princess into my care. I will require you, though, to make one more trip north to train your replacement. Only after that, are you released from service."

"When am I to depart?"

"After this letter is read and I give you a reply, you must be ready to go north, but pick your replacement well," she said

* * *

Ako – the household cat – rubbed his lithe black and grey body expectantly across Nestuwan's legs as she relaxed on a tall golden chair. Nestuwan dangled her hand lazily beside her and slowly caressed the spotted cat's head as she sat in her beige colored room. A brimming cup of red wine sat on a short gilded table

that was carved with images of scorpions across its top.
Live short papyrus stalks in black clay pots sat beside
red flowers in front of a reed covered window opening.
The scroll she held was fastened on the side by a black
clay seal with Narmer's ring impression pushed deeply
into it. She broke the seal and started reading.

* * *

Greetings Great Mother of the King, may you live
forever.

I took the Navy south and disembarked on the
western shore. I sent the ships south with barely enough
sailors to operate the boats. I then travelled north. It was
slow travelling the marshland, but due to the abundance
of fresh water pools dotting the landscape, we did not
have to waste much time searching that necessity. The
western land is full of colorful birds with beautiful
plumage I have never yet seen and strange animals
from the underworld. One fish in particular, almost
killed Re'hotep who had just reached in the water to
catch it. He screamed and had to drop this magical fish
right away since it felt like touching lightning. He was
not injured seriously, but we took it as a warning from
the gods. Before we moved on, I sacrificed to Amun to
appease him and set our hearts at ease.

I set out spies north once again, to see if Setaten
[the commander of Thesh's army] was on the move and
believed our ruse of travelling south. Weren was very
helpful in this as he knew the places to search for signs
of their movements. I must honor him when I return
home.

Nestuwan's heart skipped a beat in anticipation when she read the line about her son returning home. *Oh Amun, protect my son. Make his ways your ways and guide his steps.* She then started reading again.

Setaten had not moved from his position in Saqqara, but Thesh had moved his army away from the capital of Memphis and was heading south. This information was particularly troubling to me since he would have such a large army if they joined together. Our only hope would be to strike the smaller army first; even then we will need the god's help.

I entered Memphis at the same time as Menes had arrived and marched on to the palace right away. You should have seen this place, this is truly a land of reeds. There are papyrus plants as far as the eye can see. But right in the middle, it all of a sudden opened up to a road lined with fragrant spice trees. A large temple stood like a beacon to weary travellers at the end of this 'spiced road'. The temple's walls had colorful scenes of the cobra goddess Wadjet painted on its whitewashed bricks. On the opposite side of the temple we saw a grand palace. It is much larger than ours in Abydos – I assumed this from the start. I took my soldiers and entered the palace. The throne room is ornately decorated with many growing plants. There were impressive images of Wajet and Osiris standing on each side of a carpeted floor that was the color of a bed of burning, red-hot coals.

The guards that protected the palace started a small skirmish with my soldiers, but they were quickly subdued. I am now in complete control of the palace. Thesh has not been found anywhere though, but a priestess of Hathor was found roaming the halls. I had met her in Dashur at the temple of Hathor where she serves. Upon talking to her more, I found out that she is the daughter of Hsekui. She was set to marry her half-brother Thesh, but she ran away. Her name is princess Neithotep.

This is what my son needs! Nestuwan thought, her heart fluttering as she recalled the woman that she had just met. She had been concerned about Narmer ever since the death of Eshe; so maybe this princess will sooth his soul. She continued to read.

I have crushed the remaining army that languished here in Memphis and put them to the spear. Thesh and the leader of his army have not been located yet. I am now in pursuit of them, south.

Written in my hand,
King Narmer, Ruler of the South, Keeper of the Laws of Ma'at and Conqueror of the Land and delivered to Chisisi.

* * * *

Weneg adjusted himself on his stool and took a drink of water from a clay cup. He then bit a piece of some hard cheese that sat on a plate on a short table beside him.

"Let me tell you something else I have not thought of in a while. I had brought my 'little stone treasure' back to Abydos. Remember the one I had rescued from the river? I had now decided what I was going to do with it," Weneg said, as his face showed a sense of accomplishment by the squint of his eyes and slow nodding of his head. "I remembered the horrible state that the god's makeup grinding pallet was in, since I was the one who had to clean it. I thought I could design and carve a decorative pallet, worthy of the King.

I procured some small blocks of dolerite and different sized stone saws. I also was able to get some polishing stones and grinding grit from a stone carver. I started learning from this old artisan during the daytime – I learned quickly. Within a month I had designed and carved two fabulous creatures whose necks were entwined. The circular place between their necks was to be used as a makeup grinding platform for the god."

"Where is the pallet now?" Ist questioned.

"Is it still used?" Hayki asked.

Weneg opened his hands as he shrugged. "The last I saw of the pallet, it was being used in the temple of Horus."

The day was getting late so Weneg dismissed them, but not before asking them to return the next day.

Kah, Ist and Hayki slowly walked along the well-worn path back home. Twilight made the scrub trees cast eerie shadows across the road like the crooked fingers of hideous gods. A haunting feeling was added by a flurry of birds that exploded out of a papyrus marsh, that stood between the road and the river.

They approached Hayki's cut-off in the path, but he did not walk down it, he just followed Kah and Ist to their house. As they walked into their yard they could see something was wrong. The door to the house stood open and flower pots were dumped to the side. The gate that penned up the cow and goats was ajar and their food trough was overturned.

"What is going on here?" Kah questioned.

Inside the house, there was utter disaster as if a strong desert wind was let loose. Pots and dishes lay on the floor, as well as planted flowers were in disarray. The young couple's many clothes, were pulled out of the tiring boxes and ripped. Kah and Ist were aghast at the devastation in their bedroom.

"My clothes! Who would do such a thing to us?" Ist screamed.

Kah was stunned and slowly paced between the bed and the doorframe.

"I know who would have done this," Hayki said sadly. "My brother. Anitka."

26

AFTER FOUR DAYS TRAVELING south, Narmer and Menes discovered the backside of the army, confidently camping at the outskirts of Saqqara. Quietly they marched their army in the dead of the night when there was no moon. Narmer's army silently camped behind the Northern soldiers. As twilight broke, it was obvious that Thesh's army was unaware that they had been spotted and Narmer was right on their doorstep. The trap was set.

Narmer was glad he had sent Weneg, Princess Neithotep and Chisisi ahead many weeks ago, on a small, fast boat, flying northern colors that he had taken from the Memphis ship yards. He had hoped they were able to slip by Thesh unmolested and were on their way to Abydos.

Re, the sun god, broke free from his travel through the waters of the underworld and cast his brilliance across the land. Now was the time to spring the trap.

Four rows totalling one thousand troops, led by tall blue and white fluttering standards, marched into the cramped streets of Dashur. The soldiers were bare-chested and wore white linen loin cloths. They carried spears and leather-covered wooden shields. The outside row of men carried bows and arrows as well as stone tipped maces. They were not only greeted with open-mouthed stares from the children, but shock and anger from the adults. The soldiers marched past three gleaming white temples; one to Amun; one to Osiris and a final one to Isis in the center of town. A few soldiers from Thesh's army cried out and attacked Menes ranks – they were quickly and brutally executed. A few of the northern army soldiers ran ahead to warn the remaining men to try to stop the advance, but it was too late.

Thesh's army turned and faced Narmer's – it was much larger than the spies had reported. They totalled in excess of two thousand men strong – a much larger army than Narmer's. Narmer was dejected when he saw the size of the army in front of him. *We will be crushed! Oh Amun, give my men the strength to fight for you!* A sharp booming order came from their front lines. Narmer or Menes could not hear what was said, but the intention was very clear. Their army leveled their spears and charged. A bloody battle erupted between the two sides. Narmer slew three men in the first two minutes and Menes killed two.

"Archers, ready your arrows and fire at will!" Narmer screamed as he cut down three more men.

The soldiers on the outskirts of the ranks did just that, easily finding their marks and silencing many more men. Even though the northern army had low quality weapons, they were very proficient in using them – especially their spears. As the men advanced, the northern army began to show their proficiency and gained control of the fight and beat Menes men back. As the northern army steadily gained ground, Menes troops started to fragment.

"Take the shock troops and drive a wedge through the middle of their line, right there. Show your worth." Menes yelled at Weren during the incredible noise of the fight, as he pointed to a thinning line of opposing soldiers.

Weren rushed ahead of his band of criminal soldiers and screamed out his orders to them. Seeing that Thesh temporarily had the upper hand, the criminal soldiers turned on Menes army and began fighting against them.

"What are you cowards doing?" Weren yelled as he thrust his spear into the face of his previous friend and then into a second, showing his worthiness to Menes. The prince had been watching Weren's actions in the thick of the battle. Teremun – the prison leader – stood beside Weren and killed two of his criminal friends who had turned against Menes. After the criminals saw that their leaders were not with them, saw their mistake and switched sides again – but it was too late – they had shown their true colors. Menes spun around and continued slaughtering men as Weren was now standing beside him swinging a bloodied axe at the northern soldiers. Another criminal – this one Weren, remembered – had no ears and no tongue. He had been convicted of raping his neighbor's wife. The man stood beside Weren and began fighting. In a lull in the battle, Weren turned on him and killed him as the woman was his sister.

Five northern soldiers approached Menes with spears, but because of Menes skill, they were unable to gain the upper hand on him. They were able to stab him in his ribs – not killing him, but seriously injuring him. Weren stood beside the fallen prince protecting and defending him from further attacks.

Narmer was at the front of the quickly losing, surging battle – Minnakt fought beside him. Narmer had now lost count of the opposing soldiers he had killed – each one of them hurting his soul though. *Are you pleased, Father? Are you pleased that I am killing my countrymen*? Narmer thought with every thrust of his spear, ending someone's life. He was fighting a losing battle and he was well aware of it. Suddenly an arrow found its mark in Narmer's calf and brought Narmer to his knees. He crawled forward, across one of his dead soldier's body's and pried the mace out of the man's hand. He was now on his knees and he quickly tied the weapon to his belt. He crawled further, trying to find some sort of protection, but was unable to find any. He crawled over a northern soldier he assumed was dead, but the man was just injured and dazed. As Narmer crawled across him, he awoke, grabbed for a short dagger and slashed Narmer's chest. *I will not die this way!* he screamed in his mind. Narmer rolled closer to the man and trapped the man's hand that held the weapon between his body and the ground. As the northern soldier writhed and twisted around trying to free his arm, Narmer reached out, grabbed a broken spear tip that was only an arms-length long and shoved it into the man. He could feel the spear tip rake across each of the man's ribs and then deep into the soft inner organs – ending the man's life.

Horns blared ahead of him and the northern soldiers parted as a man stepped forward. He had long, black hair and a full, curly beard that cut to his neckline. He wore a black kilt with a white, blood-spattered belt that hung to his knees and no sandals. He carried a spear, a ram's horn and he had lines of decorative scars between bold, black tattoos covering his arms and face. A younger man followed him who wore a spotless white kilt and had a red crown with a tall curved feather. He had thick gold chains decorating his neck and a large gold and jasper pectoral. While this was happening, Menes was nursing his own injuries from a spear that had temporarily put him out of commission.

Narmer removed the arrow from his leg, keenly aware of the heavy scent of blood and sweat that was attracting vultures. The field was littered with limbs, broken bodies and injured men. His chest and leg ached in mind-searing pain as he glanced up into the sky and saw the vultures circling overhead.

"Is this the upstart pretender 'King' I have heard about?" the tattooed man's deep, gravelly voice asked.

"He is the one . . . kill him," said the man behind him.

"My pleasure, Majesty."

Narmer's mind flew into overdrive as he thought about all the things that brought him to this spot: he thought about his father King Scorpion, Nestuwan – his mother and Eshe, his dead wife. *This cannot be my end and not on my twenty-second birthday,* he said inwardly as he gritted his teeth. Narmer stood up as Setaten approached and he doubled over in pain. Setaten rushed in with his spear hoisted, seeing the opportunity and prepared to strike. "Don't fail me now Khu," he whispered under his breath. Narmer heard the man's footsteps closing the distance between them quickly. He placed his left hand on his leg and moaned out in pain, but with his right, he unlatched the stone-tipped club. When Setaten was right on top of him, Narmer spun around to the left, at the same time that the man thrust the spear. The spear was dodged and now Narmer, with a lot of momentum and a mace in his hand, was standing beside the warrior. There was a split second of shock that flashed in Setaten's eyes before the mace made contact. The warriors head exploded in a mess of blood and brain matter. Time seemed to stand still as everyone watching had to register what had just happened. Thesh was shocked and dropped his weapon to the ground. Narmer picked up a discarded spear at his feet and pointed it at Thesh.

"Do you yield!?" Narmer asked, not really needing an answer.

A northern warrior rushed ahead with his spear hoisted, but Minnakht fired an arrow into the man's chest and killed him instantly.

Thesh did not answer, he just removed his red crown and placed it on the ground along with his gold and jasper pectoral. Narmer snapped his fingers and pointed to them. Minnahkt rushed forward and picked them up, laying them at Narmer's feet. Minnakht leaned forward and whispered something into his ear. The King stepped back with a disgusted look on his face.

"Bring the criminals forward!" he yelled.

Within the half hour, all the soldiers that had been given that precious second chance, stood defiantly in front of Narmer, who by then had been bandaged and was feeling much better.

* * *

Within the hour Narmer and Menes had their injuries tended to and were standing in the town square with the army surrounding them. Thesh had his elbows tied behind his back and was kneeling in submission in front of them. Fifty remaining men who had been criminals at one time and had been given second chances, kneeled and were bound on the ground behind Thesh. Narmer walked behind Thesh and picked up a hook that was lying in the dirt and stuck its tip in the northern King's nose as a sign of absolute domination.

"I take all your lands and remove you as King. You are finished as ruler. Let it be known from here on that we are a joined people and I am your King! Furthermore, this new land will be called Kemet for we are all people united in this land, rich with black soil that the gods have provided. Unfortunately there are those of you that are not worthy of this," he said leveling his gaze at the criminals who were unworthy. "Do your duty, Minnahkt," he said as he snapped his fingers and pointed to the criminals. One-by-one the men were dispatched by spear, the only remaining left alive were Weren, Teremun and Thesh. Narmer stood tall and authoritative before these three men.

"You have shown yourselves worthy," Narmer said as he placed his hands on the criminal's shoulders. "You have not," he said when he stood in front of the disposed King. Narmer held onto King Scorpion's old war mace in one hand, grabbed Thesh's hair in the other and smashed his head in.

"Swear allegiance to me now or leave this land immediately," he yelled out to the crowd.

One-by-one the people came forward, kneeled and kissed his feet – nobody walked off the battlefield. After everyone had paid homage to their new King, Menes also approached and kneeled and kissed his brother's feet.

* * * *

In Weneg's hut, the student's still sat in a small circle amazed at the story they had just been told. Each one of them considered the inner strength that Narmer had to summon within himself, to make it through the war he had gone through. They were impressed that he had the compassion to invite all citizens and opposing soldiers into the new country he named 'Kemet'.

"That was an amazing story, Teacher," Hayki said.

Kah's eyes looked up to the ceiling as he tried to process a nagging question in his mind. "How did you know what actually happened at that final war? You said you were in Abydos at that time," he asked.

Weneg calmly took a second bite of cheese and a sip of water. "I asked the King and Menes and Minnahkt," he said flatly.

Kah felt stupid asking such an obviously answered question. His blushing face gave away the embarrassment. Right then a man burst through the door – it was Anitka!

"Anitka?" Hayki questioned fearfully.

"Hello Anitka. So nice of you to drop by, we have missed you," Weneg said cautiously.

I did not miss him, Kah thought.

"Be silent, old man!" Anitka said evenly as he seethed bitterness.

Kah stood up, but the angered teen pointed a large copper knife at him. "You – mister perfect. You have nothing to say! I have been alienated for too long. I am sick of sitting here and watching as everything gets handed to you as if you were Osiris himself. I have gone through hard times – you have not. My mother was taken from me – yours was not. A woman I loved – you stole from me. You have a beautiful house – I do not. You have a fantastic job that will provide you with food for all time – I do not. My life is crumbling around me and nobody cares. Nobody ever cares," he said as his voice got quieter and quieter.

"It is true that I have been given a much better path in life than you. I do not know how I would have reacted to the loss of my mother; our teacher has lost a mother. Remember the only woman that was a mother to him was also taken from him as well. Maybe I would have pent-up rage the same as you, maybe more, but you have done it; I have not. In that case you are better than me," Kah said quietly. "I did not know that you had been interested in Ist, so in that regard I am sorry. As far as becoming a priest . . . it is not as wonderful as you may think. I will have to start my chores, servicing the god long before anyone even awakes. I also have to wash five times a day, as well as keep my clothes spotlessly clean."

Anitka shrugged as if it was no big deal.

"Now I have not gotten there yet, but am required to go through some purification rituals. My entire body will need to be completely shaved. I have to abstain from sexual intercourse for months at a time. And on top of that, I will have to get circumcised."

Anitka seemed to lose his anger – he didn't like what was all involved in the 'wonderful life' of a priest. *I guess his life isn't all that spectacular.*

"I am sorry for my actions Kah," he said slowly. "Sorry for messing up your house Ist," he said sheepishly. "I will replace the things I have destroyed. It will take me some time, though. Please do not turn me in to the authorities," he said, as he knew the punishments he would receive would be the same as the nose less criminals he had heard about in the story.

"Your actions have done more damage than just to Kah and Ist," Weneg said. "You have not been a proper son, brother, or student, have you? Your insolence has disturbed my classroom for a long time, but all is not lost. You have repeatedly said that this life is hopeless. You may not know this, but you can make amends and benefit many generations to come . . ."

When Weneg said that; Anitka's eyes lit up with hope.

"How is your writing?"

"It is fine . . . why?"

"If you are willing to copy all of these onto scrolls," Weneg said, motioning to his baskets of tablets, "you can deliver them to every town and allow everyone to have this knowledge; not just the temples. This will take many years to spread the god's words. Are you willing to take on such a task?"

Anitka thought about this daunting mission. *Can I do this? I will be persecuted by the stanch priests that want to keep this knowledge hidden and to themselves. Maybe I can change my life around and make my world worthwhile! I can spread my religion far and wide . . . I will be a success.*

27

THREE MONTHS HAD PASSED, almost as if in a daze, for Narmer and Menes. The brothers proceeded to move the capital from their home in Abydos to Memphis. During their time at home, priest Hor-Nu died, quietly in his bed. This was not a death that upset Narmer or Menes in the slightest. They, on the other hand, were happy that a new priest who was not set in his ways would now be assisting Nakht.

Nestuwan stood in awe at the vastness of the new land after her boat finally arrived from its long trip in the south. There were new types of trees and animals that she had never seen before. The people seemed pleasant enough and as she placed her feet for the first time on the new black soil, the people sang a chorus of blessings and welcome to her. Later during the day whenever she was addressed, they called her "Great Mother of the King," – she liked that.

"This land is truly and abundantly blessed by the gods," Nestuwan said as she strolled up and down the hard-packed, dirt streets. She saw a deep stone-lined ditch that was used to remove waste water and food scraps. "This is a very clean town," she said out loud, pleasantly surprised.

The guards that walked with her were quiet as she inspected the town's amenities. As the King's mother, walking by the domed ovens that supplied the town's bread, she was given a fearful surprise; Weren was standing beside a full water canister, washing his dirty hands. His ghoulish features shocked her, forcing her to catch her breath and take a step back.

"I demand to be told your name, vile creature!"

Weren was shocked to be addressed that way, but was not unfamiliar with her surprise, bowed in respect placing his forehead on the ground.

"Great Mother of the King, my name is Weren," he said still bowing.

Nestuwan critically considered this "Weren." *Where did this man come from and why is he wearing an armband that has my son's insignia on it? He must have some importance though. I know he has the injuries that are inflicted on criminals, but why is he here?*

"You may stand, Weren. Tell me, why are you here?"

Weren found it hard to believe that she was unaware of the criminal shock troops that he was in charge of. *Does the King not place much importance in me?* he questioned.

Weren was nervous to speak to this powerful woman. *I must be careful,* he told himself trying to calm his nerves.

"I have been serving both the King and his brother for the past many seasons. Menes has placed me as the head of the King's Shock Troops. The King also has forgiven my crimes on condition that I do not return to my old ways. If I do, that will be my last day in this world. I will not let him down," he said confidently. "I have indeed paid for my crimes under Thesh's rule."

Nestuwan eyed the blemished man and suddenly felt compassion for him. She understood that he was a man who had gone off the path of the Laws of Ma'at, but was determined to claw his way back and change.

"Will you accompany me to the celebrations after you clean yourself up, Weren?" she invited.

He could not believe the absolute change in her attitude towards him; she had called him a 'vile creature' but now wanted his presence at the party. "I will be pleased to accompany you," he replied.

* * *

This great event would be the biggest that anyone had ever seen. Nestuwan and all of her staff, of course, stood pensively as coronation celebration was to take place at the new capital's town square. In the shadows of the grand temples of the gods, blue and white banners fluttered high above the citizen's heads. Musicians beat drums, rattled sistrums, tapped on tambourines, strummed on lyres and harps and blew into double pipe flutes. The people that were unable to play an instrument kept time by clapping. There were thousands of people both from the north and the south, standing and rejoicing, waiting for the festivities to begin. Narmer walked to the center of the dais that was permanently set up for any events that would arise and greeted the crowd. "Today is a life changing day in our lives, a change that brings the north and south together," he started his trumpet call.

The crowd became silent and parted. A woman dressed in the most beautiful clothes they had ever seen, stepped forward. She had a white and gold-lined dress with white leather sandals. She wore a wide, gold pectoral and a long, braided, black wig in which tiny, golden chains were woven.

Townsfolk gasped, "It's the princess!" they exclaimed.

Neithotep stood at the base, but center of the dais and bowed low to the ground in supplication. Narmer was quick in asking her to rise.

"I come to you, Neithotep – Princess of the North and I pledge myself to you from this day forward." As she said this she kneeled at his feet and kissed them.

This woman is beautiful, he thought as he soaked in her affection.

"Princess, I have talked to your friend Meresamun. I know you have served as a priestess and a pure singer in the temple of Hathor," Narmer stated. "After these many years of being inexperienced in love, do you truly want to bind yourself to me?"

"Yes I do – for the good of my people as well as for me," she said with a broad smile that allowed small cracks to appear in the makeup around her reddened mouth.

Narmer's mind brought him back to his visit with Nefrusheri – the albino dream interpreter. 'A new life and a new wife,' he remembered her saying. *She was right all along,* he thought as he pleasantly shook his head.

* * *

Maya – the new High Priest - stood flanked by the High Priests: Nakht and Meresamun. As if on queue, they raised their hands simultaneously silencing the crowd of revelers.

"This is a new day in all our lives – a day that we will tell our children about, throughout the ages to come," Nakht shouted.

Nakht was now aging. He was fifty three, he struggled with walking and standing for a long length of time. The Priest's voice was not as strong as in his youth, but he was determined to be the one who instilled Narmer as King.

"We come before the gods and ask that they would look graciously on, as we hand over the reins of power to this new King. We pledge our lives to be his servants," Nakht yelled as loud as he could.

Nakht's voice then failed and Maya took over.

"Will you uphold the Law of Ma'at as you rule us? Maya asked.

"Before I continue, I will ask that my brother be included in this ceremony, for we will rule this country together," Narmer requested.

Menes could not believe his ears. This was completely unprecedented. *Will I indeed be King after all this time,* he thought?

"Menes and I will rule Kemet as one. My law will be his law and his law will be mine! I know this is not usual, but this is an unusual time," he said as he extended his hand to Menes. "Do you accept this request, my Brother?"

Menes was euphoric and ignored the pin prick to his soul as he reached out his hand and joined it with Narmer's.

"I will wear the crown with you, Brother," he said confidently.

The doors to the temple then opened and a large contingent of priests carried the images of the gods to the town square. The gods were carried in large majestic barques. Menes noticed the priests straining under the weight of the god's boats, but did not move. The images were draped under sheer golden cloth, as wisps of sharp myrrh floated from ornate brass censers throughout the people.

"I will stand with you," Menes loudly announced.

Maya then bowed to Narmer and then to Menes. "I ask again, will you both keep the Laws of Ma'at close to your hearts for the well-being of Kemet and drive out chaos from these lands?"

In unison they both replied they would. Maya then stood in front of Narmer holding the red crown. Narmer could feel the eyes of thousands of people glued to his every move as he stood very still and the crown was placed upon his head.

"With this crown as a symbol of the north, I proclaim you King of the Northern lands." Maya shouted. A great cheer arose from the onlookers. Nakht then stepped forward holding the white crown and said, "With this symbol of the south I give you power over the Southern lands."

Narmer diligently waited as beads of sweat rolled down his face and into his eyes. The white crown was then fitted on top, yet inside of the red one, like a puzzle. *I have completed my task Father,* he said to his father as relief washed over his soul.

A deafening cheer rose up and the musicians began to play once more.

Maya then lifted his hands to silence the crowd and approached Menes holding a duplicate red crown. Tightness gripped Menes throat as emotions tempted him to let go and let his tear gates flow. He was overjoyed as Maya charged him with the same commands and placed the red crown upon his head – a crown that Narmer had requested be made previously. Menes was exhilarated when he felt the weight of the crown. He twisted his neck and cracked it.

Maya then approached again with a duplicate white crown and repeated the commands given to Narmer. Menes wholeheartedly agreed as the crown was fitted on his head. *So this is what power feels like,* he thought as an overwhelming sense of responsibility washed over him. *Now I understand what my father had said. I long to return to responsibilities that I had as a child.* His second thoughts didn't change the fact that he was going to rule. *I have to deal with this new path in my life . . . May Amun give me strength to rule with Narmer,* he cried out.

* * * *

Weneg sat calmly in the dimly lit hut as he finished the story for the day. Kah and Ist were sitting cross-legged and holding hands, completely engrossed with the tale that their teacher had just relayed. Hayki and Anitka also sat side-by-side enthralled with the story.

"Was Menes worthy of becoming King with his brother, even though he had doubts about ruling?" Weneg asked.

Kah was the first to answer. "Yes, he was worthy."

"Why do you think? I would like to know."

Anitka thought deeply then replied, "He was worthy because he had been offered the opportunity by the King and was blessed by the High Priests."

"Interesting . . ." Weneg said.

As soon as Weneg replied, Anitka knew he had been wrong.

I will continue tomorrow. Please come back for the finale."

Kah and Ist quickly stood and thanked Weneg and walked outside. Hayki and Anitka came out of the hut laughing and casually talking to one another – this was something that had been usually filled with fighting and yelling.

"They sure are getting along now," Ist said to Kah.

"I wonder what changed in Anitka's life?"

The two groups kept walking until Anitka and Hayki's path to their home split off. The two boys ran down the tree-lined road towards their house.

"I will be starting my job at the temple at the end of the week," Kah mentioned as they walked together hand-in-hand.

"I suppose our home will be a little quieter now that Hayki is gone as well," Ist said.

"That is true . . . when we arrive home, let's bake as much bread as we can, so you are well supplied during the months I will be away."

"I am not going to be a cripple," Ist said, playfully giving him a shove.

As they walked to their home they saw Kah's father standing by their house holding a large traveling bag. "You will need this," he said as he handed it to Kah.

28

WITHIN ONE YEAR, WONDERFUL news was broadcast throughout Kemet. Neithotep was pregnant with her first child. This came as a great relief to all that worried about the longevity of Narmer's rein.

Joyful days soon turned into sadness for Menes, as Hamila became sick and died from a disease that lingered in the water. Menes was so distraught that he sailed south by himself, on a fast boat to search out Nefrusheri and ask for her guidance. The sails snapped and the mast groaned under the pull of the wind, as the boat sped by any onlookers that happened to be out on the banks that day.

"Why have I had such bad fortune," he shouted to the wind in anger. "I have waited my time underneath my brother's rule! I do not deserve this," he complained aloud.

Days turned into weeks and soon he saw the border of the town of Lahun. *I remember when we first visited this town – what a mess it was!* Menes brought the image back to his mind. He was pleased at the changes that had been made, *they have really changed this place around,* he thought after he disembarked and investigated the streets. He walked into the temple to acquire guidance from the oracle, but she was not present. By now a crowd had gathered, since seeing their King was a very rare occasion. The press of people was so thick that even with soldiers holding them back; many decorative trees that had been planted got trampled.

The familiar face of the cleanly shaved Menkhaf approached Menes and prostrated himself on the ground. As he lay there waiting for permission to rise, Menes felt an overwhelming sense of guilt. A sense that he could not identify.

"Rise, Menkhaf."

"I hope that you find our town to your liking, Majesty. We employ every citizen one day a week to keep this standard," he said, as he swept his hand from one side of the town to the other.

"I do see that much has been completed. I am very pleased. I would like to meet with Nefrusheri, but I could not find her in the temple. Do you know her location?" Menes asked.

Menkhaf nodded, but had a worried look on his face – which troubled Menes. *I hope she is okay,* he thought.

"The Wise-Woman has taken ill in the last several months and now lives on the outskirts of town. We have sacrificed for her and said many a prayer, but it is of no use."

Now Menes was concerned. *Will I get the guidance I so desperately need or will I just have to ride these feelings out?*

"Let me take you to her," he said as he reached out his hand and beckoned for his King to follow.

They walked along the rich brown banks of the river until they found a small one-story, mud-bricked structure. It was unadorned and unpainted. Two small Ficus trees grew close to the door, but Menes did not know if they had been planted there or not.

"She is inside," Menkhaf said pointing to the door.

After the man left, Menes approached the door and walked in. Nefrusheri was sitting on the floor leaning up against the wall. Her legs were stretched out in front of her at an odd angle. He noticed she had blisters that blemished her shins and had not cleaned her hair in a long time. The smell in the room was that of mold mixed with old incense. Nefrusheri didn't move when Menes walked in – she just lay there with her white hair plastered across her face with sweat. Thinking she was asleep, he turned to leave, but just as he got to the door she spoke.

"I am at your service, Menes."

Menes quickly turned around and looked at her – she was still half braced against the corner wall, but slumped over.

"I have come to seek your guidance . . . I seek your wisdom."

"I know . . . Menes," she said deliberately, again not addressing him as *King*.

He was taken aback with her reply, but did not confront her about it. *How dare she address me like a commoner?*

"You feel like you do not belong."

"Yes . . . How did you . . ." he asked unable to believe what he had just heard.

"You feel lost and unworthy," she added.

Menes just stood frozen in disbelief, looking at her – she had touched on the core of his deep thoughts. "How do you know such things?"

"I know these things because the gods reveal them to me. To answer your question . . . No, you are not worthy to wear the crown," she abruptly said.

"What?!" he said furiously.

"Did your father not say Narmer was to be King, not you?"

A lump grew in his throat. *How does she know these things? Things that King Scorpion only said to me in private,* he inwardly screamed. He definitely remembered his father's words to him. He remembered the King telling him that Narmer was to be King and that he was to support him.

"Your disobedience to your father and King damned you!" she said as her voice became shrill, her back straightened and she stood up. This surprised him and he retreated backwards towards the door. "You will be knocked off your perch, OH mighty King," she said sarcastically. "You will be unseated by an inconsequential beast as a testament to the god's power and your miniscule insignificance." She then collapsed to the dirt floor in mental exhaustion.

Menes rushed out of the building in fear. He passed undetected through the outskirts of town and on to his boat. *What just happened,* he thought? Menes could hardly catch his breath as he was overwhelmed with a paralyzing fear. Menes let the river's current grab his boat and draw it along leisurely. His head began to spin, he fell to his knees crawling to the left side of the boat and then retched. His eyes blurred and he saw his father laying in the water staring up at him.

"You are not to be King! I told you this. Why did you disobey me?" the vision of his father sternly asked.

He blinked his eyes and shook his head – his father materialized into an alligator, snapped its wicked teeth, then slipped under the brown water and swam off. Menes jerked back from the edge of the boat feeling sick and guilty. He stumbled into the small cabin, opened up his tiring box and retrieved the box that held his crown taking them outside. As he walked, the box all of a sudden gained a tremendous amount of weight not only physically, but emotionally as well. With anguish of the situation he found himself in, it caused him to drop the precious cargo he held in his trembling hands.

On his hands and knees, Menes pushed the black ebony box across the deck. At the side of the boat, he attempted to open it, but was unable to. He knew that retrieving the crowns from the box was of great importance; he seemed to be stymied.

Beside him was a war axe that had been forgotten by a soldier – Menes grabbed it and used it to hack the troubling box open. Inside were the two things he had desired to wear all of his life – the red and white crowns of Kemet. As glorious and beautiful as they once were; they now looked ugly and poisonous to him.

Menes held the crowns to his chest and wept.

"Just one more time . . . I deserve to be King just one more time," he said loudly to a committee of vultures that had landed in a nearby tree and gathered on the muddy bank.

Menes placed the double crown on his head reveling in its power. He looked up at a large black vulture that was keeping pace above the boat.

"See, this isn't so bad," he said to the observing bird hovering overhead. The bird hissed, let out a high-pitched screech and flew off. He brought out a chair, sat to relax and felt much better after an hour. He listened to the gurgling river, proudly sitting on his golden chair and coasted through the town of Meydum waving to the citizens. He saw walls of papyrus ahead – he liked the plant and was pleased when the thick plants seemed to crowd the river banks. He did not enjoy his seclusion long when a bee stung him on his bare leg.

"To Set with you," he cursed and swatted the inconsequential insect.

Immediately, he felt a tightening in his chest and constricting of his throat. He was unable to swallow and an impending doom enveloped his mind. He panicked and placed his hands on his neck to somehow relieve his ever tightening throat – it didn't work. He needed air now! Menes felt the double crown now weigh evermore heavier on his brow and he craved relief. With all the strength he could muster, he pulled the crown off his head and tossed it aside. Menes held his neck and tried to call out for help, but no sound escaped his lips. He watched helplessly as a vulture – the symbol of the King's power - landed on the ship's deck and began picking at the discarded crown. Menes watched as the vulture nudged the crown into the muddy water, screeched and then flew off.

Menes mind swam with delirium as he lay face up on the deck. Just before he succumbed to lack of oxygen, a committee of vultures landed on the boat and surrounded him.

* * * *

The hut was silent, only labored breaths could be heard between the snapping of the oil lamp's wick.

"Was that how the King died?" Ist questioned.

Weneg raised his palms and shrugged. "All I know is his boat was found with the box that held the crowns, smashed apart on the deck. There were talon marks, some vulture feathers and blood on the deck. During the search I was able to question Nefrusheri. That was the story she told me; I believe that story."

"How did Narmer react to the disappearance of his brother?" Anitka asked.

He was heartbroken, but I could tell that he knew. Narmer and Neithotep had a baby boy which they named Hor-Aha. Of course you know, that after that, Narmer ruled for sixty years. His son became King – and what a great King he is."

"What about King Narmer? Were you there when he met Osiris?" Hayki asked.

"Yes I was. Stay a little longer and I will tell you," Weneg said as the memory saddened him, but he wanted to continue on with telling the story.

"I can still stay and listen," Ist said.

"As can my brother and I," Anitka replied.

"I would not miss this for the world!" Kah said.

Hayki just smiled and nodded his willingness to stay. A majority of his happiness was his pleasure with his burgeoning relationship with his brother.

NARMER WAS SIXTY YEARS old and had ruled Kemet
for many years, instructing his son Hor-Aha on
how to be a responsible and wise King, ruling the
mighty empire he had built. Narmer still missed his
twin brother Menes terribly and had built him an empty
tomb with furnishings in the desert, so that hopefully
his Ka would find it and take up residence there, not
aimlessly wandering the land.

I became very close to the King in those days. We
walked into the desert; boated on the Nile; played Sennet
and hunted lions. Nestuwan and Khu – my father – had
died many years previously. I unfortunately had been
unable to give him any grandchildren. Neithotep also

died and had been buried in a grand, mud-brick tomb beside Menes empty tomb.

* * *

"One day, the King and I took his boat along the river to do some exploring in the papyrus forests that blanketed the banks, in and around the capital. The King's security kept pace on land and retrieved any ducks we felled in the papyrus.

'You have been a great friend to me, Weneg. I never feel alone when you are with me,' the King confessed to me.

'Thank you for giving me that opportunity to serve you, so many years ago,' I said. I remember rubbing the tattoo he gave me on my arm out of habit.

'It is my pleasure to have you as a friend,' he said. 'Remember what you have seen and what you have heard these last several years. The knowledge might come in handy in the future.'

'Got one, Majesty!' a guard called out from the reeds.

'Just hold on to it for now,' I called back, 'We will swing around and pick it up later.'

The King grabbed an oar, guided the boat in a large arc around an uprooted stump and headed back to the bank. I saw many crocodiles in the water at this part of the muddy river and made some stupid comment about not wanting to go in there. Without realizing it, there were at least forty hippopotami surrounding the boat. I was scared to death.

'Easy now,' the King said warily.

The boat completed its arc in the river and was now parallel with the uprooted tree. Right then, our boat contacted a submerged hippo. Time seemed to slow. As if almost in unison, the river exploded in a fury of animals with one desire – to destroy everything.

'Help me, Weneg!' the King screamed.

'I'm coming, Your Majesty!' I yelled back.

'Save the King!' the soldiers yelled from the bank.

The boat split in half as a large hippo reared up and landed full force on the deck of our boat. The King was thrown to the front of the ship and managed to hold onto the ship's tall curving prow. I scrambled ahead trying to reach the King, but my foot broke through the splintered deck.

'Help me!' the King called again, panicking.

My leg was stuck in the boards now and I was unable to free it. As I pulled on my leg, the splintered wood dug into my calf, trapping my leg even tighter. As I looked around I saw several crocodiles warily keeping their distance – this was a good thing too, as I saw my leg dribbling out blood. A larger hippopotamus made a quick line towards me. I prayed for mine and the King's protection to any god that would hear me. The hippo reared up and smashed into the ship. I thought I was at my end, but that jarring loosened up the boards enough for me to free my leg. Just as I thought I was safe, a large crocodile that was very close, hissed at me from the river. He must have known that I was injured and would have made an easy meal. The large beast's mouth snapped shut multiple times making an uncomfortable warning sound. All of a sudden, one of the smaller crocodiles launched itself out of the water and partially onto the boat. The reptile wormed back and forth trying to wiggle onto the ship. After one minute it was successful. Now I was trapped again, but this time, at least, my leg was free. Blood was still flowing from my wound as the beast got closer.

'Weneg!' The King was barely able to call my name.

The pain that seared through my leg never abated, but it did give me a new energy to continue on. I bounded over the crocodile to a safer place, just as the animal rushed at me. I mounted what was left of the ship's deck and searched for my friend, the King – I saw him floating helplessly, surrounded by hippos.

'Your Majesty!' I called.

The soldiers in the papyrus plants yelled to him as well. By now the current had moved the broken boat towards the uprooted tree. Still calling to him, I grabbed what was left of the rotting, protruding tree and pulled myself onto it. Just as more crocodiles started swimming towards me, I managed to get a stronger hold and climbed up the tree as high as I could. The broken ship slowly sank into the river. When that happened, the beast on the deck returned to the river and quickly joined the hunt. At this time the hippos seemed to crowd together into a large circle.

'My King!' I called out.

I never took my eyes off of my friend and called to him again. He did not respond. Then in an outrage, the beasts stomped Narmer again and again.

'No!' I cried out. 'Damn you beasts of the underworld.' They did not stop pulverizing my friend until all that remained was his partial corpse."

* * * *

313

Weneg stopped speaking – he was crying. "Give me some time," he said breaking up. "That concludes my lesson; I hope you have enjoyed the story. Take the lessons to heart, ponder them, and learn from them."

Anitka opened a leather satchel and pulled out new leaves of papyrus and sat beside the basket of clay tablets. He dipped his reed into an ink pot and began copying. Kah watched the young man writing the wisdom and his heart softened to him.

"Anitka!" Kah said. "I will be the High Priest one of these days. You and I could have this knowledge available for all, just like King Narmer wanted. Would you join me in this?"

A broad smile lined Anitka's face. "This will be a great adventure Kah; and a meaning to our life!" Anitka said as he offered his hand to Kah.

A minister of the gods was born, ready to spread their message to all who could and would hear. No longer would the truths of the gods be hidden behind the temple walls. Now it was free for all to learn.

EPILOGUE

THE COT WAS DAMP from sweat as Ist rolled over onto her back. Her back had been aching for many days now, but however Meretseger propped the blankets or cushions, it did not help.

"Take comfort, my daughter," Ist's mother calmly said soothing the girl while rubbing her back.

Her mother managed to relieve some discomfort and the pregnant girl was then able to close her weary eyes, sleeping for a very brief period of time. *Oh I wanted to have children, but now . . . I think it was a mistake,* she thought, still half asleep.

A gush of water rushed out between Ist's legs, waking the girl. She panicked – she didn't know what was happening to her body. Even though she had seen a birth before; she had never had firsthand experience. Soon after her water broke, her contractions began. She felt her abdominal walls spasm in a fury of pain that she could not control.

"I hate him!" she sobbed almost incoherently.

"You do not hate him, Daughter, this is child birth. Your emotions are out of control right now," Meretseger said with a chuckle as she remembered her own experience.

Meretseger motioned to a midwife. "My daughter will require the birthing blocks now," she said calmly. The contractions came regularly, throwing Ist in to fits of unbearable pain. She could not hold her composure any longer and threw up. A contraction cramped her body once more. Meretseger sat beside the cot, calmly stroked Ist's hair and rubbed her temples.

"Oh!" the girl cried out as another contraction came and went.

The midwives helped Ist to her feet and helped her stand on the birthing blocks. Within the hour the new mother delivered her first child. It was a girl, but then the midwife looked up at Ist with a smile radiating from her face just as another contraction was gripping her.

"I have a pleasant surprise for you, my dear. You are having another child!"

Within minutes, Ist had given birth to twin girls.

BIBLIOGRAPHY

http://www.nndb.com/people/540/000163051/
http://www.kingtutone.com/pharaohs/menes/
http://www.reshafim.org.il/ad/egypt/timelines/topics/
navigation.htm
http://www.touregypt.net/featurestories/birding.htm
http://www.ancient-egypt-priests.com/AE-Life-english.htm
http://en.wikipedia.org/wiki/
Ancient_Egyptian_concept_of_the_soul
http://www.predatorturnedprey.com/Egyptian%20
Names.html
http://en.wikipedia.org/wiki/
Clothing_in_ancient_Egypt
http://www.behindtheName.com/Names/usage/
ancient-egyptian
http://www.reshafim.org.il/ad/egypt/timelines/topics/
navigation.htm
http://www.touregypt.net/featurestories/marriage.htm
http://www.touregypt.net/featurestories/priests.htm

http://www.touregypt.net/featurestories/law.htm

http://en.wikipedia.org/wiki/Capital_punishment_in_Egypt

http://www.levity.com/alchemy/islam24.html

http://www.touregypt.net/featurestories/hunting.htm

http://en.wikipedia.org/wiki/Beauty_and_cosmetics_in_ancient_Egypt

http://allthingswildlyconsidered.blogspot.ca/2010/09/i-am-not-beside-you-where-will-set-your.html

http://www.touregypt.net/featurestories/taweret.htm

http://www.ancient.eu.com/article/87/

http://www.touregypt.net/featurestories/dream.htm

http://en.wikipedia.org/wiki/4th_millennium_BC

http://www.touregypt.net/egypt-info/magazine-mag11012000-mag4.htm

http://www.reshafim.org.il/ad/egypt/timelines/topics/vegetables.htm

http://www.catNamesmeow.com/egyptian-cat-Names.htm

http://www.electricshock.org/electric-animals.html

http://www.oocities.org/unforbidden_geology/ancient_egyptian_stone_vase_making.html

http://www.ancient-egypt.org/index.html

http://en.wikipedia.org/wiki/Military_of_ancient_Egypt

http://www.touregypt.net/featurestories/kmt.htm

http://www.ancient-egypt-priests.com/AE-Life-english.htm

http://www.crystalinks.com/egyptpriests.html

http://www.reshafim.org.il/ad/egypt/history.htm

http://www.tropicalfloridagardens.com/2010/09/13/have-you-seen-the-flower-of-a-ficus-tree/

http://www.reshafim.org.il/ad/egypt/trade/roads.htm

http://www.reshafim.org.il/ad/egypt/timelines/topics/wood.htm

http://en.wikipedia.org/wiki/Egyptian_vulture

http://ancientfoods.wordpress.com/2011/08/12/ancient-egypt-bread/

http://historylink101.com/n/egypt_1/
religion_role_of_priest.htm
http://en.wikipedia.org/wiki/High_Priest_of_Ptah
http://www.ancient-egypt-priests.com/AE-Life-english.htm
http://en.wikipedia.org/wiki/Date_palm
http://www.italtoursudan.com/itsudanpage.
php?pg=nileriver
http://www.ask-aladdin.com/Egypt-Sites/Nubia-
Monuments/nubia.htm
http://www.reshafim.org.il/ad/egypt/ceremonies/
http://en.wikipedia.org/wiki/Sekhmet
[2]http://houseofanubis.webs.com/Selections%20of%20
Ancient%20Egyptian%20Prayer1M701.pdf

Egypt – World of the Pharaohs – Könemann
Egyptian Book of the Dead
History of Ancient Egypt with Professor Bob Brier